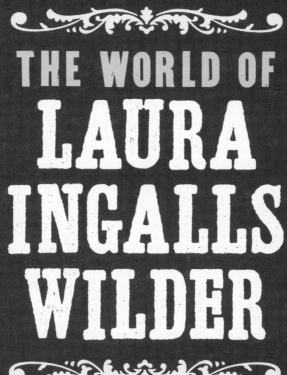

THE WORLD OF
LAURA INGALLS WILDER

THE FRONTIER LANDSCAPES THAT INSPIRED

The Little House Books

BY MARTA McDOWELL

Timber Press
Portland, Oregon

Frontispiece: Laura Ingalls Wilder picking peas in her Missouri garden.

Dedication: Laura Ingalls Wilder's life and works are laced with wildflowers, including this 1953 Garth Williams illustration for *These Happy Golden Years*.

Sources and Citations appear on page 358.

Photo and Illustration Credits appear on page 380.

Handling and eating wild plants is inherently risky. Plants can be easily mistaken and individuals vary in their physiological reactions to plants that are touched or consumed. The information in this book is true and complete to the best of our knowledge but it is provided without guarantee on the part of the author or Timber Press. The author and publisher disclaim any liability in connection with the use of this information.

Published in 2017 by Timber Press, Inc.
The Haseltine Building
133 S.W. Second Avenue, Suite 450
Portland, Oregon 97204-3527
timberpress.com

Printed in China
Text design by Anne Kenady
Jacket design by Jarrod Taylor

Library of Congress Cataloging-in-Publication Data

Names: McDowell, Marta, author.
Title: A Wilder world: Laura Ingalls Wilder and the landscapes of the American frontier /
    by Marta McDowell.
Other titles: Laura Ingalls Wilder and the landscapes of the American frontier
Description: First edition. | Portland, Oregon: Timber Press, 2017. | "Prologue—A Life
    on the Land—Clearing the Land: The Wisconsin Woods—Preparing the Soil: A
    New York Farm—Harrowing: The Prairie of Kansas, Indian Territory—Making a
    Better Garden: Creekside in Minnesota and Iowa—Ripening: The Dakota Prairie—
    Reaping: Settled Farm and Settled Town—Threshing: From Great Plains to Ozark
    Ridges—Saving Seed: Rocky Ridge Farm—Putting Food By: The Rock House and
    the Farmhouse—Wilder Gardens—Visiting Wilder Gardens—Growing a Wilder
    Garden—Source Abbreviations—Plants for a Wilder Garden—Recommended
    Reading. | Includes bibliographical references and index.
Identifiers: LCCN 2016057864 | ISBN 9781604697278 (hardcover)
Subjects: LCSH: Wilder, Laura Ingalls, 1867–1957—Homes and haunts. | Wilder,
    Laura Ingalls, 1867–1957. Little house books. | Wilder, Laura Ingalls, 1867–1957—
    Knowledge—Botany. | Authors, American—20th century—Biography. | Women
    pioneers—United States—Biography. | Frontier and pioneer life—United States. |
    Family farms—United States. | Gardening—United States. | Gardens in literature. |
    Nature in literature.
Classification: LCC PS3545.I342 Z7685 2017 | DDC 813/.52—dc23 LC record available at
    https://lccn.loc.gov/2016057864

ISBN 13: 978-1-60469-727-8

A catalog record for this book is also available from the British Library.

For Kay and Pat who remember,
and to Ginger and Lucia who will.

It is a beautiful world.

—THESE HAPPY GOLDEN YEARS

The voices of nature do not speak so plainly
to us as we grow older, but I think it is
because, in our busy lives, we neglect her
until we grow out of sympathy. Our ears and
eyes grow dull and beauties are lost to us
that we should still enjoy.

—MISSOURI RURALIST

Contents

PREFACE

Some decades ago when I fit the criteria of Young Adult reader, I was Laura Ingalls. That is, when I wasn't Nancy Drew or, somewhat later, a foot-stamping Scarlett O'Hara. Laura spoke her mind, rode black ponies bareback, helped Pa with the haying, and pushed off her sunbonnet. Besides, I had the genetic creds for Laura. My mother grew up in the middle of the Illinois prairie, became a teacher, and taught in a one-room country schoolhouse, just like Laura and Ma Ingalls. Her family inspired my love of gardening and my confidence with canning jars. My father was a farm boy from Henry County, Kentucky, whose stories included the Christmas crate of oranges—the single gift shared among his family of nine—and walking to school unless the creek was too high, in which case they rode the mule. It wasn't until I was well into adulthood that I realized that the first family car of my memory, a mammoth black Hudson sedan dubbed "Old Jenny," had been named after a mule of his youth.

Born in 1867, Laura Ingalls Wilder wrote a bumper crop of books for young readers. Farming, gardening, and nature were backdrops and key plot elements for every volume in the series. Originally published between 1932 and 1943, the eight novels chronicle growing up in the Wisconsin woods and on the prairies of Kansas, Minnesota, and South Dakota over a twenty-year period starting in the late 1860s. It was a coming of age story for a girl and reflected the coming of age of a nation, as homesteaders spread west from the Mississippi.

Beyond history, her books were about natural history. Laura discussed weather and land forms. She observed plants and the animals that depended on them. She foraged wild berries and picked wildflowers. And long before she was a writer, Laura Ingalls Wilder was a gardener and farmer, growing food for the table and raising crops for sale. She lived the farmer's covenant with the wider natural world, tending soil, plants, and animals to sustain herself and her family.

For many of us, Wilder's books introduced us to a life in and dependent on nature. Never was germination so eagerly awaited or crop failure so devastating. Her stories, predating reality TV by decades, often read like some sort of *Survivor: Prairie Edition*. Yet despite grasshopper plague, drought, fire, twister, and blizzard, her love of nature shines through, buoyant with optimism. Nature, in her world, is its own character, one with a definite if sometimes unstable personality.

It isn't too much of a stretch to group Laura Ingalls Wilder with America's nature writers. Nature was her home, as well as little houses. Readers of her books become budding naturalists. The actions of the Ingalls and Wilder families take place in different parts of the country with different ecosystems, and the stories demonstrate the results of changes to the land. The series sows a deep appreciation for the world outside one's own door. Now that I am approaching the age at which Laura Ingalls Wilder started writing her memoir and novels, I found that exploring her works became a personal time machine. She opened a portal into my own melting pot of memory as I explored the places and plants of her life.

I've organized this book in two parts. After a short prologue, "A Life on the Land" follows the trail of Wilder's plant, farm, and garden interests intertwined with her life story. If you're a Wilder fan, you will find a familiar order, as it follows the sequence of the *Little House* books chronologically and geographically. I urge you to read or reread them alongside. Three additional chapters cover the Wilders at Rocky Ridge Farm in Mansfield, Missouri, and the other places that her daughter, Rose Wilder Lane, gardened. The second part of the book, "Wilder Gardens," is for the traveler who wants to hop into the wagon and travel to Wilder and "wilder" gardens across America, and for the gardener—aspirational or experienced—who would like to grow the plants that Laura grew and knew, with a catalog of specifics including botanical names.

And speaking of "Laura," I hope she would excuse the familiarity. In her day, even Almanzo did not address her by her first name until after they were engaged. After that, Miss Ingalls became Mrs. Wilder. But because she shared herself with so many who got to know her character first-hand, a chapter at a time, Laura is the name I will use when referring to her as a person, reserving Wilder for her professional name as a writer.

PROLOGUE

An imagined scene in Mansfield, Missouri
Late autumn, 1894

She is bone-tired, and sits down on the stump. Every inch of the just over five feet of her still pulses with the rhythm of the crosscut saw that she and Almanzo just put aside. It feels good to take a break. She watches her husband limping downhill toward the cabin to check on Rose. Their prairie Rose. She would be eight soon, as bright as a shiny penny. The other day she wanted to know why her mama was out working with Papa, since the new place is in *Mans*-field. Well, this may be Mansfield, but this woman would do her share to make this farm a go.

Almanzo says he'd rather have her at the other end of the crosscut saw than any man he's ever worked with. If only he could sell some loads of wood in town, that would be enough cash money to make it through the winter with the supplies they had packed along. It was a good thing they'd brought those chickens on the back of the wagon.

She looks around at the trees—so many trees—and the funny tilts and angles of their new land. It is a rocky ridge, and Rocky Ridge Farm it will be called. She thinks of what it could be: stretches of orchard blooming in spring and bearing in fall, corn for the horses, a pig, a cow of course. And more chickens. She could turn a profit with poultry, especially if Almanzo grew the feed.

The cabin will do for now—good thing it was here already. But she imagines a white farmhouse with porches and windows to gather up this beauty. She will plant her garden nearby. A big garden with peas and such. The barn should be close too, as Almanzo still needs help hitching the team.

Stretching, she looks down and sees patches of leaves growing here and there. Violets. The promise of their flowers makes the coming winter tolerable. Even with the shortening days, there are plenty of wild birds, and the trees have already set buds for next spring's leaves. Their new land infects her with an enthusiasm she hasn't felt in some time. She is smitten with the place, the ravine and the long hill up to the high field where dawn lights up its edge. The water from the spring is sweet. There is no shortage of wood to burn. Rose even caught a rabbit the other day.

Leaning back on the stump, she thinks back to other stumps and other trees—big trees—and to Pa and Ma. Her parents had made so many farms, so many gardens over the years. They just kept at it. She would too.

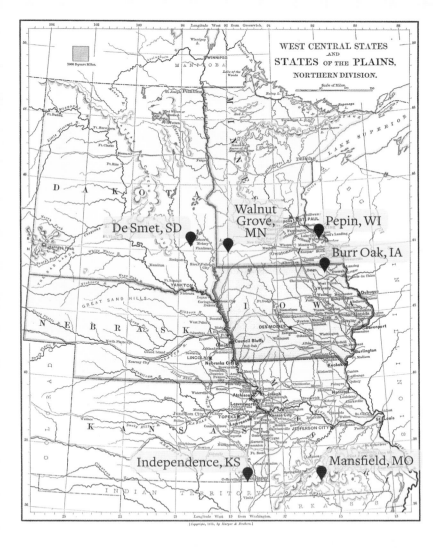

The places where Laura and Almanzo lived the majority of their lives are overlaid on this 1875 map.

Ma took charge of the day's work for the rest of them, and best of all Laura liked the days when she said, "I must work in the garden."

—LITTLE TOWN ON THE PRAIRIE

A LIFE ON THE LAND

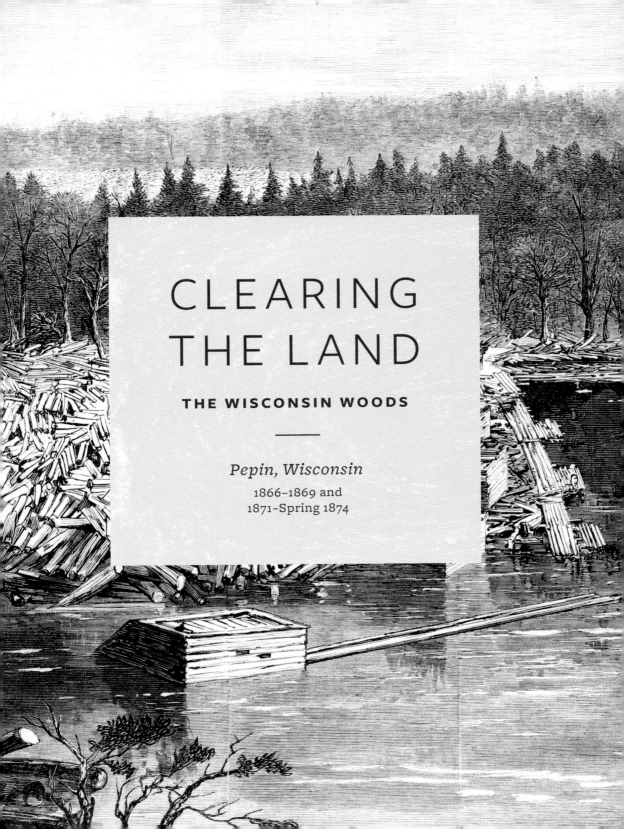

CLEARING THE LAND

THE WISCONSIN WOODS

—

Pepin, Wisconsin

1866–1869 and
1871–Spring 1874

The natural world surrounds Laura and Mary as they peek out of the log cabin in Helen Sewell's cover illustration for the first edition of *Little House in the Big Woods*, published in 1932.

The sap, you know, is the
blood of the tree.

—LITTLE HOUSE IN THE BIG WOODS

"Once upon a time." Like many children's stories, Laura Ingalls Wilder opened *Little House in the Big Woods* with this quiet invitation to readers to turn their thoughts back in time. Hers was a long story, rooted in with her father's and her husband's, tales of family and farms and nature—a nature that was sometimes inviting and sometimes ferocious. It began in Wisconsin.

On an unseasonably mild Thursday, February 7, 1867, Laura Elizabeth Ingalls entered the world. Her parents, Charles and Caroline Quiner Ingalls, were pioneers, eking out a living from the land in a clearing of their own making in the vast Wisconsin woods. There were two daughters in the Ingalls household now, with infant Laura joining Mary, a toddling two-year-old, one girl for each great oak that shaded the house.

The first little house of Laura's life was in the forest and of the forest. She was born in a log cabin, that quintessential American beginning. Seven U.S.

presidents, including Abraham Lincoln who was assassinated just two years before her birth, are called "log cabin presidents" due to their own rough-hewn birthplaces. Log cabins are the ultimate in local building techniques. Step one: enter settlers. Step two: fell trees and trim logs. Step three: use logs to build house, barn, and fences.

By the time Laura was born, her parents were already experienced farmers. Both had their roots in old Yankee families, with ancestors who had boarded ships and crossed the Atlantic from England to promised lands in America. Charles Ingalls had grown up on farms as his pioneering parents moved their family in several stages, from western New York to Concord, Wisconsin, in the southeast corner of the state. In his youth, Charles learned the rudiments of agriculture, carpentry, and hunting, skills that would support him throughout his life.

He met and married Caroline Quiner, a young schoolteacher from a neighboring farm. They first lived near, or perhaps with, her mother and stepfather. They grew hops, breweries being a big regional business even then. In October 1861, Caroline Ingalls, now in her second year of marriage, wrote a letter to one of her sisters, painting a portrait of the couple as young farmers:

> And now about Charles and Caroline. We are well and enjoying ourselves. You will think I am healthy when I tell you how much I weigh. I weigh 138 pounds. Charles is well but he has worked very hard this summer and is about tired out now. We have got our hops picked and pressed. It took three weeks with 20 pickers to pick them. We have sold $250 worth and have about as many more to sell as we have sold; but we do not expect to get as much for the remainder, as the price is reduced.

Caroline and Charles Ingalls, drawn from a photograph taken circa 1860.

Farming was the standard way for strong, independent young Americans to get ahead. But it wasn't easy. About the same time Caroline wrote her letter, her in-laws' Concord farm failed—the reasons are unclear—and Charles's parents moved to new land further north and west in Wisconsin.

Charles and Caroline soon followed. They bought land in a little dipper of a county called Pepin some seven miles from a town called Pepin and a body of water called the same. It is one of the many French place names in the area, going back to a time when kings named Louis could grant lands to gentlemen-explorers. Laura once wrote that she was born near the "legend-haunted Lake Pepin."

Legend-haunted? Ah yes, Lake Pepin shares folklore (or fakelore, depending on your point of view) with Loch Ness, in that a giant sea creature, nicknamed Pepie, has been reported there on and off for the past hundred years. Legends of quarreling Indian deities have also clung to the region, including one that lent a name, Maiden Rock, to a bluff above its eastern shore. Perhaps the stories were among Pa's repertoire, but if so, Wilder did not record them. And don't tell the lake, but Lake Pepin is really just a wide place in the Mississippi River, an expansion about two miles wide and twenty or so miles long. The delta deposited at the confluence of the swift Chippewa River just to the south made a natural dam that formed the lake. From its pebbly Wisconsin shore, one looks west to Minnesota.

The Mississippi divides the continent in more ways than one. It is an immense drainage system that encompasses the central basin, from the east-

A view of Lake Pepin and Maiden Rock, circa 1874. In her writing Wilder did not mention steamboats, their ticket prices likely beyond the means of her family.

ern Rockies to the western Appalachians. It was the transportation superhighway of its day, the waterway that was a major driver of the Louisiana Purchase in 1803 and the motivation behind hard-fought Civil War campaigns. For Charles Ingalls and like-minded antebellum settlers, easy access to transportation for both crops like wheat and trade goods like animal pelts made the wooded acreage around Pepin County attractive. Stay tuned. The river will figure prominently as the Ingalls family embarks on its way west in the years to come.

The changes that Laura Ingalls saw in Wisconsin—as forest went to farmland—were at the western edge of a line of clearing that had been underway in America since the seventeenth century. Starting at the Atlantic coast, this process of clearing and cultivation had moved with a steady drumbeat across the continent for two hundred years. It was all-American, encouraged by the Founding Fathers. Benjamin Franklin, in his inimitable fashion, had listed the three ways a nation might grow:

> The first is by War ... This is Robbery
> The second is by Commerce, which is generally Cheating
> The third by Agriculture the only honest way.

Honest agriculture required that the land be "improved," and first, as was the case for Charles Ingalls's Wisconsin farm, the trees had to go. In early America, trees owned the east. If you pick up a green marker and color in a map of the continental United States with the extent of forestation in the year 1600, you would basically fill in everything from the Atlantic seaboard across the Appalachians to a wiggly line halfway to the Rockies. The old saying that a squirrel could have moved through the trees from Maine to Mississippi and never touch its feet to the ground is not hyperbole. Those same forests stretched far to the north. Of a stranger who had been lost in the Wisconsin woods, Pa said, "if he had gone on the way he was headed, there was nothing but woods between him and the North Pole."

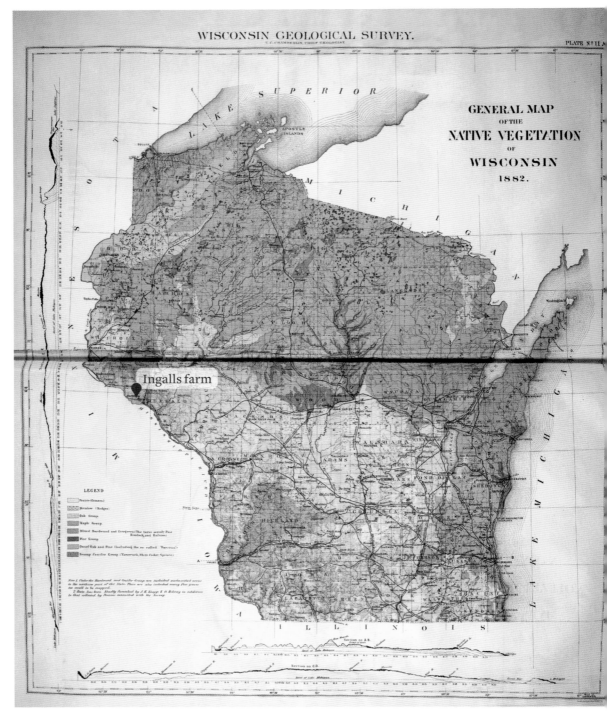

An 1882 study of Wisconsin vegetation shows with shades of green how the woods got bigger as one proceeded north. The Ingalls farm was located in a region labeled the "Oak Group."

In the 1830s, a French gentleman, Gustave de Beaumont, traveling with the more celebrated Alexis de Tocqueville, wrote his sister Eugenie from the wilds of western New York. He might as well have been talking about Pa and his little farm in the Wisconsin forest. By Beaumont's observation, Americans young and old were wood-hard. They made up an ax-wielding populace, sharing "a widespread hatred of trees . . . whereas they find charm in a field of wheat." Their farms were clogged with rough-chopped, waist-high stumps and vegetation that grew back "so rapidly that it thwarts man's initiatives." He concluded:

> There is no doubt that the natural state of the land here is to be blanketed with forest. This is the untamed state of nature, and untamed nature remains sovereign in these parts, which civilization first touched only forty or fifty years ago. The woods symbolize the *wildness* of the place . . . . Accordingly, all of civilized man's energy seems to be directed against the forest.

Some of this outlay of the nation's energy was directed toward extracting resources, rather than against the forests per se, and that plays into the Ingalls-Quiner story as well. While most of their family members were drawn to Wisconsin for farmland, some of Caroline's kin came for the trees. As the easy-to-access timber in New England forests had been depleted, the Big Woods and pineries of western Wisconsin beckoned the timber industry. Mammoth white pines, topping 150 feet tall and four centuries old, were common to its virgin forests. Loggers worked up the tributaries from their confluence with the Mississippi—the Chippewa River principal among them. They floated rafts of logs to the larger lumber mills and markets of downstream cities like St. Louis. Caroline's brother Tom Quiner—who, Laura remembered, "came to make us a visit . . . [and] brought Ma a book called 'Millbank'"—worked for years at the Laird, Norton Lumber Company in Winona, Minnesota, some forty miles downriver.

SCENE IN ONE OF THE MAGNIFICENT FORESTS OF NORTHERN WISCONSIN,
NORTH OF CHIPPEWA FALLS.

These forests have yielded far more wealth than the gold mines of California.

But most of the Ingalls-Quiner clan stuck to farming, and farming meant clearing trees. It demanded steady effort, sweat and sinew. It's no accident that popular tools for sale at the Pepin store in Laura's day included ax and saw. A drive through their parts of Wisconsin today also requires effort—but only of imagination—to picture the forest that once grew there.

If you have ever cut down a tree of any size, or watched one being cut down, consider the time, even with gasoline power, that it takes to remove it. What Charles Ingalls along with his pioneer cohort accomplished seems unbelievable. He chopped down trees with hand tools. To save time, he also would have girdled trees, cutting through a layer of bark around the tree's circumference. If we use Grandpa Ingalls's metaphor, that sap is the blood of the tree, girdling severs its veins. It kills the tree in a season or two, making it easier to remove. The stumps too big to take out were left, and Laura remembered, summer and winter, many games that involved childhood acrobatics from them.

Around the stumps, Charles plowed and planted. The seeds he sowed for cash crops were grains—wheat, oats, corn, but wheat was foremost. That was typical for Wisconsin farmers in those days. In the 1860s, when the Ingallses farmed there, the state was in the midst of a wheat boom, driven in good measure by the Civil War. For a brief time, Wisconsin was the top wheat producer in the nation. Huge grist milling operations were set up along the Mississippi, and some of the brands—Gold Medal flour, for one—persist on supermarket shelves today.

Why wheat? Well, if you were a new farmer, it made sense. The capital outlay was low. It was easy to store and nutritious. Two harvests a year were possible in Wisconsin, if you had enough land cleared. Plant winter wheat in fall and harvest in early summer, with hard red "spring" wheat sown in spring and cut in the fall.

Wheat tells a long tale, as one of the first plants domesticated for agriculture in the Middle East some twelve thousand years ago—about the same time as the last glacial remnant of the Ice Age was in its final retreat from Wisconsin and the last American mastodon died. Small grains like wheat had been cut with sickles and scythes and threshed with handheld flails for eons. When Charles grew wheat on his late-nineteenth-century farm, he was carrying on a tradition that was practically Paleolithic.

Pa had advantages over his forebears. Charles Ingalls used a somewhat newer innovation, the hay cradle, to cut his grain. Wilder would later describe it as "a steel blade fastened to a wooden frame with slats that caught the grain as it was cut and a curved handle to swing it by." The cradle was invented sometime in the mid-1700s—George Washington used it on his farm properties—and the first U.S. patent was issued in 1823. But better things were in the hopper.

During Pa's lifetime, the Industrial Revolution made it to the farm. He witnessed the commercial debut of equipment including the horse-driven thresh-

Wheat was the principal grain for Wisconsin farmers like Charles Ingalls.
Shown here are corn (1), two types of wheat (2 and 3), barley (4), rye (5), millet (6), rice (7), and oats (8). »

This hay cradle was found in the cellar of Laura's last home, Rocky Ridge Farm, in Mansfield, Missouri.

ing machine, so slick at separating the grain from the straw and chaff. Yes, it was noisy, yes, it spewed dust, but that combination of belt, steel cylinder, and mechanical teeth spelled progress. Pa was all for it.

Plus, his freshly cleared land seemed custom-made for wheat. Its alluvial soil, deposited by the old Wisconsin glacier, was fertile and well-drained, and capped with a layer of forest debris worked by past armies of ants, worms, microorganisms, and weather. Opened with the plow, it was perfect for first crops, full of nitrogen and other minerals. Yields were high, as were expectations.

Of course, the land had to be *kept* clear. Stumps re-sprouted. The seed bank, tree seeds dormant in the soil, woke up when the dense canopy of the old north woods was replaced with sunlight and rainwater. Year after year the sprouts and saplings rose up against him, the bane of Pa's existence. If he didn't keep "everlasting at it" the woods would take over again.

Charles went at these endless rounds of clearing with a grubbing hoe borrowed from his brother-in-law Henry Quiner, who lived and worked the adjacent forty-acre farm. (Caroline's brother Henry had married Charles's sister Polly, one of three Ingalls-Quiner marriages in this intricately braided family tree.) A grubbing or grub hoe is a long-handled tool with a heavy blade that runs perpendicular to the wooden handle. Forged and sharpened, it is a weapon against tree roots. With endless hacking, it is understandable why Pa looks out from his few extant photographs as a thin, sinewy man.

THE PIONEER'S HOME.
ON THE WESTERN FRONTIER.

A Currier & Ives print published in 1867 celebrates the pioneer life and the bounty of farm and forest.

3306. Leaves and acorns of various oaks. 1, Q. Phellos; 2, Q. alba; 3, Q. velutina; 4, Q. rubra; 5, Q. montana; 6, Q. mac o-carpa; 7, Q. bicolor.

Oaks, botanically *Quercus*, are familiar trees across North America. Shown here are the acorns and leaves of six species of American oak.

And yet, Pa loved the woods. He had the true hunter's love for wild places, and he instilled that love in his daughters. Their part of Wisconsin was the northern edge of the broadleaf forest, dominated by oaks and hickories. Oaks get a prominent place in *Little House in the Big Woods*, with two in front of the log cabin providing a play space for Laura and Mary, complete with tree swing. Hickory chips are Ma and Pa's preference for smoking meat. Black cherry and walnut trees, and the shrubby hazel, Wisconsin natives all, make appearances in the novel.

North and east of Pepin, the mix of trees changed to the boreal forest that sweeps far into Canada. Here the conifers—pine, tamarack, and spruce—go to the front of the class, along with birch, beech and maple. So when the Ingallses drove north to Grandpa Ingalls's farm for maple sugaring in late winter, their journey followed the actual distribution of tree species in the woods.

The woods were a dark place in summer, as the canopy closed in when the trees leafed out. The wild things that inhabited the woods were not magical beasts, but carnivores—panthers and wolves and bears (oh my!)—and the herbivores they fed on—rabbits, deer, and muskrats. Pa hunted, loading his rifle with homemade bullets. There were tracks in the snow and shrieks in the night. Between actual bears and bear-shaped stumps, it must have seemed a growling, howling wilderness.

While Pa hunted, farmed, and fished, the distaff side of the family tended to the house, laundry, poultry, dairy, and garden. The Ingalls garden was fenced and close to the house. Given the needs of the family and the harvest that Laura remembered, it must have been an ample plot. The brindle bulldog, Jack, patrolled at night to keep the garden deer-free, becoming the hero of every gardener who battles Bambi and his lot. With the exception of the heavy digging, Ma, Mary, and Laura handled the garden chores.

A word of warning. If you spend any time comparing the *Little House* books with Wilder's autobiography *Pioneer Girl*, you may be tempted to ask "Will the real Laura Ingalls Wilder please stand up?" It turns out that with a close reading of the latter, the first vegetable garden mentioned in the series was planted not by Laura's parents, but by interim owners of the log cabin. The Ingallses lived in the little house in Wisconsin not once but twice, with Kansas, the Indian Territory of *Little House on the Prairie*, sandwiched in between. It is a reminder that while fact-based, Wilder's work is fiction. The character Laura is sometimes different from the real Laura, like Peter Pan and his shadow, although readers know in their hearts that the Laura on the page and the Laura who was a person have the same character, the same values. The sometimes-blurred line between fact and fiction adds texture to the tale of Laura Ingalls Wilder.

Regardless, the vegetable garden behind the log cabin was the first to appear in the series and, we suppose, the first she remembered. It isn't sur-

Nature is full of surprises.

prising what bubbled up as Laura's garden recollections: weeding—not every child's favorite part of growing vegetables—and harvesting, which is much more fun. While collecting the dusty potatoes that Pa had dug sounds vaguely mundane, Laura's description of pulling the skinny carrots and the round turnips from their underground homes is rousing. The girls helped carry the root crops back underground, "down cellar," as she later calls it, for careful storage in bins and barrels. With the night temperatures taking a dive, the cellar with its insulation of earth-controlled humidity and temperature kept the vegetables viable. The dried leaves and straw that Pa banked around the exterior foundation would have helped too. And Caroline Ingalls would have checked the stored vegetables regularly all winter to guard against rot and to parcel out the supply to make it last until spring.

Like the settlers flooding into Wisconsin during the Ingallses' day, many of the vegetables harvested from their garden were European migrants. Beets, for example, originated as wild plants that grew on the sand and rocky shingle around the temperate coastlines of the Mediterranean. An almost four-thousand-year-old cuneiform tablet in Yale University's collection includes a Babylonian recipe for broth made from beets. Ancients cultivated them for the leaves, and these ancestral beets looked more like chard—a close relative. Root beets came somewhat later, during the Roman era, selected and bred to favor swollen, nutritious roots. By the 1650s, beets had made it to the Plymouth Colony, along with Laura's forebears. Governor William Bradford inscribed this vegetative verse in 1654, capturing the beet for posterity:

All sorts of roots and herbs in gardens grow,
Parsnips, carrots, turnips, or what you'll sow,
Onions, melons, cucumbers, radishes,
Skirrets, beets, coleworts, and fair cabbages.

(Skirret, a relative of the carrot, was a popular root vegetable in England and its colonies, but was supplanted by the prolific and easier-to-prepare potato. Colewort was a name applied to leaf, as opposed to head, cabbage. Collards are a modern approximation.)

Laura wrote about the energy-packed beet, a vegetable that has been a part of American gardens since colonial days.

While the beets that Laura and Mary helped harvest went to cool storage in the cellar, other produce was lugged to the attic. Braids of onions and strings of red peppers festooned the rafters. The pumpkins and their squash kin, including the thick-skinned Hubbards, furnished a winter playroom for Laura and Mary, at least until Ma cooked them. The attic, while still cold, would have been a bit warmer and drier than the cellar, thanks to heat rising from the stove and radiating from the chimney. Winter nights Pa banked the fire in the cookstove, gathering the hot coals, compacting the heat, maybe adding a green log. He covered the embers with ash so that that fire would burn low, smoldering till sunrise.

The attic was also the storehouse for culinary and medicinal herbs, making the space fragrant as well as burgeoning. It is disappointing—at least to a garden writer—not to find an itemized list of herbs in Wilder's novels. For cooking herbs, only sage gets specific mention, unless you count the horehound in the candy that Pa brought home in *On the Banks of Plum Creek*. Ma used sage leaves, dried from the garden, as an ingredient in her pork sausage in *Big Woods*. Sage was stored in the Wilders' attic in *Farmer Boy*. And in *By the Shores of Silver Lake*, a sibling argument—Mary wanted sage in the stuffing and Laura didn't—was moot as they didn't have sage anyway.

An attic hung with herbs and onions and furnished with winter squash made a perfect playroom.

One useful plant did merit an offhand acknowledgment. Laura's Christmas doll, Charlotte, sported eyes drawn with pokeberry ink. Some people even call it "inkberry." Pokeberry is the deep purple fruit of pokeweed, an enthusiastic native that, in a single season, grows to tremendous proportions. Its green shoots push through the ground in early spring; by the time the berries ripen in autumn, its stems easily reach to seven or eight feet. The berries are poisonous to humans, but favored fare of birds. They eat, process, and poop the seeds—with an effective coat of organic fertilizer—thus ensuring that pokeweed will poke up in many more places each spring. While Wilder only cites one use of the plant—juice from its purple fruit as an ink substitute—its spring shoots and greens are edible if carefully prepared. (If you want to try poke at home, be sure to study up in a reliable manual, such as those recommended in the back of this book. The shoots must be harvested while young and boiled in multiple changes of water to eliminate toxicity.)

One of the beauties of Wilder's books is that they encompass the arc of the year. In spring, the woods came to life. She wrote, "Birds sang in the leafing hazel bushes along the crooked rail fence. The grass grew green again and the woods were full of wild flowers." Then she left a litany of the flowers she saw, "Buttercups and violets, thimble flowers and tiny starry grassflowers were everywhere." All children like buttercups and violets. Thimble flowers are small, white anemones, each with a stippled seed head that could pass for a dimpled sewing thimble, at least to a child. Laura's grassflowers were probably a type of blue-eyed grass, a miniature member of the iris family that looks like grass with tiny blooms at the ends of the blades.

After the dark greens of summer, days shortened as late September's equinox approached. Laura saw the sumac along the zigzag fence near the cabin ignite with flaming leaves and dark pyramids of berries. As daylight retreated and the temperatures cooled, more leaves colored, and nuts ripened and fell from the trees. The girls collected black walnuts, with pungent green husks protecting durable shells.

⩚ Laura's doll, Charlotte, had eyes painted with the purple juice from pokeberries.

⩚ A damselfly rests on a thimble flower—also called wild anemone—a flower Laura remembered from several places including Wisconsin.

Pl. 30.

P.J Redouté del.

Besson Sculp.

Black Walnut.

Juglans nigra.

I wonder if Pa cracked the walnuts that Laura and Mary collected. Why do I wonder? The secret to how my own father extracted black walnut meat intact from their shells died with him. Dad gathered the nuts each fall from around town. He was small, a wiry man with strong, deft hands that gnarled with arthritis as he aged. Outside the garage, he spread the nuts on his soil sifter to dry, covered with an old window screen to foil the squirrels. I know he husked the nuts outdoors, removing their fragrant outer cases, then brought them—still in their shells—down into the basement to cure. At that point, the veil of mystery descends. My next memory of black walnuts was the smell and flavor of my mother's nut ball cookies, a part of Christmas as much as the tree and the manger scene.

The first time I tried to harvest black walnuts was the autumn after we had buried my father. Collecting them was easy as black walnut trees are relatively common in New Jersey, just as they were for the Ingallses in Wisconsin. In removing the husks, I stained my fingers what seemed a permanent greenish brown, as I learned an up-close-and-personal lesson in the strength of natural dyes.

After the nuts had cured in the basement for about a month, I assembled a small arsenal: nutcrackers of various sizes and shapes, including one specially advertised for black walnuts, and nut picks. Nut extraction day had arrived. If someone had been recording—at the time it would have been VHS—they would have had something worthy of America's Funniest Home Videos. Nuts bounced and ricocheted, but the shells didn't budge. They were so hard I wondered if they might substitute for gravel in resurfacing roads. I graduated to a claw hammer, then a small sledge, and eventually managed to smash open a few nuts, pulverizing the nutmeats at the same time. The result was a thick paste of walnut imbedded with tiny shards of shell. I picked up the phone, but neither my brother nor my two sisters could shed light on Dad's techniques. I gave up. Two weeks later, a high-priced bag of shelled black walnuts from a Midwest supplier arrived in the mailbox. They just didn't taste the same.

—MM

The elegant but tough black walnut, as illustrated in an early book about trees entitled *The North American Sylva*.

Laura's childhood reading material included *The Youth's Companion*. Issues included a regular puzzle feature called "Nuts to Crack."

An acorn is a nut unique to oak trees—this one from a scarlet oak—with a cap or "cupule" that protects the seed as it grows.

In addition to the walnut trees providing food, the oak trees supplied toys for the two girls. Laura and Mary used acorns in their games of pretend. The acorn seems purpose-built for small fingers. Most varieties of oak produce acorns with little caps that separate from the nuts to make perfect saucers.

Acorns are small warehouses of concentrated energy, a sort of Red Bull for tree sprouts. The fact that "mighty oaks from little acorns grow" is a result. Animals leverage this botanical vitality. Squirrels hoard acorns, as Laura noted, collecting them in an anxious autumnal rush. They deposit stockpiles in hollow trees and bury them like treasure for the hungry months ahead. (This caching behavior helps spread the seeds, since squirrels rarely eat all their reserves.) Squirrels aren't alone—mice and jays, woodpeckers and ducks, and especially large mammals—all have seasonal menus that feature quantities of acorns. It is an oak-driven food chain.

The two deer that Pa shot and hung in the trees in front of the little house would have fattened up on autumn acorns. The amount of acorns produced by oaks each year varies by growing conditions and natural cycles, and the annual volume of mast—crops of seeds produced by oak, beech, and the like—has a direct relationship with animal life. Mammals, birds, even some insect populations fluctuate in unison with the mast. Like financial markets, these are cycles of boom and bust, but what drives the mast cycles is not entirely clear. They vary by genus—beech and oaks often alternate from year to year. Tree species seem to take turns too—an autumn when the red oaks bear heavily might coincide with a thin crop of white oak acorns.

Hunting by the beam of the full moon, Pa perched in the wide, strong branches of an oak, watching the salt lick he had placed in the clearing to attract game. But sometimes when they walked into range—doe and fawn, even buck or bear—he couldn't bring himself to take them. He was not a tenderfoot, but did have a tender heart.

It seems that Charles Ingalls was so sweet that even bees didn't sting him. When Pa found a bee tree and came home with a wagon full of honey and comb, Laura worried that the bees would not have enough food to keep up their busy work. But Pa assured his daughter that he had left them plenty. There even was a hollow tree nearby so that the hive could relocate. Pa said it was time for the bees to move. It was time for the Ingalls family to have a new home too. But first we will take a detour to Malone, New York, led by Laura Ingalls Wilder.

PREPARING
THE SOIL

A NEW YORK FARM

Malone, New York

1866

> Don't forget it was axes and plows
> that made this country.
>
> — FARMER BOY

If you read the *Little House* books in order, when you open *Farmer Boy* you may think, as I did, "Where's Laura?" She is missing, replaced by a young boy, Almanzo, on his family's place in New York State. But soon the story catches hold, and you suspend your questions to get to know a new person and a new place. With her second novel, author Laura Ingalls Wilder set up a long series, introducing her future husband in his childhood home.

If Almanzo Wilder was born to be a farmer, he arrived at the right time and place. He was the fifth and penultimate child of a prosperous farm couple, James and Angeline Wilder. Some of Almanzo's older siblings are part of the cast of *Farmer Boy*—brother Royal and sister Eliza Jane, both of whom reappear in later books, and Alice, the closest in age to Almanzo. (The first-born Wilder, Laura Ann, remains offstage in the story, and the youngest, Perley, arrived after the timeframe of the novel.)

The Wilder farm was on the rich acreage stretching into New York from the banks of the St. Lawrence River. Some fifty years earlier, Almanzo's grandparents had moved from Vermont to settle in the North Country. They chose Malone, a town twenty-five miles south of the river that drains the Great Lakes and divides New York from Ontario, Canada. As did other New England farmers, the Wilders brought with them their Yankee attitudes—patriotism, civic improvement, hard work—and their beliefs in democratic government, education, and religion. Through some combination of nature and nurture, they passed these values to their son, James, who in turn passed them to his son, Almanzo.

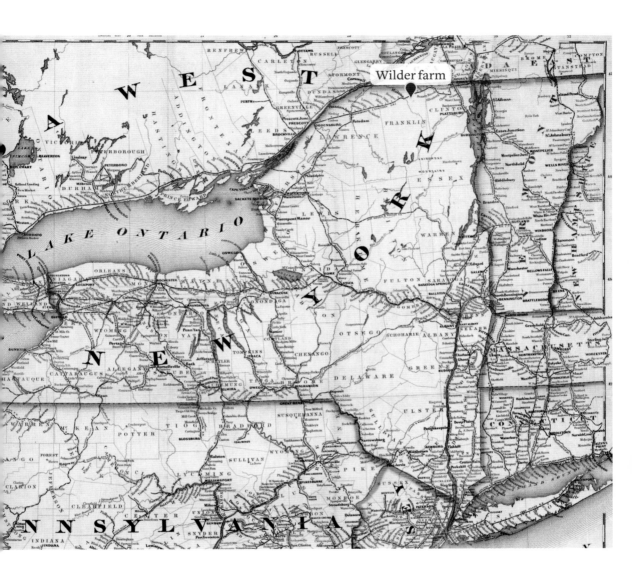

Almanzo Wilder spent his boyhood on a farm in far upstate New York.

Almanzo's birthday, February 13, 1857, was ten years minus a week before Laura Ingalls's. His story, *Farmer Boy*, is set in 1866, the year he turned nine. He was old enough to help with many chores but still too young for his heart's desire—to train the pedigreed Morgan colts that were his father's pride and one source of the farm's income.

The Wilders had a flourishing farm in a flourishing town. Their home was about five miles from Malone center, physically located in the adjacent community of Burke, but Malone was their hub of church, commerce, and school. When Almanzo was growing up there, Malone was well past its frontier days. It was an established place. Civilized. Steeples dominated the skyline. The Salmon River divides the main road into East and West Main Streets. By the late 1860s the town's commercial center bustled with a two-towered depot for the Northern Railroad, the prominent First National Bank, and a department store, along with the county courthouse. Malone was the seat of Franklin County, named in honor of Benjamin Franklin.

One sure sign of civilization was Malone's "square," actually a triangular park enclosed by an iron fence and adorned with trees and flowers and places to sit. It also boasted an extensive "arsenal green," a combination parade ground and town common. The mid-nineteenth century saw a great surge in town beautification in America with the establishment of village improvement societies, the planting of street trees, and the creation of public spaces. Andrew Jackson Downing, an American landscape designer and another native son of New York State, saw the public park as a key institution for an emerging nation. People of all social classes could assemble there. In 1848, he wrote that parks were "better preachers of temperance than temperance societies, better refiners of national manners than dancing schools, and better promoters of general good feeling than any lectures on the philosophy of happiness."

In addition to its public spaces, Malone in the 1860s got high marks for education. Almanzo attended a village school, then possibly went on to Franklin Academy, an early private secondary school. His older siblings definitely went there, though there is no proof that Almanzo attended. It was coeducational and progressive, housed in an up-to-date brick building at the top of Academy Hill. Students learned the fundamentals of botany from the

AREA OF ENLARGEMENT

Malone, N.Y.

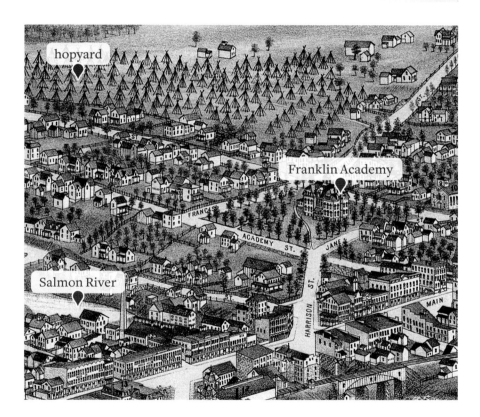

hopyard

Franklin Academy

Salmon River

FRANC

ACADEMY ST.

JANE

HARRISON ST.

MAIN

This 1886 map of Malone shows a bustling town with a prevalence of hopyards. Note the pyramidal trellising for the perennial vines. According to the census of 1870, James Wilder was growing hops too.

MAIN STREET.

Malone prospered in the late nineteenth century during and after the period that the Wilders lived there. These circa 1890 photographs include, on the top left, Triangle Park with a Civil War monument installed.

The Class-Book of Botany showed various types of edible roots: the sweet potato, the Jerusalem artichoke, and the potato.

popular *Class-Book of Botany* by Alphonso Wood, an aptly named and Dartmouth-trained minister, botanist, and educator. First published in 1845, the book went through so many editions and printings that it was, for a schoolbook, a bestseller.

Alphonso Wood told students that "botany combines pleasure with improvement." He exhorted them to get outdoors, to explore forests and fields, from "charming retreats of Nature in her wild luxuriance" to where she "patiently smiles under the improving hand of cultivation." As Almanzo could attest, roaming the riverbanks, woods, and farmland provided "vigorous exercise, both of body and mind, which is no less salutary than agreeable, and its subjects of investigation are all such as are adapted to please the eye, refine the taste, and improve the heart."

Wood's textbook favored experimental methods and included practical information for a farmer-to-be. "Thus if wheat be grown in the same soil with the pea, the former will select the *silica* along with the water which it absorbs in preference to the lime; the pea selects the *lime* in preference to the silica. Buckwheat will take chiefly *magnesia*, cabbage and beans, *potash*. This fact shows the importance of the *rotation of crops* in agriculture." Crop rotation was a new, almost revolutionary, idea in the mid-nineteenth century. Almanzo would apply what we now call sustainable practices throughout his farming life.

Of course, his father provided many of Almanzo's day-to-day lessons in agriculture. And in many ways *Farmer Boy* reads like lessons for Future Farmers of America. Furrows should be straight, carrots should be thinned to two inches apart, and once corn is big enough it can be "laid by"—left alone—because the plants will outcompete the weeds. Plants hit with a late frost can be saved by wetting them down before sunrise—the water raises the temperature in the plant cells and the air around them to keep them just above freezing—although today's growers are more likely to use automated irrigation systems than to carry around buckets and ladles. And if you have good seed, by all means plant it quickly. Procrastination was not a word that worked in the Wilder vocabulary, gardening or otherwise.

Take, for instance, the potato, a crop that served the Wilders well. In later life, Almanzo remembered winters of his youth when his father sorted five hundred bushels of them. Every night after supper Father descended into the cellar of the house and worked by lantern light. The result: a marketable crop ready for spring sale. In addition to sorting the potatoes for size—even today there are potato size standards that determine price per bushel—Almanzo's father would have been looking for some potentially lethal signposts.

There are many plusses to the potato. A clever package, it grows and stores with ease. It is hardly an exaggeration to call it a miracle food—vitamin rich and packing a wallop of carbohydrates. But there is one minus to the potent potato. If invented by big pharma today, it might have to be approved by the FDA. As a member of the nightshade family, potatoes contain strong alkaloids, solanine and chaconine, that can kill.

From the point of view of the plant, this dose of poison is a good thing, a defense mechanism combating disease and putting off predators. Nor does it mean you need to forego your fries. Our digestive systems easily cope with

A small Almanzo wielded a big hoe to cultivate between the rows of corn seedlings.

Potato eyes quickly form shoots when exposed to light.

potatoes properly grown and stored. Scientists estimate that you would have to eat about one hundred properly stored potatoes to succumb. But beware the green or sprouted spud. With prolonged light exposure or stress, toxin levels soar. Thus a green skin is an early warning system, as the color develops when the potato is exposed to sunlight. See some green, peel it clean. And if an errant potato found its way to the back of the Wilders' cellar bin and started to sprout, Father would have known that those shoots were a bad thing, packing a higher concentration of solanine. See a sprout, cut it out. Unless.

Unless you want to plant a new crop of potatoes. As Almanzo knew, potatoes have eyes, not to see with but to grow. Cut a potato in pieces with a few of these eyes on each piece and—shazam!—you have expanded your potato crop. Thus a "seed potato" isn't seed at all, but a tuber, an amazing underground stem that puts out shoots from the nodes that spiral around it, shoots that morph into leaves or roots depending on their orientation in the soil. It is likely that the Wilders would have "chit" their seed potatoes, placing them upright in a bright, frost-free place to encourage their green shoots to get a head start a few weeks before planting.

At nine years old, Almanzo knew the fundamentals of potato farming. He'd been helping in the fields more or less since he was old enough to walk. So when Father wanted to underscore how money equals work, he asked his son to enumerate the process of producing potatoes: plowing, harrowing, planting, hoeing, digging, sorting, and storing. The moral of the story: half a bushel of potatoes equals fifty cents.

Almanzo learned the best ways to grow, harvest, and sell potatoes.

Farmer Boy is a trove of information about other plants, but call me skeptical about the milk-fed pumpkin. In the story, Almanzo raises a pumpkin of enormous proportions for the agricultural fair by slicing the vine and having it wick over time from a pan of milk, replenished daily. Pumpkins are heavy feeders and respond to good soil, generous watering, and nutrients, including the lactose that milk would provide. But feeding the vine directly using osmosis, while botanically possible, doesn't seem to be the magic answer to producing the Great Pumpkin.

Still, the idea of the "suckling squash" appeared in newspapers in the Northeast as early as the 1870s. In December 1875, the *American Agriculturist* reported a Maine farmer "has been for some time feeding a squash, in the hope of being able to bring it up to 200 pounds. The feeding is done by cutting off the vine about six feet from the squash, and placing the end in a pan into which fresh milk is daily poured." The magazine's editor was dubious. He suggested that if the vine were fastened to the cow's udder, the plant trained over its back, and the squash stuck between the horns, it could "somehow be fed on eggs with the milk, and thus furnish pumpkin pies ready grown." So it's possible that Almanzo experimented with this somewhat scientific approach. The pursuit of giant pumpkins still stokes the competitive spirit of American gardeners, with the latest U.S. record holder's entry weighing in at over a ton. (Check out the postings on BigPumpkins.com if you are still in doubt.)

A giant like this heir-
loom Connecticut
Field pumpkin is still
a child magnet.

Not all of the Wilders' plants were for food. While the Wilder family had
little leisure, they did manage to carve out enough time and space to grow
some plants that were purely for beauty. Geraniums bloomed bright red on
the windowsills, rivaling the color of Mother's red dress. Outdoors, maple
trees shaded the house. Both lilac shrubs and snowball bushes grew in sunny
spots nearby.

Lilacs were relatively early arrivals in colonial times, and why not? They
seem to want to multiply, suckering as they do, pushing up new stems from the
base of the shrub. Dig out a fresh shoot or two from the parent plant with roots
attached—a grub hoe would come in handy for the job—and you will have
created an offspring. Have patience. A new plant limits itself to heart-shaped
leaves for a few years, but eventually it will set bud and produce the heavily
scented, panicled flowers that seem synonymous with spring.

Geraniums originated in South Africa and became popular plants for American homes starting in the early decades of the nineteenth century. By the 1860s many different varieties of geraniums were available from American nurseries.

Lilacs were among the first hardy ornamental shrubs brought to American gardens from Europe.

Snowball bushes bloomed at the same time as the lilacs, according to *Farmer Boy*. The Wilders' snowball bushes were a type of viburnum, *Viburnum opulus*, another immigrant from Europe that proved adaptable to a wide range of American growing conditions including the cold winters of Malone. Its pompoms of flowers open lime green and fade to white, giving months of beauty for almost no work. Both lilacs and snowball bushes are reliable and undemanding as well as pretty. Perfect for a busy farm family, and a bright contrast against the red ochre siding of the Wilders' home and barn complex.

In 1871, the local newspaper described James Wilder as "a well-known, industrious, thrifty and intelligent farmer," and the barn complex was a testament to his success. Big Barn, the Horse Barn, and the South Barn, all described in detail in the novel, loomed large in Almanzo's memory and in the daily existence of his childhood. The barns were connected to the house with a passage down one of the hallways, allowing easy access during harsh weather.

Walk with Almanzo through the barn passage into the house. The Wilders' comfortable clapboard farmhouse was luxurious compared to the Ingallses' cabin. Imagine having a parlor just for guests! It included, among other enticements, a cabinet of curiosities with some of the wonders of nature: shells, unusual rocks, petrified wood. The Wilders' curio collection was also a social device. Visitors ushered into the house could see, via this display of the world's marvels, a demonstrated interest in higher pursuits.

The presence of these curios in the Wilders' parlor was a barometer of their interest in science. Science, or "natural philosophy" as it was called in their day, was a popular hobby, encouraged by educators and ministers. It appeared to embody the universal design of the "Great Architect," with His pencil in every flower or seashell or rock. An appreciation of nature, and the inclination to collect interesting bits of it, was something Almanzo continued for the rest of his life.

As important as the parlor was to the psyche of the farmhouse inhabitants, the kitchen was its heart. *Farmer Boy* stands alone among the Laura Ingalls Wilder books since Almanzo rather than Laura is its focus. Yet it is a frequent favorite among readers, likely due to its burgeoning cornucopia of food—comfort food—and Almanzo's enthusiastic intake thereof. The Wilder dining

The size of the house was modest in comparison with the barns.

tables are groaning boards: pancake towers, heaping platters of meat, vegetables, bread, potatoes, and plenty of Mother's butter. Of course, on an average day of farm work, the Wilders expended around five thousand calories apiece.

The kitchen in summer steamed with boiling pots of fruit and sugar, reducing into jellies and jams. *Farmer Boy* is something of a directory to Mother Wilder's pantry, mentioning preserves of crabapple, strawberry, and grape, plus watermelon-rind pickles. From that we can infer some of the fruits

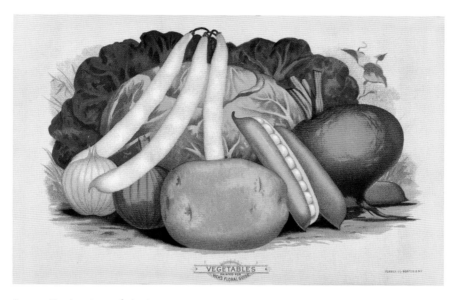

Farmer Boy is a story of plenty.

the Wilders grew, and indeed that part of New York is still known for its excellent fruit.

Apples were everywhere. Almanzo ate them whole and as part of his favorite "fried apples 'n' onions." They were sliced and dried in the sun. The cores were saved for vinegar, a reminder—if one were necessary—that nothing was wasted on the Wilder farm. We aren't told the types of apples that Almanzo picked from their trees, but popular varieties that flourished in upstate New York in those days included local favorites like 'St. Lawrence', a few that are still familiar ('Northern Spy', 'Baldwin', 'Winesap'), and one that should make a comeback based on the marketing potential of its name—'Rambo'. 'Baldwin', with its winter hardiness and heavy crops, was originally a chance seedling on an eighteenth-century Massachusetts farm. It started with more colorful monikers—because its trunks attracted sapsuckers, it had been known as 'Pecker' or 'Woodpecker' before General Baldwin's success at promoting it. The tart 'Winesap' was an especially good cider apple, and the Wilders took their apples to a local mill to be pressed. On winter evenings in the family parlor Almanzo liked to drink sweet cider, especially with popcorn, his all-time favorite snack.

The Wilders grew apples, and 'Rambo' was a commonly grown variety in northern New York at the time.

While Almanzo was busy eating popcorn in front of the fireplace, his mother's hands were never idle. I can almost hear the percussion of Angeline Wilder's knitting needles, knit stitch and purl, fashioning garments for her family in the evenings by the fire, while Eliza Jane read the newspaper aloud. "She knit all our socks and mittens," an adult Almanzo later told his wife, "Shag mittens for the men folks, do you remember, all fuzzy on the outside?" But Mother's handiwork at clothing went well beyond accessories.

As a thought experiment, open your closet and dresser drawers and consider making the garments from scratch. For this brainteaser, you are not constructing your attire solely from store-bought bolts. Start instead with the earth. From field and pasture, you grow the flax, raise the sheep, harvest, and shear. You now have fiber—unruly piles—and proceed to do what Almanzo's mother did: card the wool, dress the flax, spin yarn and thread, dye, warp the loom, and then weave the fabric. The spinning wheel whirred. The shuttle and heddle clacked, turning one-dimensional string into fabric of length and width. Then came scissors, pattern pieces, and construction. Almanzo's mother sewed clothes for the entire family, from the undergarments out.

An aside on Angeline Wilder's dyeing process, as it was also plant-based. In the Wilders' day, natural dyes were the norm. (Today, they are expensive chic, as any knitter who buys high-end yarns can attest.) In *Farmer Boy*, we are told that Angeline Wilder dyed the wool cloth for Almanzo's coat and trousers with butternut hulls. Butternut is a forest tree, a member of the hickory family. Each of its nuts has an extra layer of protection—a fleshy husk around the shell that will turn your fingers brown if you pull it off. This color transfer works on fabric too, and it is so strong that it doesn't need a mordant—a treatment that fixes color to fiber.

The Wilder girls collected various roots and barks from the woods, though the novel doesn't specify from which plants. What they gathered was destined for Mother's great cauldrons simmering in the yard, resulting in dye baths for her skeins and lengths of wool and linen. One candidate for the red—the red of the waistband of Almanzo's school trousers—is bloodroot, a spring wildflower with roots of arterial hue. (Bloodroot's botanical name, *Sanguinaria,* also means "of the blood.") The Algonquin people who first inhabited the region used it as a colorant, prizing its orange-red dye, and settlers soon adopted the practice.

For its taste rather than its color, Almanzo and Alice collected the leaves and berries of another woodland native. It is easy to wax poetic about this diminutive plant that carpets the ground with shiny evergreen leaves. Almanzo knew it as wintergreen; you might know it as teaberry or checkerberry. To avoid confusion, if you decide to order it from a nursery, its official name is *Gaultheria procumbens.* (Jean-François Gaulthier was a French-Canadian naturalist; "procumbent" means to grow along the ground.) It slowly spreads, forming colonies of miniature shrubs. Almanzo and his sister Alice knew where to find the best patches.

Bloodroot, as illustrated in Helen Sharp's *Water-color sketches of plants of North America* (1888), produces a natural dye long used in America. »

Wintergreen is related to blueberry and mountain laurel, but forms a low-growing network of small plants. » »

Papaveraceae. Poppy†.
Sanguinaria Blood-root.
S. Canadensis, L.

Pepperell May 6 '92

Ericaceae.

Gaultheria procumbens, L.

Teaberry, Checkerberry. Creeping Wintergreen.

Taunton
July 26. 1899.

Wild fruit like raspberries
are welcome in summer.

I can see my own father setting out in his old clothes early on summer mornings to pick wild raspberries and blackberries among their dense patches of arching, thorny canes. He was tight-lipped about his destinations—secret spots where the berries grew—along the train tracks, under the power lines, in old vacant spaces that had once been farms but that nature was reclaiming. His only tools were a bucket and an old coffee can, with the ingenious addition of a neck strap of sorts, made of heavy cotton string knotted into two nail holes that he'd punched on opposite sides of the rim.

We children could go with him if we asked, out into the humidity and brambles and bugs. His only injunction was that we "pick 'em clean." It didn't make sense to me then, why he cared if we missed a few ripe berries. There were so many that we couldn't get them all. But now, when I come across one of his old strung coffee cans on the basement shelves, I realize that mine had been a childhood of plenty, his of scarcity. Yes, fresh berries taste great. But for him they had helped keep the wolves of hunger at bay.

—MM

The ripe red berries of wintergreen appealed to Almanzo and Alice as well as local wildlife.

For the Wilders, berry picking was part of a habit of thrift. Ripe fruit was gathered by season. Unlike raspberries and blackberries—and most fruit for that matter—which came on in summer, Almanzo's wintergreen ripened in the autumn and stayed viable under snow. With bright red berries ranging from pea- to marble-sized, they were tasty enough to inspire a little boy to take off his warm woolen mittens and dig through a snowbank for them. Their cycle is inverted, making them a source of lean-season fruit for wild animals too.

When Alice came home from school, she could smell the wintergreen berries on her brother's breath. The wintergreen plant is one of nature's chemistry labs, pumping its leaves and berries full of methyl salicylate. It is a smell most of us would recognize, flavoring chewing gum, toothpaste, and after dinner mints. It is decidedly minty, though the plant isn't remotely related to those familiar occupiers of the herb garden. As a member of the Ericaceae, the heath and heather family, it is much closer kin to rhododendron than to peppermint or spearmint.

Pick a wintergreen leaf, crush it, and inhale. Your nose will know why Mother Wilder worked to capture its essence for cooking. She and Alice took their pail of wintergreen leaves, cleaned and crammed them into a jar, then topped it up with whiskey. (I would substitute vodka for whiskey, as it imparts less flavor of its own.) Wait six weeks, strain out the leaves, and bottle the result. Almanzo said his mother measured it out for her baking. Wintergreen thus extracted was also used to flavor candy, to concoct—along with sassafras—root beer, and to rub in as a medicine, since it shares properties with aspirin. In its synthetic form, wintergreen is still a key ingredient in commercial muscle rubs like Bengay. They must have needed anti-inflammatories, given the heavy work they were doing in the woods.

For James Wilder, the forest provided a cash crop. Father taught Almanzo how to work his fledgling yoke of oxen to haul wood, though the lessons were sometime precarious. (A log slipped as Almanzo and the hired men were levering it onto his sledge, pinning him under it. Luckily he came out unscathed.) Father harvested lumber for sale, for fuel to fill the woodshed, and for raw material. A man of many talents, James Wilder used various kinds of wood to fashion products ranging from simple items like shingles or axe handles to fine furniture and toys. He had his choice of local trees. *Farmer Boy* itemizes oak and sugar maple, beech, cedar, and spruce, hickory and ash, the strong but pliable elm.

Trees can teach lessons. Selecting two saplings to use for the hickory runners on Almanzo's new sled becomes the basis for his father's instruction in careful observation. There is variation in a population of plants. No two trees are alike and no two individuals are the same. The parable applies to people too. Do we need a new flail for beating grain on the threshing floor? For the handle, perhaps oak would do, but the beater—the business end— should be made of ironwood, a tree with limbs that look like the arms of a weight lifter. That is why some people call it "musclewood."

Laura Ingalls Wilder was accurate in her portrayal of plants. In *Farmer Boy*, when father taught son how to make a little whip for training his calves, Star and Bright, James Wilder selected moosewood. Almanzo then braided his little "ox persuader" from strips of the tree's inner and outer bark, working it

Forest timber was a part of the harvest on the Wilder farm.

to just the right consistency. Moosewood is a small maple that grows in the forest understory, in the shelter of larger trees. It is easy to spot with many of its branches sporting pea green bark with vertical bright white stripes. As the limbs grow, its outer bark splits and the inner bark shows through, resulting in the characteristic striping. It is a beacon for moose and deer, as they browse the tender branches of moosewood in winter.

The Wilder farmland was the source of other parental lessons, a sort of mini-agricultural history of America. "Don't forget it was axes and plows that made this country," Father told Almanzo. He enlisted his son as a small soldier in this fight for a nation that, by 1866, now stretched from sea to sea, if one included territories like Dakota. James Wilder also made history come alive when he cut his grain the old-fashioned way. "Father harvested his grain by hand with a sickle and cut his hay with a scythe," Almanzo later mused, "I do wonder how he ever got it done."

Part of the way Father got things done was by using natural phenomena as a way to schedule his farm activities. Corn, for example, was planted in spring when the leaf buds on the ash trees opened to the size of a squirrel's ear. This adage reads like something out of the Old Farmer's Almanac. The earliest citation I've found is from an English book dated 1816. It noted that "some tribes of American Indians . . . plant their corn when the wild Plum blooms, or when the leaves of the Oak are about as large as a squirrel's ears," substituting oak for Almanzo's ash trees. By the 1860s, when Almanzo was a boy, New York publisher A. J. Johnson issued similar advice in a popular book called *Facts for Farmers*. Some sources employ the ears of a mouse instead of a squirrel as the animal indication, and perhaps with the help of a barn cat it would have been easier for Almanzo to get a close-up look at the ear of a mouse. But regardless of which rodent or which hardwood tree, this type of homey advice employs a branch of biology known as phenology. By monitoring the emergence of leaves and flowers, the migrations of birds, and other natural phenomena, scientists can test hypotheses about larger questions like climate change.

Without knowing them as such, as Laura Ingalls Wilder chronicled these

The patterned bark of moosewood is easy to identify in eastern forests where it grows.

boyhood tales she described several distinct plant communities. The Salmon and Trout Rivers were in a riverine system, a linear ecology that supported and still supports fish—the joy of Almanzo's rainy days—as well as aquatic plants and such. The wintergreen berries, low-bush blueberries, and huckleberries he picked in their season were all related members of a plant community known as "successional heath," a mix of low shrubs that buddy up in acidic soil cleared for farming or logging. The heath didn't last long. Over the course of a few decades it was reabsorbed by the forest, but in the meantime it provided a rich habitat for the native berries that attracted the Wilder siblings.

Laura Ingalls Wilder was about to describe a very different biome, as ecologists call it, in her next book, *Little House on the Prairie*.

Father Wilder had a talent for sowing corn evenly by hand when the time was right for planting.

HARROWING

THE PRAIRIE OF KANSAS, INDIAN TERRITORY

—

Rutland Township, Indian Territory,
in present-day Kansas

1869–Spring 1871

Changes to the American West in the years before and after the Civil War were depicted metaphorically in this 1873 painting, "American Progress."

The land that you couldn't see the end of.

—LITTLE HOUSE ON THE PRAIRIE

Some things in life cast long shadows: trees, late afternoons, autumn days, parents. Some settings in history cast long shadows too. In America the West is one. In the nineteenth century western fever was an epidemic, and Charles Ingalls had a serious case. The grass would be greener, the skies would be bigger on the other side of the Mississippi. In Wisconsin the sound of other people's axes was an annoyance. The little road that ran by his farm was getting downright well-traveled. And in terms of hunting—a key part of the family's finances—it was becoming a case of where the wild things were. It was time to head west.

I wonder if Caroline agreed. After finishing *Little House in the Big Woods* with her second-grade daughter, my niece Jenny posed a reasonable question. "Why *did* Pa drag them from their cozy Wisconsin farm?" she asked, a little put out. With its comfortable house and full larder, it seems a strange decision. But Charles Ingalls was not much on long-term planning. "Pa was no businessman," Wilder wrote in later life. "He was a hunter and trapper; a musician and poet." We don't know how willingly Ma accompanied her poetic frontiersman of a spouse, but in late winter of 1869, it was westward ho for the Ingalls family.

When Charles and Caroline Ingalls left to head west, they were replaying a scene familiar to many and portrayed in ballads and paintings like this one, "Leaving the Old Homestead," painted in the 1850s.

To get to their new home, they first had to cross the Mississippi River, an almost mythic border between "back east" and the prairies and plains of the West. Pa fitted out their buckboard wagon with bows made of hickory—soaked, bent to shape, covered with canvas. With wagon loaded and hitched he drove them across the frozen river. In the novel, two snowy ruts show where other wagons had gone before them. What was the pull?

Politically, the timing seemed solid. The years between 1854, when the federal government officially "opened" the Kansas Territory to settlement, and 1861, when the state of Kansas came into the Union, had been violent. Vigilantes—the "Free Staters" and the Missouri-based "Border Ruffians"—warred over slavery. In the wake of the Civil War all that was settled, and the bleeding in Kansas was stanched. There were rumors of land, free for the taking. Treeless, flat, and fertile, the land whispered to Charles Ingalls.

The railroads had started to build at a great pace across Kansas in the late 1860s and were putting a new spin on the prairies. Forty years earlier, Major Stephen Long, after a two-year expedition to the area between the Mississippi and Rockies, pronounced the broad midsection of the continent "almost wholly unfit for cultivation, and, of course, uninhabitable by a people depending on agriculture." A map in his published account labeled it the "Great Desert." But by mid-century, in a significant public relations turnabout, the word "desert" was dropped, or at least shifted further south and west. As the rail network expanded, railroad companies distributed literature far and wide extolling the farming potential of the Great Plains.

Other commercial and political boosters touted the region. It was the second Eden. An agriculture writer of the day summed it up as the "Garden of America" ready for the taking:

[H]er prairies, her limestone hills and broad levels; her sandy alluvial bottoms, located in almost as many different climates as positions, abound with all of nature's food, stored for years in the production of tree, fruit, and flower, to such extent that she may yet be said to be in her infancy. And no one who has not visited and traversed her wide borders . . . can have, but by traveling over it, any conception of the wealth stored up in the soil of the West.

You'd be crazy not to go farm there.

Laura Ingalls was too young to remember much of her Indian Territory days firsthand, as she was only three years old when they arrived, but other pioneer diaries corroborate her family's attitudes. Another Kansas settler, twenty-two-year-old Abbie Bright, joined her brother near Clearwater sometime in 1870. She wrote a diary entry the following July:

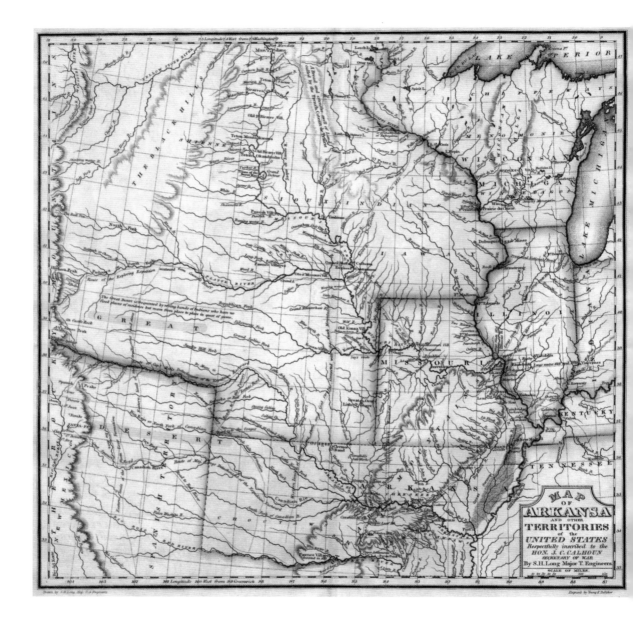

In 1822, Major Stephen Long and his expedition explored territory that later became Oklahoma, eastern Colorado, and Nebraska. He popularized the term "Great Desert" for the shortgrass prairie east of the Rockies.

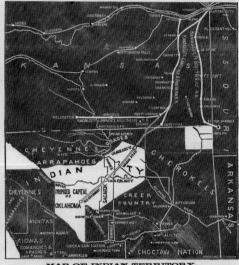

THE PRESIDENT

In his last message to Congress, strongly recommends that the Indian Territory be opened for settlement, and there is no doubt but that Congress at its present session will pass the necessary act declaring the unoccupied lands in

INDIAN TERRITORY

THAT

GARDEN OF THE WORLD,

OPEN FOR

HOMESTEAD AND PRE-EMPTION

MAP OF INDIAN TERRITORY,

Showing the Lands that will be subject to Homestead Entry and How to Reach Them.
White indicates Homestead Lands, of which there will be over 10,000,000 Acres.

In view of the early opening of the Territory, it is necessary for those who would improve the opportunity to secure Free Land and Homes in this magnificent country, to be prepared to start as soon as the lands are declared by Congress to be subject to Homestead Entry. The rush will be great, and early comers will have every advantage.

Every Person 21 Years of Age or Over will be ENTITLED TO 160 ACRES.

COFFEYVILLE & INDEPENDENCE

The two large towns on the Border, and the nearest points to the Public Lands will be the

GREAT OUTFITTING POINTS

FOR

Immigrants to the Indian Territory.

The Old Government Wagon Road starts from both these points. Plenty of Wood and Water on the route, and all large streams and bad crossings are avoided.

THE GOVERNMENT LAND OFFICE IS AT INDEPENDENCE.

THE KANSAS CITY, LAWRENCE & SOUTHERN R. R.

Being the Short, Direct and only Good Route to the Public Lands in the Territory, are making every preparation necessary to accommodate the rush, and will make

Special Low Rates for EMIGRANTS and their HOUSEHOLD GOODS

J. E. LOCKWOOD, General Ticket Agent, Kansas City, Mo.

Ramsey, Millett & Hudson, Printers.

A promotional poster from around 1880 drew new settlers to a "Garden of the World" in Indian Territory that had, by then, been pushed south of the Kansas state line.

You know my object in coming here was a desire to cross the Mississippi and a love of traveling. Well when I came, every body had taken a claim, or was going to. So brother said I should take one too. It was the fashion—and fashion has a great influence on some people.

There was romance in the west, but there was a dark side too. "This is the Osage Indian Land," Abbie wrote. "There is splendid land here, and a prospect of a railroad near, so some think the claims will become valuable in time." But Abbie Bright and her brother, like Charles Ingalls, had no legal right to the land they occupied.

By squatting, accidentally or on purpose, inside what was then Indian Territory, Charles Ingalls and his neighbors had the possibility of a real estate windfall. A bonanza. Pa stopped the wagon, built a log house, dug a well, plowed, and planted inside one of the ancestral lands of the people of the Osage Nation in hope that it would soon come under the umbrella of the Homestead Act of 1862. If so, his "claim" might be grandfathered. The question of the Osage Diminished Reserve that, in 1869, cut a fifty-mile swath across the state of Kansas was a political hot potato in far-off Washington. There was a treaty, there wasn't a treaty. It simply wasn't clear.

From the days of the Puritans, European immigrants had seen the Indian use of land as something less than ownership. Their agriculture was more portable. They tended their fields communally in ways that the colonists perceived as haphazard. "In a vacant soyle," wrote seventeenth-century Massachusetts minister John Cotton, "hee that taketh possession of it and bestoweth culture and husbandry upon it, his Right it is." If the Indians weren't going to stick to one place and farm—"improve" their land—the colonists rationalized, they did not have valid property rights.

Added to this entrenched attitude, the anticipation of favorable Congressional votes and railroad construction became something of a tradition in the West in the decades following the Civil War. In getting there first, pioneers aimed to get the best land at the best price.

Take out the familiar paperback edition of *Little House on the Prairie*, and look at the cover. The Garth Williams illustration tells the story of the

The Osage women tended the children and the traditional crops of corn, beans, and squash.

Ingallses' move. Two little girls stare out from the back of a moving wagon with their parents in front on the seat of the buckboard. The canvas cover frames the family. Sunbonnets frame the sisters' faces. Blond-haired Mary, a little bigger, is on the left. Always the better angel, Mary looks accepting but somewhat stunned. In the dead center is frowning, alert Laura, projecting her inner bad girl along with a consuming curiosity.

An ax handle and wooden water barrel jut out on one side, a hay fork and rake on the other, signaling the type of work anticipated for the journey and for creating a farm from scratch. A wooden yoke is chained on the back, ready for plowing. The loyal brindle bulldog, Jack, trots in the moving shade under the wooden axles and between the wheels.

The flat landscape is a contradiction. It seems endless, yet during the day it feels like they are trapped inside a bowl. The sun glazes hard and bright, with strange optical effects. A constant wind shushes through the grass and tousles Mary's curls. At night, Laura looks through the opening in the canvas. She can see Ma and Pa sitting nearby, lit by the campfire. "It was lonesome and so still with the stars shining down on the great, flat land where no one lived." By "no one," she meant settlers, of course.

While they camp along the way, the sisters pick wildflowers. Their mother sets their little bouquets in a tin cup filled with water on the lip of the wagon, beautifying their temporary abode. Ma minds more than manners for the girls. She models an aesthetic appreciation of beautiful things, including these delicate floral offerings.

I am in a car driving into southeastern Kansas, the first time I've traversed this part of the Laura Ingalls Wilder trail and this part of the country. Once across the Missouri River, I'm pleased to be in the rectangle states, as I've christened them. These are the ones that had always stumped me—a child of the Eastern Seaboard—grappling with my wooden puzzle of the lower forty-eight. The rental car's navigation system suddenly looks like it's flat-lining. Each intersection is at tidy angles like the corners of a log cabin.

The water in the landscape surprises me. For some reason I expected Kansas to be dry—perhaps from working on brown backdrops for a long-ago production of Oklahoma!—*but this area is crisscrossed with creeks and rivers, just as Wilder portrayed it in both autobiography and novel. As I check out the topographical map courtesy of Google Earth in my hotel room that night—something that would, I think, have delighted Pa and Laura—I learn that the area drains first into the Arkansas River and then, further south, into the Missouri.*

My destination is Rutland Township, the location of the Ingalls farm. To get there I have to cross the Verdigris River at a bridge in Independence, some dozen

« Laura and Mary stare out at the vast prairie from the back of the moving wagon.

miles away. The river, low and slow, traverses the county from north to south. To get a closer look at it, I pull off the road and slide unceremoniously down the wooded bank on my posterior. The current is languid, though the Verdigris has been subject at intervals to disastrous flooding. Gathered at the river are plenty of trees large enough for log cabin construction, and a generous layer of sandstone protruding along the eastern bank would have been more than adequate for the fireplace that Pa added on. Road sounds are muffled, and I can imagine fording the river in a horse-drawn wagon.

—MM

High water held perils for the Ingalls family. An unnamed creek in a spring spate presented a frightening episode, but, as Pa rightly reckoned, water also translated to trees. The North American prairies are in great part treeless, and the sudden break from the density of the eastern forests was a matter of comment for explorers, pioneers, and eventually scientists. In 1884, Charles Sprague Sargent, founding director of Harvard's Arnold Arboretum, called the prairie "a strip of debatable ground where a continuous struggle between the forest and the plain takes place." The plain seemed to be winning the debate, since in eastern Kansas where the Ingallses settled, the "arborescent vegetation is confined to the river bottoms." Laura Ingalls Wilder seconded him, writing in *Pioneer Girl*, "Pa built a house of logs from the trees in the nearby creek bottom."

She was accurate in her portrayal of trees; those appearing in her novel are native to eastern Kansas. Willows proved their usefulness. Ma swept the earthen floor with a broom made of willow boughs, and Pa built her a willow rocking chair, weaving its seat out of stripped sprouts. He probably used black willow, the most common species in that part of the state. It still grows along Walnut Creek, to the east of where Charles and Caroline raised their log house. If you want to make your own rustic rocker, black willow would serve nicely.

Willow was not alone on the creek edge. It had the company of swamp oak and sycamore, walnut and cottonwood. This is the first appearance of

Cottonwoods congregate in places with water.

the cottonwood in Wilder's books, but far from the last. This denizen of the prairies is, in botanical terms, *Populus deltoides*, and if you like words as Laura did you will see that the name suits. *Populus* is the Latin for people—as in "population"—and is the genus, the umbrella name for all species of poplars. *Deltoides* means shaped like a delta—the Greek letter Δ. The leaves of this specific cottonwood are fluttering triangles that capture the wind, green in summer and gold in fall.

Cottonwoods populate stream edges and anywhere with adequate water on the plains and prairies of the West along with their cousins, the willows. They multiply on muddy banks, like those Kansas creeks and rivers forded— and in one case, swum—by the indomitable Ingalls band. The trees sucker, throwing up shoots from roots of existing plants, with the lucky side effect of stabilizing the soil on creek banks and bottoms. They seed with abandon, distributed on cottony puffs by the wind, covering the ground like summer snow.

The cottonwood that the Ingallses encountered is an all-American tree in terms of its credentials. William Bartram, whose father, John, created the first botanical garden in America, described the tree on his explorations of what is now Alabama during the Revolutionary War. Meriwether Lewis added to the mix in Missouri. In his diary of the Corps of Discovery, he described cotton-wood in detail on the 25th of May 1804, with his somewhat random spelling and punctuation:

> [It] is so abundant in this country, it has now arrived at maturity and the wind when blowing strong drives it through the air to a great distance being supported by a parrishoot [parachute] of this cottonlike substance which gives the name to the tree in some seasons it is so abundant as to be troublesome to the traveler— this tree arrives at great sise, grows extreemly quick the wood is of a white colour, soft spungey and light, perogues are most usu-ally made of these trees, the wood is not durable nor do I know any othe[r] valuable purpose which it can answer except that just mentioned—

While Charles Ingalls was not in the market for a pirogue—a canoe, that is—regardless of spelling, it was a relief to the eyes to see trees on the prairie. He might have recognized cottonwoods from his Wisconsin years. Cotton-woods and other similar poplars did (and still do) grow in the north, partic-ularly in wet, sunny spots, but they faded into the background compared to the great stands of hardwoods and pines. In Kansas the cottonwood stepped forward, thriving in a landscape harsh to trees.

These open spaces were also lush with another kind of plant life. It was the western extent of the tallgrass prairie, what Laura called the "High Prai-rie." This great grassland once covered around 300,000 square miles of the continent, about the size of Texas, stretching north into Canada and south past Oklahoma. Early French explorers thought the open country looked like a great expanse of hay, a field ready for mowing. They christened it *praierie*, a French word for meadow. The root systems of grasses and other perennials

An 1874 newspaper reported farmers battling a prairie fire.

are so extensive that the prairie has been compared to a forest turned upside-down, with most of the activity underground.

The closer you get to the Rockies, the shorter the grass gets, its height in direct proportion to the average annual rainfall. Pa settled in an area that gets on average about thirty-eight inches of rain a year. Western Kansas gets less than half of that—around a foot and a half. The variation is caused by a rain shadow cast by the Rocky Mountains, diverting Pacific moisture further east. Thus, closest to the mountains is the shortgrass prairie, then mixed grass, and then tallgrass, a living rain gauge. But more than precipitation, or lack thereof, caused the prairies to form. The three other key and elemental ingredients were wind, fire, and mammals—lots of ruminant mammals.

Prevailing winds scoured the flat lands. Laura noticed the wind, its whorls and eddies, moving the grass. Fire, set by lightning or man, cleared brush and thatch with wide pyres that engulfed the land. Prairie fires loom large in Wilder's plot lines. "I saw the prairie fire coming," she wrote. "The wind was blowing hard and the dead grass burned quickly." Fire could spell disaster for a farmer, but in many ways the prairie profits. The deep-rooted grasses burn but bounce back with extra vigor.

Grazing also contributed to the prairie's health, grazing that for centuries had been dominated by vast herds of American bison, or buffalo. These great furry lawnmowers, eating prairie grasses on one end and producing organic fertilizer on the other, were a part of making and maintaining the prairie environment. In Wilder's writings the buffalo only appears offstage. The Osage Indians ride off to hunt them, long gone from Kansas. In Wisconsin,

Plate 81.

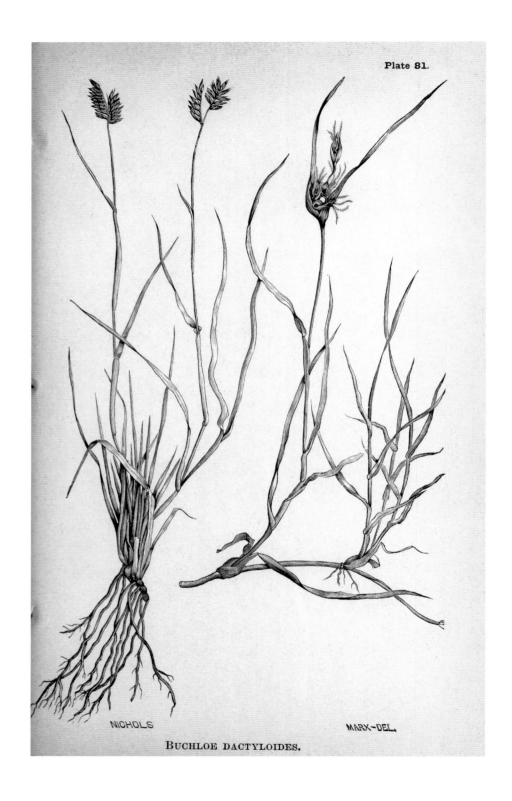

NICHOLS

MARX–DEL.

BUCHLOE DACTYLOIDES.

The landscape dwarfed their little prairie house.

Curly buffalo grass is more prevalent in the drier shortgrass prairie.

buffalo skins were mentioned. Later in the series, a buffalo robe or coat sometimes shows up. The buffalo had been almost entirely exterminated by the time Laura was growing up, a decades-long slaughter driven by ambitions for national expansion, demand for hides, and the desire of western railroads to speed up trains slowed by roaming herds. The railroads also contracted with buffalo hunters to provide meat to feed to construction workers.

By the Ingallses' Kansas interlude, longhorn cattle had replaced the buffalo and the cowman replaced the buffalo hunter. After the Civil War, Texas drovers began moving thousands of cattle north each year, across Oklahoma and southern Kansas to reach the train lines that took their herds to market. The cattle made their temporary home on the range, eating the dense stands of buffalo grass along the way, becoming the latest generation of prairie grazers. When Wilder wrote of Indian Territory in autumn, she pointed out buffalo grass, "Now it [the prairie] was dark yellow, almost brown, and red streaks of sumac lay across it. The wind wailed in the tan grass, and it whispered softly across the curly, short buffalo grass."

By 1867 the Kansas Pacific Railroad had reached Abilene, and the drive that Laura saw was likely on its way there. (The book says the cattle drive was headed to Fort Dodge, but the train didn't arrive in Dodge City until 1872.) Pa picked up some cowboy work and was paid in kind with a big piece of beef and, even better, a feisty cow and her calf to provide milk for his growing family.

The site of the Ingalls cabin, located by a determined researcher in the 1960s, lies on prairie that is rolling rather than flat. The land undulates, softened still more by the waving grasses and wildflowers. North and west of the homesite are a series of low ridges, like large waves on an ocean horizon. An early historian of Montgomery County described them in 1883:

> Elevated mounds, with steep declivitous sides, are found in places, rising abruptly out of the midst of a plain, to considerable heights. These are, in some instances, peak shaped, while in others they are capped with an almost level plain, comprising, in some cases, several acres in extent. . . . These elevations are in no way connected with the "Mound Builders," but in their native magnificence bespeak the workmanship of a mightier hand, and wiser builder.

These mini-escarpments are cuestas, geological relics of the seacoast of Kansas, reminders in landscape form of the age of dinosaurs. Some 250 million years ago, a great shallow sea covered today's continental prairies, so comparisons between prairie and ocean—think "sea of grass"—are especially apt. Sea levels rose and fell, rose and fell. The attenuated seesaw action over millennia carved the gentle slopes and ridges of the Osage Cuesta region, including those that filled Laura's view to the north.

The door and single window of the Ingalls cabin faced the opposite way, due south, where the sun lent the best natural light to the interior. Caroline Ingalls could accomplish her fastidious housekeeping without burning precious fuel to light the single room. From the doorway, Laura saw sunrise and sunset lighting the prairie and could track the arc of the sun over the course of a day. She also could have seen the census taker coming.

Asa Hargrove, the United States census taker for Rutland Township, Kansas, came through the Ingallses' door on August 13, 1870. On his sheets he penned the names of Charles, Caroline, Mary, and Laura on successive rows across the bottom of page nine, then ran out of room. He had to start at the top of a fresh sheet to fit in the newest member of the family, Caroline Celestia Ingalls. Carrie squeaked into the 1870 census, having arrived on Wednesday,

Watermelons do not cause malaria.

August 3, 1870. It is also telling that, in the column labeled "Profession," most of his male neighbors were listed as farmer, but Charles Ingalls was termed a carpenter. The census documents a pioneer community, small but stalwart. Edward Mason, a twenty-five-year-old unmarried farmer, is there, and scholars think that it was Mason whom Wilder immortalized as "Mr. Edwards" in the novel. George Tann, the African-American doctor who most likely delivered baby Carrie, is on the census too, listed as a physician and living with his parents.

Dr. Tann also treated the Ingallses during their bouts of fever and ague, which brings up the strange case of the watermelon. In both fictional and autobiographical accounts, Wilder had one of her characters suggest watermelon as a possible cause of ague, the shivering chills that are a classic symptom of malaria. Eat watermelons; suffer the ague. Wilder was not the first writer to record this fruity folk quackery, linking watermelon to malaria. In the late 1740s, Peter Kalm, a Swedish scientist studying plants in colonial Pennsylvania, reported that German settlers blamed malaria on eating too much watermelon. By the time Wilder took pencil to paper in the 1930s, the true culprit for malaria was widely known. It was not bad air—*mala aria*, as the Italians had put it—nor watermelons, but a blood-borne parasite transmitted by mosquitoes. That Wilder knew this she makes obvious in the novel, dwelling at length on the mosquito-infested creek bottom where she and Ma picked wild blackberries and on the swarms that tormented them all on calm evenings.

Like Pa, these brothers in Nebraska knew that watermelons were healthy and refreshing.

Blackberries were abundant near the creek, but so were the mosquitoes. »

Of course prairie pleasures balanced prairie pests. Laura loved wildflowers. Wilder's descriptions let the reader experience some of the flora through her eyes. Prairie larkspur bloomed in hues of blue to pinkish white, its individual florets each spurred with a long tube that must delight its pollinators. Goldenrod plumes were butterfly magnets. But what were "starry daisies"? This general description is a puzzle, at least for the plant-obsessed among us. Was it a fleabane perhaps? Boltonia is another possibility, which has the appealing alternate name of white doll's daisy. It is impossible to be sure. The prairie hosts so many members of the Asteraceae family—those with daisy-like, composite flowers—that one writer suggested that the prairie be rebranded as "daisyland."

There were new plants, bugs, birds, and animals to look at on the prairie.

The pleasures of the place went beyond flora to fauna. One of Laura's favorite childhood pastimes was looking at the illustrations in the family Bible, particularly the ones of Adam naming the animals and Noah's ark. Laura's outdoor explorations were populated with snakes and frogs, rabbits and squirrels. She and Mary played catch-me-if-you-can with the thirteen-lined ground squirrels—what she called gophers. Some Kansas pioneers called them "picket pins" because these curious little rodents sit up straight and, from a distance, look like the stakes that are driven into the ground to tether horses or cows.

Wilder captured a prairie soundtrack. There were birds galore. Meadowlarks soared, singing the harmony of morning in their ascents. Dickcissels—"dickie birds"—swung from the ends of prairie grasses, tsking "dick" as they bounced. There were phoebes and bluejays. The mockingbird imitated so many songs that in a rare instance of misidentification in the *Little House* books, Wilder called it a nightingale. In Laura's day there were prairie chickens aplenty, and some of them ended up on the Ingallses' supper table. Hawks hunted by day, owls by night. Curlews, killdeer, and sandpipers waded in creek bottoms.

In a land that first appeared empty, the prairie bestiary was so rich that Charles Ingalls the hunter saw a land of plenty. There were deer, rabbits and beavers, minks and muskrats, wolves and foxes. He could hunt and trade the furs, turning pelts into plowshares, if you will, as well as seeds and little luxuries for his family. They could live, if not like kings, at least like comfortable, up-and-coming Americans.

For trading his furs, Pa went off to Independence. He came home with seeds. For farm crops, he had purchased wheat and corn along with a plow and, in an irony of agricultural history, after busting sod Pa and his fellow farmers would replace the diverse wild grasses of the prairie with these two very tame members of the grass family. He bought seed potatoes. For the garden he bought seeds: turnip, carrot, onion, cabbage, pea, bean, the infamous watermelon, plus, for himself, tobacco. The cabbage seeds got special treatment. Ma sowed them in wooden flats indoors, getting a head start on the season. She got the sweet potatoes going too.

In the many gardens of varying locales that Laura Ingalls Wilder described through the years, the sweet potato appears only on the farm in Indian Territory.

The meadowlark singing its song atop
a post entwined with a morning glory
vine. Illustration by American artist
Louis Agassiz Fuertes in *The Burgess
Bird Book for Children*, 1919.

Ma raised her cabbage seedlings in
wooden flats.

Sweet potatoes are a warm-weather crop and are linked in the book to the
energetic Mr. Edwards, that "wildcat," whose Tennessee home state remains
a center for fine sweet potatoes. In the story, it was Edwards who, crossing the
flooded creek to assist Santa Claus, delivered gifts for the girls' stockings and
nine sweet potatoes to go along with the Christmas turkey. Seventy-five pages
later, we learn that his sweet potatoes were the gift that kept on giving. Ma held
one of the sweet potatoes back and planted it indoors in late winter.

Unlike the Irish potato, the sweet potato is a tuberous root. It doesn't
have eyes per se, but give it some moisture and green shoots will pop out from
growth points around the bulbous mass. Caroline Ingalls could have easily propagated her held-back holiday sweet potato into a substantial field of
vines for the following summer. She would have set the root end of her sweet
potato in moist soil or water and been rewarded with sturdy shoots. When
the shoots had strong stems and leaves, she would have popped these slips

from the mother plant and planted each one to develop roots of its own. Each healthy slip could produce up to ten pounds of sweet potatoes. A miracle of multiplication.

For the Ingalls family, gardening was a necessity. They were always operating on a shoestring. So, in May of 1871 when Pa brought word that the government was going to evict the settlers from Indian Territory, it must have been crushing. They had been on their place less than two years, and had nothing to show for it. Pulling up stakes meant abandoning things or giving them to neighbors: the precious plow, the cow and its calf, and the burgeoning garden. They even ate their seed potatoes, the reserve saved from the harvest for next year's planting. As Charles Ingalls drove the wagon away, Laura and Mary must have watched the house with its garden plot and sod-strewn fields get smaller and smaller, with the pang of once-dear places left behind. But the Ingallses had each other, and Pa was unsinkable. He looked forward to the next garden, a better garden.

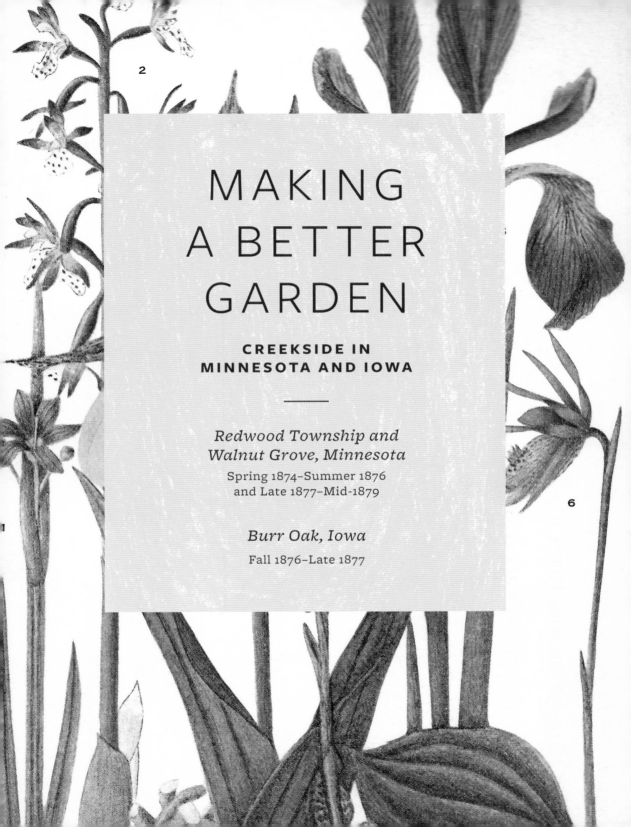

MAKING
A BETTER
GARDEN

CREEKSIDE IN
MINNESOTA AND IOWA

———

Redwood Township and
Walnut Grove, Minnesota
Spring 1874–Summer 1876
and Late 1877–Mid-1879

Burr Oak, Iowa
Fall 1876–Late 1877

Rich, level land, with not a tree or
a rock to contend with.

— ON THE BANKS OF PLUM CREEK

Back in Wisconsin, time passed for the Ingallses, sowing and reaping. But less than three years after their return from Kansas, Pa turned his team west once more. The family was back in the covered wagon headed to Minnesota by Laura's seventh birthday. Her father presented her with a gift to mark the day, *The Floweret*, a child's book of poetry. She kept it for the rest of her life.

Published in Boston in 1842, the book is full of sentimental, instructional rhymes for girls and boys. Anna Maria Wells was a Massachusetts poet, and I like to think that Pa planted a small seed of authorial ambition by giving his daughter this book by a woman writer. *The Floweret* is alive with birds, bugs, and especially, as the title indicates, flowers. Roses and violets are prominent, two flowers that Laura Ingalls Wilder will employ over and over again in her novels. The protagonists of the poems model behaviors that she will echo. Anna, for example, shows good comportment:

> Anna, with a smiling face,
> Came from the garden bowers,
> And brought, to put in mother's vase,
> An apron full of flowers.

Another poem scorns Miss Nelly who sits in the parlor in her "muslin and lace" with "simpering face" rather than running in the fields in a calico frock. And in a third selection, a little girl named Lucy gets a lesson from Mother Nature:

> Bird and insect, flower and tree
> Know they must not idle be;
> Each has something it must do,
> Little Lucy, so must you.

The never-idle Ingallses were making their way west after winter dissolved into spring, around April 1874. They drove "on and on" through the green world of a prairie spring, jostling and jouncing on the rutted roads by day, seeking out a campsite each night, in some nook along a stream with ample water for the team and adequate fuel for a fire. Laura and her sisters drifted off to sleep with reassuring sounds. Pa's fiddle. Chittering night birds. Horses chewing their oats. During that trip Laura was pulled from the edge of sleep for the first time by the pure, far-off call of a train. "I thought it was calling me," she wrote, "and Ma laughed."

The train was, in a real sense, calling Charles Ingalls and his pioneer peers who spread across the upper Midwest in the 1870s. In those years the Winona and St. Peter Railroad was pushing its way into western Minnesota, altering the landscape as it went. The Ingalls wagon followed the recently built train line through New Ulm to the spanking new railroad village of Walnut Grove. Laid out in the spring of 1874, just as Charles Ingalls was pulling in, the town was officially incorporated in 1879.

A Currier & Ives print from 1868 shows the dominance of the train with symbols of settlement on the left and wilderness on the right.

The town took its name from a hundred-acre stand of trees rich in black walnuts a mile or so south of the depot. In the prairie states, trees were anomalous enough that the word "grove" appended itself to many place names. And, black walnuts themselves are something of a rarity this far north as the region is on the upper fringe of its distribution in the United States.

Walnut Grove is in the Minnesota River basin, a wide swath of the state networked with water. It was astride two townships, Springdale and North Hero in Redwood County. By May of 1874, the Ingallses had settled on their new land north of the town. Pa filed a preemption claim—a federally sanctioned "right of first refusal" for public land developed into a farm—eighty acres of land in North Hero Township. Charles, Caroline, and the girls now had a stream to call their own. Their neighbors on an adjoining parcel were Eleck and Olena Nelson, Norwegian immigrants who had arrived three years earlier. Perhaps the Nelsons had built the dugout house that the Ingallses found along the stream.

"Such a pretty place," Wilder wrote of their new spot on Plum Creek. Willows crowded the banks, interspersed with thickets of wild plum. When Laura and her family arrived, the plums were so heavy with blossom, they must have looked like snow. No wonder Laura thought the creek was the nicest they had ever seen. The house was set into the bank, with small steps leading down to the creek's edge and a wooden bridge. To Laura and Mary it seemed more a play house than a real one.

It was tiny. It had, Wilder wrote, "not much more room than in the wagon." Made of sod, it was as if the house were playing hide-and-seek. It blended back into the prairie. The little girls could stand on its roof—constructed of willow and sod—and, with the exception of the protruding stovepipe, not even know it was there. The door and window emerged from the grass walls as if the house had its own story to tell.

Sod houses—"soddies" to their friends—were the result of practical application of available building materials combined with imported know-how. Scandinavian immigrants like Mr. Nelson, renamed Mr. Hanson in *On the Banks of Plum Creek*, from whom Pa purchased the land, had arrived with skills in sod building. In Norway, traditional houses had been roofed with sod since

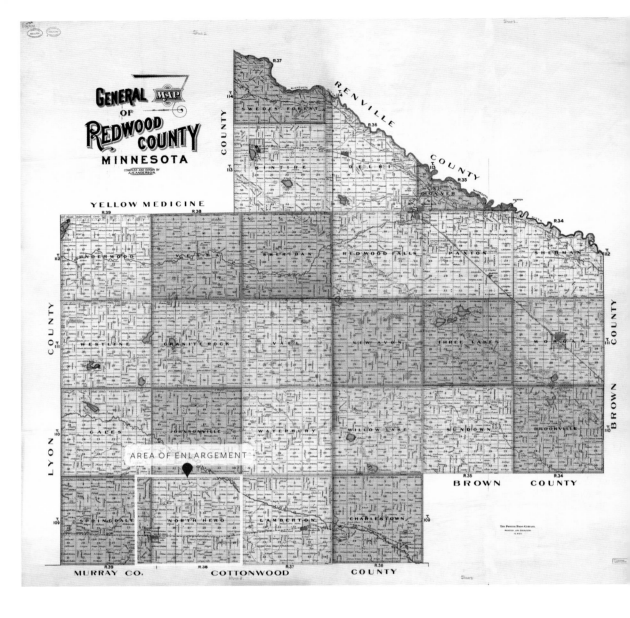

An 1898 map of Redwood County.

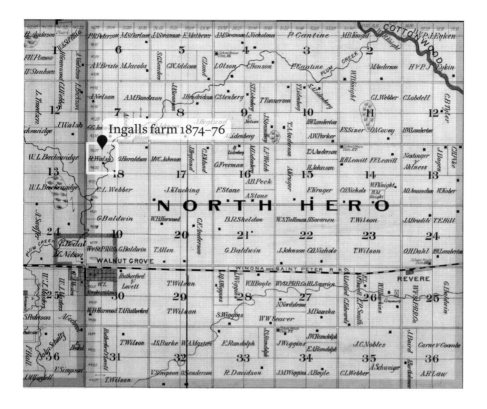

Ingalls farm 1874–76

Note the railroad, the symmetrical town plan of Walnut Grove, and Plum Creek as it winds northeast. The location of the Ingalls farm is shown, though by this time Charles and his family had moved away, and Mr. Nelson had moved into town.

A Nebraska family poses in front of a creek in 1887 with their free-standing sod house and dugout barn in the background.

the time of the Vikings. In their newly adopted country—on its prairies—grass was everywhere. Wood, not so much. These new Americans were intent on plowing up the prairie anyway, so why not put part of the results to good use?

Settlers cut their sod bricks while they were opening or "breaking" their land, cutting the virgin prairie. The sod did not yield easily. Pioneer journals record loud tearing sounds when the tenacious roots finally gave way to the breaking plow and team. As the farmer plowed up long strips, he cut them into heavy bricks with a straight-edge spade, creating a store of living building blocks. The bricks were about a foot wide, four to six inches thick, three feet long, and weighed about fifty pounds each. Wild hay—a.k.a. sloughgrass—and

The length of the roots in this display at the United States Botanic Garden shows why prairie plants are so hardy.

buffalo grass worked best, with their dense, interlocking root systems. They had to be used while moist, so that the bricks would hold together.

In construction, sod bricks often covered the outside of a free-standing frame shanty or, as in the dugout the Ingallses moved into, faced the exterior wall. Mr. Nelson had excavated a hole in the bank of Plum Creek and shored it up with joists to make up three walls of his house; the fourth was likely framed with wood to hold the window and door, then bricked with sod. The roof was constructed with willow poles that held a flat layer of sod. As sod bricks settled in, they grew together, creating a living outside wall and roof for the Ingallses' dugout, a predecessor to the vertical gardens, green roofs, and LEED-certified construction currently in vogue. Plus, the structure was solid. As William Marin, an early settler in Minnesota's Red River Valley, remembered, "a well-built sod shanty or stable is a black, fortress-like bit of architecture." While other pioneer diaries mention rain dripping through roofs and infestations of various kinds of vermin, Laura thought their place snug. Hunkered down into the hillside, it was out of the wind and tightly insulated. It was a part of the landscape.

And then there were the morning glories. The doorway of this house in the ground was alive with a chorus of color. The funnel-shaped flowers of the morning glory vines sang their harmonies, pink and purple, red and blue— some of the petals were even striped. In the heat of the summer their coiling stems shot up, creating a living screen of heart-shaped leaves and bright blossoms. While the prairie had many of its own flowers to offer, one can hardly blame the Nelsons for wanting to grow something more familiar.

Morning glories are close cousins to the sweet potatoes from Mr. Edwards, sharing the genus *Ipomoea* and hailing from Mexico and thereabouts. The seeds probably moved from south of the border to the Ingalls dugout by a more circuitous route. Morning glory seeds are large, easy to save, and as hardy as a pioneer, or an explorer. By the sixteenth century, the Spanish conquistadors had carried them to Europe, and Europeans brought them back full circle to America. They were common enough in Minnesota that, by 1870, a promoter highlighting the many attractions of the new state wrote of the adornments of a farm in Becker County where "the wife or daughter" had planted "round the door a living wreath of morning glories." Perhaps Mr. (or Mrs.) Nelson carried a little packet of seeds with them from Norway to create their own living wreath. American gardening is something of a smorgasbord, a story of migration, of exchange, and of transmission.

Wilder took some artistic license in the spring timing of her morning glory bloom. In the book, Laura finds morning glories blooming on the dugout when they arrive in May. Morning glory seeds require heat to germinate, so they wouldn't start to flower until later in summer in the Minnesota growing season. But she had everything else right. They open like magic each morning and close in the afternoon. And the morning glory is a perfect plant to enchant a child. As so often occurs with Laura Ingalls Wilder's writings, her memories evoke my own.

Morning glories have been grown in America at least since the 1780s.

❧ ❦ ❧

I have few memories of my maternal Illinois grandfather as he died when I was six, but I remember his morning glories. Louis J. Ryan—Louie to his cronies, Poppy to his grandchildren—was tall, round, and jovial. He had a bald head, a Santa Claus belly with a smile to match, and he smoked a stogie cigar. His back garden was a wonder to a child on summer vacation from the suburbs of New Jersey. Canna lilies towered overhead reaching toward that Illinois sun. Tomatoes as big as the prairie ripened in his vegetable garden behind the house in Angel Valley, as their neighborhood was called, though it was really just a dip in the prairie. To the green rows of his garden, I embarked—barefoot in the soil—to pick a mess of green beans into my grandmother's big colander. When it was full I would sit, muddy-footed and pleased

Morning glories trumpet in each day.

with myself, on the back stoop with my mother, her mother, and my sisters, topping and tailing beans for dinner. Bright blue morning glories wound up the wire fence that separated their big corner lot from Aunt Em's next door. Every morning the previous day's blooms had puckered up and the new day's batch announced itself, a blue reveille. I'd love to ask Poppy where those morning glory seeds came from, and whether he had planted them to screen his sister-in-law's view of his garden on purpose.

—MM

Morning glories or no, Charles and Caroline Ingalls didn't want to stay in the little sod house under the prairie over the long term. So Pa got busy building them a new wooden house. For this project he acquired pine lumber—sawn, not hewn—"boughten" doors with metal hardware, glass windows, and a new cookstove for Ma, bought on credit at one of Walnut Grove's two general stores. All this acquisitive optimism was founded on a dream of wheat.

Charles Ingalls indulged in magical thinking. It was as if he thought he could turn wheat into gold, as if under the soil there was an aquifer of ready money that he could tap into with his careful husbandry. His intent, and the intent of Midwestern agriculture of the post-bellum era, was to grow a high-value commodity crop. The land was perfect, level and open. In *The History of Redwood County*, the Walnut Grove soil was extolled as "a dark rich loam from two to three feet deep resting on a clay subsoil." Even better, "on account of the numerous creeks that traverse both townships the land is well drained, and excepting in some localities ditching was not needed." Across parts of the tallgrass prairie, digging ditches and installing endless drainage tiles was prerequisite to planting, but not in Walnut Grove. Pa's land may not have had poor drainage, rocks, or trees to contend with, but to break the sod he needed some special equipment: a purpose-built plow and a team to pull it. (Remember he had left the Kansas plow behind.)

John Deere, a Vermont blacksmith who moved west to the Illinois prairie, invented a steel plow in the 1830s. Until then, agriculture on the vast continental grasslands had been stuck on the surface, not to mention in the mud. Even if a farmer managed to penetrate the sod with an iron plow, he spent half his time scraping off the sticky soil from the plowshare and moldboard. Start the team and stop, start and stop, a backbreaking study in interruption. All that improved with the low-slung, "self-cleaning" steel of John Deere's breaking plow. It sliced through the dense root mass and shed the soil, making sodbusting possible, though far from easy. By the time Charles Ingalls was in the market for a plow in Minnesota, Deere and his competitors had been mass-producing steel plows for three decades.

While Pa was plowing with his new team of oxen, Mary and Laura were busy with chores and with play. And what a playground. Haystacks made perfect slides, though that was soon forbidden. The girls could climb up the dirt bank and keep climbing, to a "perfectly round table land there of about half an acre, Pa said, that rose straight up on the sides about six feet from the lower ground." Up they would scale to the top of this world with a view to a distant horizon that was as straight as the selvage on a bolt of calico cloth.

But wait, there's more. "Mary and I each had a big flat rock for a play house up on top of the bank," Wilder recalled, "then down in the creek bottom was a wonderful place to play." The bank rose and fell on the east side of Plum Creek, making the path to Mr. Nelson's house look as if it was going off to infinity. On their side of the footbridge, a big willow grew, shading a deep pool. The fishing was good there, though Laura never could get Mary to bait her own hook. Below the bridge, the sandy creek bed was clean and perfect for wading. Nature was their playground.

Wilder described the willows along Plum Creek as having yellow-green leaves, so they were likely the peach-leafed willow, a species that grows in Minnesota and loves the water's edge. Its foliage is brighter with a dash more yellow. Willows proved once again useful to the Ingallses: as material for bedsteads and bobsleds, replacement timbers for a sod roof broken by a runaway ox, and, always important, a source of firewood along with cottonwood and plum.

Apropos of the place name, wild plums are a main event in the natural history of Plum Creek. They are a boon to butterflies, with leaves that provide a caterpillar buffet, and their flowers attract many, many species of bees. Small shrubby trees, wild plums seem to like close neighbors. Like cottonwoods, they sucker with basal shoots, establishing their own congregations. Thicket is the right word for the result, especially if you are trying to make your way through them with a small pail. Their twiggy branches scratch up little girls' arms and legs. On the other hand, filling one's bucket with the warm oval fruit is easy. The ripe plums have sturdy red skins with the reward of sweet yellow flesh inside. They make delicious preserves. The birds have a taste for them too, so one must be prompt in the picking.

It was so much fun sliding down the haystacks until Pa forbade it. »

Rosaceae

Prunus. Plum, Cherry &c

Probably   P. Americana. Marshall.

wild Yellow or Red Plum.

Wild plums, ready to be picked and eaten, cooked, or dried.

Plum trees made a fruity thicket along Plum Creek.

Wilder used plum picking as one of the activities that distinguished the two older girls. Mary preferred to sit still, sewing or reading. Laura wanted to be on the go, go, go, and picking plums was a perfect task for a warm August or September day. Plus, she could dispense with her sunbonnet at least until she lugged the pails back to Ma, who made plum butter and dried many plums. Now we call them prunes, then, as now, excellent "peristaltic persuaders," as a Dr. Chapman wrote in his 1839 monograph "On Constipation."

In sunny places along Plum Creek, smaller plants grew. Blue flags—native irises—that populated the edges of the pools gave Wilder range to flex her descriptive powers:

Each blue flag had three velvet petals that curved down like a lady's dress over hoops. From its waist three ruffled silky petals stood up and curved together. When Laura looked down inside them, she saw three narrow pale tongues, and each tongue had a strip of golden fur on it.

Blue flag iris (5) grows along many creeks across the Midwest.

Blue flags
are always in
fashion.

Small wonder that the bees came calling to irises dressed in such fashion. With her analogy, it is easy to picture the structure of the iris petals: the spreading falls, the upright standards, even the narrow "style arms" with their fuzzy stamens.

Blue flag irises seem to invite comparisons to ladies' attire. Henry David Thoreau, coming across a similar plant on one of his Massachusetts walks in 1852, thought the flower seemed to sport "fringed, recurved parasols over its anthers." He found the iris a bit much, "a little too showy and gaudy, like some women's bonnets," but there's no accounting for taste. Laura loved them, and the girls brought bouquets to Ma for the table. It didn't take Laura long to discover that, like the morning glories, the blue flag buds bloom for one day only. When she was grounded indoors—punished for venturing unaccompanied to the deep water of the swimming hole—she mourned the loss of that day's blue flag and morning glory blossoms. They are ephemeral, like childhood.

Near the sword-leaved irises, the girls found clumps of jointed rushes perfect for pretending. Because their stems are hollow, the girls repurposed them as straws to blow bubbles in the water. Their segments served as beads for play necklaces. Wilder distinguishes rushes from similar plants and elaborates on their characteristics as if she is instructing her readers on plant identification. Instead of soft, bendable grasses, flat like ribbons, she points out the roundness of rushes, their sleek, hard texture, even their squeakiness.

The plants and water supported abundant wildlife in and around Plum Creek, and many animals are used as plot devices in Wilder's fiction. Waterbugs scoot on the stream's surface and dragonflies hover above it, each perfectly adapted to its respective medium. "A big old crab"—a crayfish—nestled under a stone in the creek, and leeches, those "nasty things," made their shady domicile in a mud-bottomed pool. A badger with a den in the bank terrified Laura. When Pa found his hole, the badger disappeared, at least from the storyline. One might extrapolate that the badger became one of Pa's pelts.

In the creek Charles Ingalls also installed an efficient but sustainable method of harvesting fish. He made a trap of lath, set near the waterfall to catch buffalo fish, pickerels, catfish, shiners, and more. "Pa never took more than a few to eat and would let the others go," Wilder takes pains to explain, "He said there were so many fish in the creek, it was all right to take some, but it was wicked to kill anything one didn't need."

The creek and the prairie beckoned many birds. You can learn to recognize birdcalls, using *On the Banks of Plum Creek* to test your knowledge. Wilder included several birds identified only by their songs. "Tweet, tweet, oh twitter twee twit" belongs to the tail-bobbing northern waterthrush, a small bird with a very large voice. "Chee chee chee" is the song of the bobolink, a black and white bird in clerical garb. A third, "Ha ha ha, tiraloo," is the call of a western willet, a wading bird that breeds and feeds on Minnesota's well-watered prairies. Laura spotted willets with their long beaks and longer legs probing the edges of Plum Creek for morsels like baby crabs, leeches, and the occasional small fish. Willets are in the snipe family, and it is splendid that Wilder

"What is it about water that always affects a person?" Wilder later wrote. »

« A long-legged snipe as shown in the *American Agriculturist Cyclopedia of Natural History* (1887).

Laura's party featured Ma's vanity cakes, a white tablecloth, and a bouquet of wildflowers. »

included their laughing song. Mary and Laura, in their short dresses, are taunted as "long-legged snipes" in the schoolyard by the horrid little brother of that fictional arch villain, Nellie Oleson.

Mary and Laura, the fictional characters, go to school for the first time in *On the Banks of Plum Creek*. In real life they had also attended the Barry Corner School back in Wisconsin where Laura had learned to read and spell. Of her Minnesota schooldays, Wilder shared vivid memories of recess. The boys played boy games, while girls played their own and wandered through the prairie grass picking wildflowers.

Bouquets of wildflowers are tiny indulgences. Like a cloth on the table or Ma's china shepherdess, a posy arranged in a blue pitcher bespoke pride of place. Early in the year there were violets and buttercups, along with the charming edible sheep sorrel with lavender flowers and leaves that tasted like springtime. As summer arrived there were black-eyed Susans and goldenrod to pick. Posies also take their metaphorical place in Wilder's descriptions. When the girls dressed for the town party, Ma said they looked as pretty as posies. Caroline got the same compliment from Charles regarding her stylish black-and-white calico dress on Sunday. She had just finished making it. That's Ma, stylish and practical.

Turnips are among the root vegetables stored in the cellar for use as a table vegetable and to feed the animals over the winter.

During the growing season Pa dragged himself in from the fields at night—a farmer's fatigue—too tired to fiddle. He sowed and howed: the wheat, oats, potatoes, and turnips. Of the turnips, he quoted an old planting rhyme, to "sow the turnips the twenty-fifth of July, wet or dry." This advice had appeared a decade earlier in the July 1865 issue of *The Wisconsin Farmer and Northwestern Cultivator*, so perhaps Charles Ingalls had read it there. But even then the editor, J. W. Hoyt, discounted the saying. "We would not recommend so rigid an adherence to any particular day," he wrote. "They will usually do well, if properly put in, even though as early as the first or as late as the last of July." Still they needed to go in, to keep the livestock as well as the people adequately fed during the off-season.

Nature and the farmer seem in a constant tug of war. As fast as Charles Ingalls put in his potatoes, pocket gophers made off with them, leaving mounds of dirt that appeared "as large as a half bushel scattered here and there in the grass where Pa had planted potatoes." They carried the seed potatoes off, stuffed in their cheek pockets, the way chipmunks carry around nuts. Pa, with his excellent aim, killed one with a clot of dirt. But the gophers were nothing new. As early as the 1860s, Redwood County had already issued cash bounties for them.

But no bounty could control the grasshoppers. Starting in 1873, they descended on the area around Walnut Grove. When the Ingallses arrived the

An 1875 stereoscopic image, entitled "Suspense," from a series showing the grasshoppers arriving in Nebraska.

following year, Wilder remembered their return, a "light-colored fleecy cloud… their wings a shiny white." For a moment, it was almost angelic. Their translucent mass screened the sun, a living, quivering halo, but when they dropped to the ground it was "like hail in a hailstorm." Other sources agree. In *Early Days Near Walnut Grove*, the author, Charles Howe, recalled those plagues. "We stood helpless at the side and saw the field change from green to black in so short a time," he wrote. "It really did seem that while we were looking on, the edge of the green field moved slowly along not only destroying the crops, but destroying our peace of mind, almost." The grasshoppers ate everything, clearing not just the field crops and gardens, but "every particle of grass." And, as Laura observed, all the plums, all the leaves, every last bit along Plum Creek.

The migratory grasshoppers were nomads that were a perfect storm for the farmers who unknowingly prepared the way for them. Wheat created a sudden spike in food supply, like a giant supermarket opening in a neighborhood that had previously gotten by with a convenience store. And newly plowed land—just like Pa's—was the perfect repository for laying eggs. It was heaven for hoppers.

Nothing seemed to control them, not flails, not ditches, not smudge from burning straw or manure, not even "hopperdozers"—sheets of iron covered in coal tar and dragged across the fields—seemed to make a dent in their numbers. Only the chickens were happy, eating their fill, though some reported that the all-grasshopper diet tainted the taste of the meat.

In late summer of 1875, Charles Ingalls walked miles to eastern Minnesota, driven to seek work on the grain harvest in a part of the state unscathed by insects. "He walked because there was no money to pay for a ride on the train," Laura wrote, "and he must go where he could get work in the harvest fields to earn money for us to live on through the winter." In modern parlance, we might call him a migrant worker. He left his then-pregnant wife and daughters in Walnut Grove to manage the farm. They had the help of Mr. Nelson, a good neighbor who, among other things, plowed a much-needed firebreak on the west side of the new house and barn. The prairie fire came and was frightening, but Nelson's careful plowing saved the Ingalls home and livestock.

Pa returned some months later, again by foot, wages in hand. We can hope he made it back in time for the birth of his son, Charles Frederick, "Freddie," born on the 1st of November, 1875. The next spring Laura remembered her father getting his seed wheat off the train. Both the state and county governments sponsored some sporadic farm relief efforts to citizens in need during the years of infestation. But when grasshoppers hatched again, "Pa said he'd had enough. He wouldn't stay in such a [erasure] 'blasted country!'"

Sad to say, Charles Ingalls was a master of bad timing. He sold his farm in early July 1876, almost breaking even with his initial investment but with little to show for his two years of backbreaking work. The next year, the grasshoppers departed. Walnut Grove farmers took in a record crop in 1877, but the Ingallses were not there to see it.

While Laura was unhappy to leave her Plum Creek playground, she was ready to move. In *Pioneer Girl*, Wilder wrote, "The wagon was covered; our things were loaded and early on a bright morning the horses were hitched on, we all climbed in and started east." East!?! Yes, while in her novels Wilder focuses on the westward march of her family, they actually moved back and forth, less like a beeline and more like the track of a butterfly.

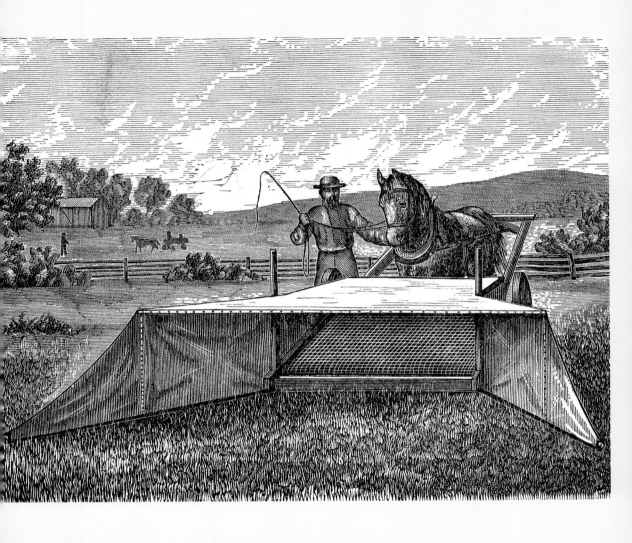

Hopperdozers scraped grasshoppers into pans filled with coal tar in an image from the 1883 *Report of the Commissioner of Agriculture*.

Laura remembered their neighbor Eleck Nelson plowing their firebreak while Pa was working in eastern Minnesota.

In this case they moved to Iowa, with an extended stay en route in eastern Minnesota with Uncle Peter Ingalls, Charles's older brother, and Aunt Eliza Ann, Caroline's younger sister, who had settled in Wabasha County along the Zumbro River. It was, for a time, a happy interlude. Laura got reacquainted with her double cousins, especially Ella and Peter who were closest to her in age. The trio was charged with tending the cows, and they made the most of it, enjoying the shady, flowered riverbanks. Forty years later, Wilder would write:

> All through the tall grass were scattered purple and white flag blossoms and I have stood in that peaceful grassland corner, with the red cow and the spotted cow and the roan taking their goodnight mouthfuls of the sweet grass, and watched the sun setting behind the hilltop and loved the purple flags and the rippling brook and wondered at the beauty of the world, while I wriggled my bare toes down into the soft grass.

The Rocky Mountain locust, now extinct, that once swarmed across the Great Plains, in a photograph from the 1870s.

The three cousins would stuff themselves on wild plums, including the frost plum—"a big, beautiful purple kind with a dusting of white that made it look as if it were frosted." The frost plum is likely a damson, introduced from the Old World, or a hybrid of European and American varieties. Some of these plant crosses were manmade, bred by colonial nurserymen as early as the eighteenth century to create new cultivars suited to local conditions. Others were the result of plum blossoms and their insect pollinators doing what comes naturally. Seeds of some of these plums leaped the orchard fence and escaped into the wild, spreading to places like Minnesota for Laura and her cousins to sample. The authors of *The Fruits and Fruit Trees of America*, published in 1857, give the frost plum a succulent review as "a late plum, scarcely yielding to any other late variety in the excellence of its flavor . . . juicy, sweet, rich and melting."

But with the sweet, there was bitter for the Ingalls family. By the time the frost came, baby Freddie had died. The Ingallses left Minnesota. While Wilder never discussed the family's grief, it had to have shadowed their trip as well as their stint in Burr Oak, Iowa.

This illustration of a creek, a girl, and her imagination appeared in the
Independent Fifth Reader that Mary and Laura used in school.

There Charles Ingalls took a break from farming and tried his hand at two new ventures. But the hotel business didn't suit him, and the grain mill, which he operated for a season, was disappointing. Still, the place had its compensations, especially the birth of Grace Pearl Ingalls, who arrived on May 23, 1877. While there could be no replacing their lost child, the golden-haired, blue-eyed newborn was a blessing.

Burr Oak was a settled place, but the Ingallses were not. In their two years in town, Charles and Caroline moved their family three times. First they lived downstairs in the Masters Hotel where they worked, along with Mary and Laura who waited table and washed dishes. Then they took rooms above Kimball's Grocery two doors down, next to the saloon. A saloon does not a good neighbor make. Between the drinking and the noise, it was too Wild West—though perhaps we should say Wild Midwest—for the Ingallses. (Ma became a supporter of the temperance movement.)

After the saloon almost burned down one night, they relocated once again, to a small brick house that they rented two blocks away. It was on the edge of town, not far from a pasture for their new cow and adjacent to an oak wood "that was filled with sunshine and shadows, where birds sang and wildflowers grew." The oaks were likely those for which the town was named.

The bur oak, spelled with a single "r," is a rugged prairie species named for its distinctive seeds. If you think of the expression "a burr under the saddle," meaning something or someone who is persistently annoying, you will have an idea of the prickliness of the caps on the bur oak's enormous acorns. Its botanical name, *Quercus macrocarpa*, points to the acorn's dimensions—"large" (*macro-*) "seed" (*-carpa*).

As in Minnesota, Laura delighted in fetching the family cow from its pasture and picking flowers there. The meadow was greened by Silver Creek which wound through it, edged by flag irises. Sweet Williams opened pink among the grasses. If you grow flowers or buy them at the market, you may think of the sweet William as a small carnation with clustered flowers, gathered like small bouquets on its wiry stems. But sweet William is a common name shared by several different plants with similar structures. In this case, Wilder is referring to the graceful spotted meadow phlox, *Phlox maculata*, which blooms in moist places in Iowa at the same time as the iris.

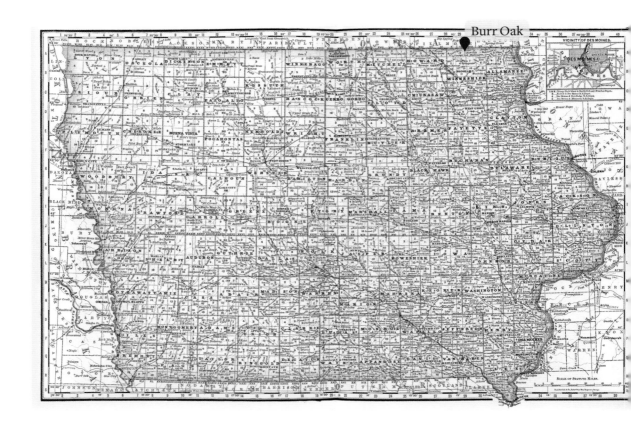

Burr Oak, Iowa, is just over the state line from Minnesota, and not far from the Mississippi River.

Pl. 3.

P.J Redouté

I

Renard Sc.

QUERCUS macrocarpa.
Over Cup White Oak.

The bur oak (though with a different common name) was included in *The North American Sylva* (1812), the first work encompassing western tree species.

While Laura was gathering flowers, her father was gathering steam to hit the road again. Burr Oak was no longer to his liking, "[A] dead town, he said it was, without even a railroad." The ten-year-old Laura started hearing the "lonesome, longing music" from Pa's fiddle and bow during the spring of 1877, his regular moving-on refrain. In addition to his wanderlust, Charles Ingalls was a young man with a cash flow problem and creditors who wouldn't listen to reason. So he packed the family into the wagon and left one night under cover of darkness— "between two days" as it is sometimes said—with debts outstanding.

Heading west once more, Pa brought his wife and four girls temporarily back to Walnut Grove. He picked up work as a butcher and a carpenter. He built a little house on a lot near town and, with a borrowed team, plowed a good-sized garden behind it. Two years passed in Walnut Grove. Two gardens yielded their harvests. The girls went to school, and Laura excelled in sports, though Mary called her a tomboy.

The spring after her twelfth birthday Laura helped her father get the new season's garden started, and then "Mary and I made some flower beds and planted seeds and set out plants that Missouri Pool gave us." Missouri Pool was a young, pipe-smoking neighbor whose life and garden left a vivid impression on Laura. Missouri Pool's flowering garden was full of fragrant mignonette, bright moss roses—another name for portulaca—and hollyhocks standing tall against a fence. For Laura, one flower had special allure. "I loved the poppies best, with their wonderful colors and the texture of their petals, the blossoms were like silken banners blowing in the wind."

In *Pioneer Girl*, Wilder remembered that her sister Mary liked to dig in the flowerbeds, while she—Laura—"did hate to get my fingers in the dirt." Is this a turnabout on the sibling personality front? Laura, by this time on the brink of her teen years, seems to have developed a temporary aversion to soil. Or maybe she just couldn't be bothered growing flowers when wildflowers abound on the prairie. But soon it would be a different prairie yet again.

⌃ Soft petals waving on wiry stems make poppies look like "silken banners," rain or shine.

⌄ Laura's wild sweet William is a type of phlox with spotted stems.

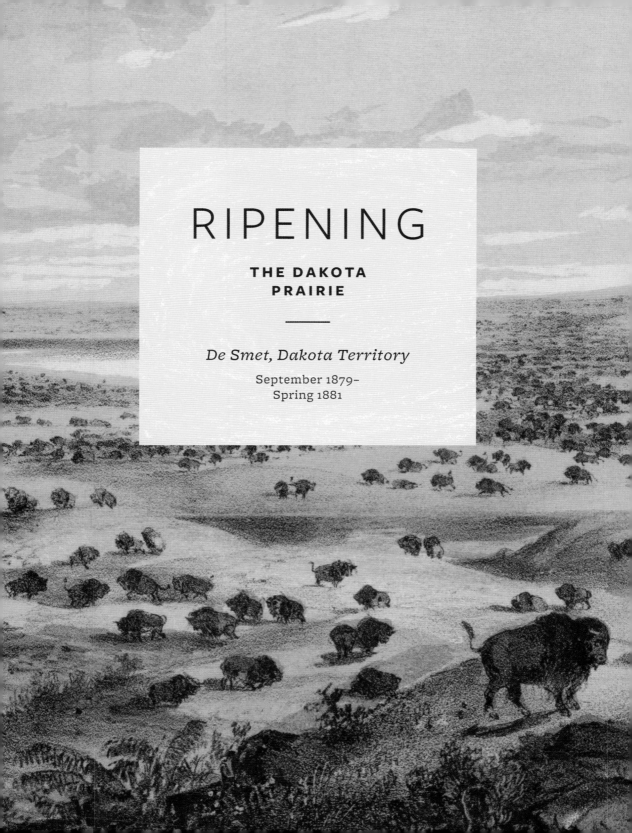

RIPENING

THE DAKOTA
PRAIRIE

———

De Smet, Dakota Territory

September 1879–
Spring 1881

The earliest known image of the three older Ingalls sisters. From left to right: Carrie, Mary, and Laura.

We're west of Minnesota, and north of
Indian Territory, so naturally the flowers
and grasses are not the same.

— BY THE SHORES OF SILVER LAKE

Growing up has never been easy, but the two eldest Ingalls girls had extra cares. In the spring of 1879, Laura found herself assuming a different role in the family. Fourteen-year-old Mary was struck blind. An attack of meningitis temporarily paralyzed half of her face and permanently damaged her optic nerves. It was a bolt of lightning, like the one that had struck an oak tree in front of their Wisconsin log cabin nearly a decade before. Laura remembered Mary's tree, "out in the yard, with her play things under it, was struck by lightening one day in a storm. The tree wasn't killed but one side of it was made dead and the branches broken off." Like the oak, Mary survived with lasting scars.

The changes to Mary's life also changed the trajectory of Laura's. She took on many of the roles of senior sibling—in school, in the garden, and eventually as wage earner. She became Mary's eyes, describing everything in detail to her sister. This process of seeing out loud cemented Laura's memories, etching impressions in her mind and honing her skills as a narrator.

It was a thrill for Laura to see the landscape moving at the speed of a locomotive. This picture was taken in Tracy circa 1880.

With the family's next move, Laura had plenty of new things to see and describe for Mary. The offer of employment with the Dakota Central Railway, part of the expanding Chicago & North Western system, and the lure of unsettled land, led Charles Ingalls to uproot his family once more. Traveling ahead, he went further west into Dakota Territory, farther than he'd been before, leaving Caroline to pack and settle up in Walnut Grove.

Then, as Wilder described in *By the Shores of Silver Lake*, Ma and the girls boarded the train, bag and baggage. Caroline, wearing a hat adorned with lily-of-the-valley, held baby Grace. The older girls, in their flowered calico dresses, were awed with the wonders of the passenger car. They took the train to its terminus at Tracy, Minnesota, where Pa met them with the wagon to continue on to the railroad camp.

This railroad camp in 1875 gives an idea of the rough-and-ready setting Caroline and the girls found at the end of their journey. (The Northern Pacific line, shown here, passed 200 miles north of De Smet.)

Charles Ingalls would play a part in what train buffs now label as the "Great Dakota Railroad Boom." In the late 1870s, the big three companies of the region—the North Western, the Milwaukee Road, and the Omaha Road—pounced on the Territory, laying rails for passenger and freight traffic and the spread of permanent settlement that would forever alter the prairie. The time was right. Economic conditions in the country were bouncing back from the depression that followed a panic in 1873. The Black Hills gold rush that started in 1874 had put the Dakotas on the map. Transportation by river and stage was slow, so trains seemed the perfect investment. In 1879, Charles Ingalls was hired to keep the books and act as paymaster for one camp of workers extending the train line from Tracy into the Dakota Territory.

Traveling by railroad, one sees a different view of the landscape, a landscape galloping by at speed. In *By the Shores of Silver Lake*, Laura has her first

At first glance, a prairie might seem monotonous.

train ride. She was a girl whose experience of velocity thus far had been horse-drawn rather than steam-powered. She tried to paint word pictures of the views out the window for Mary but found it hard to catch at twenty miles per hour. The telegraph poles zoomed by. Clumps of trees growing near houses, haystacks, and stubble fields were dashes of color—green, yellow-brown, rust-red.

Wilder was among the many contemporary writers who described these sensations. Willa Cather opened *My Ántonia* with a summer railway journey across the Iowa plains, "[T]he train flashed through the never-ending miles of ripe wheat, by country town and bright colored pastures and oak groves wilting in the sun." Victor Hugo, describing the French countryside from a train window, wrote, "The flowers by the side of the road are no longer flowers but flecks, or rather streaks, of red or white; there are no longer any points, everything becomes a streak; the grain fields are great shocks of yellow hair; fields of alfalfa, long green tresses; the towns, the steeples, and the trees perform a crazy, mingling dance." For Laura, the plants and places she saw were untethered, a moving picture, until the train stopped.

When the women of the Ingalls family disembarked and rendezvoused with Pa, everything slowed to its familiar pace as they journeyed west by wagon. The tide of Laura's adolescent hormones seemed to rise during this plodding ride. The terrain was tedious. Everything was boring. She moaned that "nothing happened on the way and the road looked all the same." You can almost hear her say, "Are we there yet?"

I first experienced the prairie through a car window. The year was 1960-something and the automobile was a new AMC Rambler station wagon, big enough to hold two parents and four children, plus cooler, thermos, and suitcases. It was late summer. Before dawn the prior day, my father had herded us into the car to start west from New Jersey to my mother's hometown of Lincoln, Illinois, for a vacation with grandparents, aunts, uncles, and many, many cousins. The Ryans were a prolific clan.

Day one, Dad drove us across the Pennsylvania Turnpike, with its roadside picnic tables and mountain tunnels, and pushed on as far as Columbus, Ohio, stopping at a motel with a pool in the parking lot and a Big Boy restaurant next door. Far different from the Ingallses' accommodations when they were Dakota-bound. The next day the land widened out. Mountains, hills, and trees, gone. From western Ohio across Indiana and into the heart of the Land of Lincoln, we saw sky and flat land with corn, corn, corn, soybeans, and corn. The view seemed boring to me, but Mom said it was beautiful.

To pass the time, she had let each of us choose one activity book from Woolworth's, the dime store, to bring along on the trip so we could play hangman, connect the dots, and the like. As the prairie rolled by, there were endless group games of I Spy and license plate spotting, and, in later years, Slug-A-Bug—a modestly violent pastime involving Volkswagen Beetles and shoulder blows—which had to be played with stealth to stay under the maternal radar. When Dad got drowsy he sang, just as Charles Ingalls had sung as their wagon jolted along. The car echoed with our father's deep baritone, rendering folksongs, hymns, and ditties. "Old Dan Tucker," "That Old Rugged Cross," and "The Bear Went Over the Mountain" come to mind.

I was the baby—our brother Jerry, the eldest, sat up front—so my designated

spot was middle of the backseat, the filling in the older-sister sandwich. Pat had an
intense allergy to corn pollen and wanted the windows rolled up tight. Kay liked fresh
air and wanted to crank them down. Did I mention there was no air-conditioning?
In truth, I can't complain. My stoic sisters would let me sleep stretched out with my
head on one lap and my feet on the other. Travel methods may have changed since the
1870s, but family dynamics? Immutable.

—MM

The immense Dakota prairie that Laura and her sisters experienced from
their board bench in the back of the wagon was at the frontier of settlement,
where, as Wilder later wrote, the West began. Laura had a strange feeling once
they got beyond the Big Sioux River, or, as she noted during the dry season of
1879, the not-so-big Big Sioux. She and her family seemed to shrink under that
stretching sky. The prairie seemed different too, and Ma stated in her mat-
ter-of-fact way, "We're west of Minnesota, and north of Indian Territory, so
naturally the flowers and grasses are not the same." In one sentence, Wilder
provided a combination geography-botany lesson in her mother's voice. Consider where you are, then look—really look—at the plants around you.

You have got to give Ma credit. While by today's standards her attitudes
toward Indians, as depicted in her daughter's novels, are cringe-worthy ste-
reotypes, Caroline Ingalls offered her family other lessons that still ring true,
including environmental responsibility. On the ride Pa had stopped the wagon
so that the family could eat its simple repast of buttered bread and boiled eggs.
When everyone was finished, Ma instructed them to tidy up the eggshells and
the papers (they had folded up salt and pepper for the eggs in little paper pack-
ets). An Ingalls did not litter.

Not far from their Silver Lake destination, they came to a solitary tree.
Pa expected it, seemed to look for it, saying that the Lone Cottonwood was
the only tree between the two rivers—the Big Sioux, which they had crossed,
and the Jim, or James, that was some thirty miles west beyond their railroad

The prairie seems a landscape of sameness, but it is full of surprises.

camp destination. Large lone cottonwoods were arboreal landmarks, navigation beacons for the indigenous people of the plains and the pioneers on their
prairie crossings. A famous one in Nebraska along the Platte River was a tribal
meeting place, a known marker on the Oregon Trail, and eventually the site of
the Lone Tree stagecoach stop. (There is a granite monument at the site near
present-day Central City.) Another, the Landmark Cottonwood, is still alive,
though struggling, in the Texas panhandle's Black Kettle National Grasslands.

These giants were tenacious trees, exceptional for their size in treeless
surrounds. Pa was ready to propagate, declaring that he'd get some of the seeds
of the Lone Cottonwood. This was a great idea horticulturally, as its size and
vigor indicate good genetic makeup, though Mendel's ideas on inheritance
weren't known yet. But before the Ingallses were ready to plant trees, they
would need to find a homestead in their new locale.

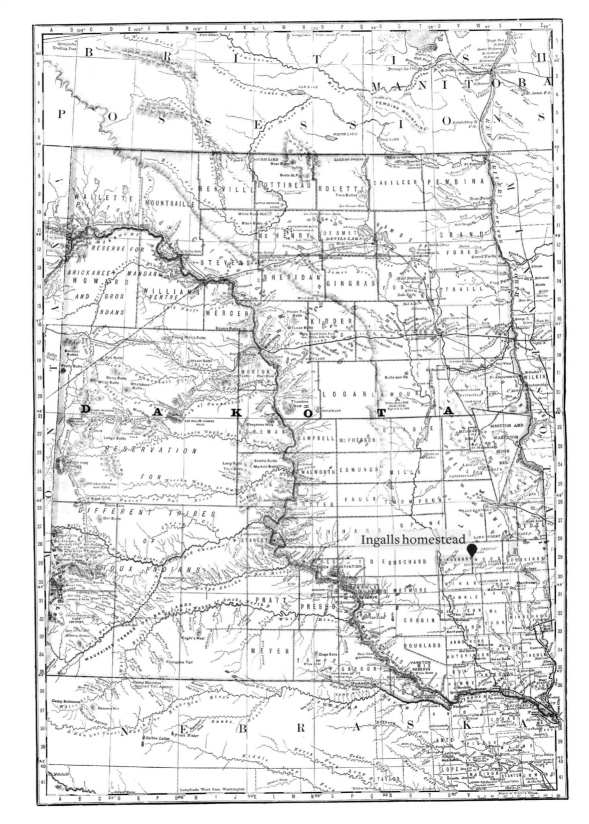

Ingalls homestead

Sloughgrass grows to mammoth size in prairie wetlands.

The place where the Ingalls family finally landed was in the Prairie Pothole Region, an area that stretches across parts of the Dakotas, Minnesota, and north into the Canadian provinces. It is a mecca for fresh water, a wide, undulating grassland polka-dotted with ponds, lakes, and marshes that are left over from the Pleistocene.

At the end of the last Ice Age, the ancient glacier abandoned cargo as it withdrew northward. Huge chunks of ice got left behind like land-locked icebergs. As the stagnant blocks of dead ice melted, some created kettle depressions filled with water, later christened Silver Lake, Spirit Lake, and the Twin Lakes, Henry and Thompson. Others dissipated into smaller channels and loose wetlands. In prairie parlance, this type of marshy fen is termed a slough (pronounced "sloo," rhymes with dew). The glacier also left sand and gravel deposits forming a substrate that, given sufficient precipitation, recharges this liquid patchwork. This was a land with easy access to water for people, plants, and animals, tailor-made for wildlife and an aspiring farmer. "Good water, good wells and plenty of them at De Smet," reported the *Daily Press*, a Yankton, South Dakota, paper, on May 20, 1880. Charles Ingalls always liked a place where there was a good and ample water supply.

An 1878 map of Dakota Territory shows Kingsbury County before it officially absorbed its neighbor, Wood County, in 1880. The Ingalls family crossed the Big Sioux River on their way to the railroad camp in De Smet.

He had finally gotten his wish and made it beyond the settled area. When the railroad workers withdrew before the winter of 1879, the Ingallses had a rare leisurely break at the company's invitation. They spent the season in the comfortable house the railroad had built for its surveyors. Not only was it furnished with a good cookstove, it also had a full larder. Nineteenth-century food preservation techniques—salt, sun, sugar—were well-represented in this larder stocked with salted fish, cucumber pickles, dried apples, and canned peaches.

If, when reading *By the Shores of Silver Lake*, you were surprised that Ma found canned peaches when she plumbed the offerings of the surveyors' pantry, you needn't be. The federal government issued the first U.S. patent for a tin-plated can during the 1820s. By mid-century, hermetically sealed cans of meats and fish—oysters were a popular product from the start—were standard fare for overland journeys and sea voyages. Civil War soldiers used cans of condensed milk to lighten their coffee. By the Ingallses' Dakota days, small factories across the country put out an array of canned goods, including vegetables and fruit, distributed through grocers in big towns and small. A recipe for fritters on the front page of *The Canton Advocate* (Canton is south of Brookings and Sioux Falls), September 18, 1879, noted, "Delicious if made of canned peaches and the juice of the peaches well sweetened and poured over them when served, for sauce." The recipe was in a column entitled "Domestic Interlude."

The Ingallses' domestic interlude was enhanced that December by the arrival of a friend, Robert Boast, who had worked with Pa on the railroad and then gone back to Iowa at the end of the work season. He returned with his wife, Ella. The Boasts were a jolly couple, bringing games and music, recipes and reading material with them. In the novel, the fictional Ella Boast also brought seeds from home that she gladly shared with Caroline. I like to think that the real Ella Boast did too, though there is no record of it.

The Homestead Act of 1862 and a set of related laws were social- and landscape-engineering enacted on a continental scale. Thomas Jefferson was one of the concept's original architects. Well before he was president, not long after the end of the Revolutionary War, he and some of his fellow congressmen crafted the Public Land Survey System to divvy up the west—at that time, the Ohio Valley and the areas bordering the Great Lakes—into square townships, six miles to a side, each composed of 36 one-mile-square sections.

Pa's land was only free if you don't count labor.

These gentlemen of Congress seemed in love with the right angle. They hadn't invented the grid plan; it had been an urban planning standard at least as far back as Biblical times, employed by Hammurabi in Babylon and beloved of the builders of the Roman Empire. In the new United States, territorial land sales from the Land Ordinance of 1785 funded the nascent government and supported Jefferson's ideal of a democracy of yeoman citizens. These citizens would also be educated, as the sale of one section in each township supported local public schools. If you fly over the Great Plains and look down at the land from an airplane window you will see the concept extended and writ large by generations of farmers. Fields are rectilinear. Roads edge the section boundaries. State and county lines generally do too. Only natural features—creeks, rivers, and the like—run counter to this regularity.

Charles Ingalls filed his patent—made his bet with the government—in Brookings in February 1880, on a parcel in Section 3. The standard unit of a land claim in the Homestead Act was 160 acres, or one quarter of a 640-acre (one square mile) section, but the quarter he selected was 159.24 acres. This might be because the surveyor couldn't or wouldn't wade out into the Big Slough, resulting in one boundary line that meandered slightly. Or it might have been a calculated fractional section, required at intervals because, lest we forget, the earth is not flat. Meridians converge.

Homesteaders converged on the Dakota Territory to get a good deal. Under the Homestead Act, with the exception of small filing fees, the land would be free—transferred from the public domain to private deed—if an applicant like Charles Ingalls built a home, grew crops, and lived there for five years.

To encourage settlement, which in turn would increase commerce, ridership, and profits, the Chicago & North Western lent a hand. In the spring of 1880, Arthur Jacobi, a Wisconsin civil engineer hired as a surveyor for the railroad, returned and staked out a new town directly south of the tracks and just west of Pa's claim. It was one of many towns Jacobi and his counterparts laid out, strung like square beads at regular intervals along the Dakota Territory's new rail lines.

The lots, blocks, streets, and alleys in the town near Pa's claim followed a simple grid plan. The main street ran perpendicular from the train tracks

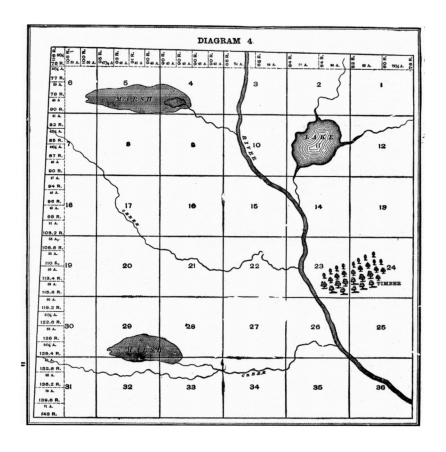

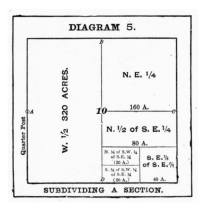

The land survey applied a grid-based system of sections and townships across much of the United States.

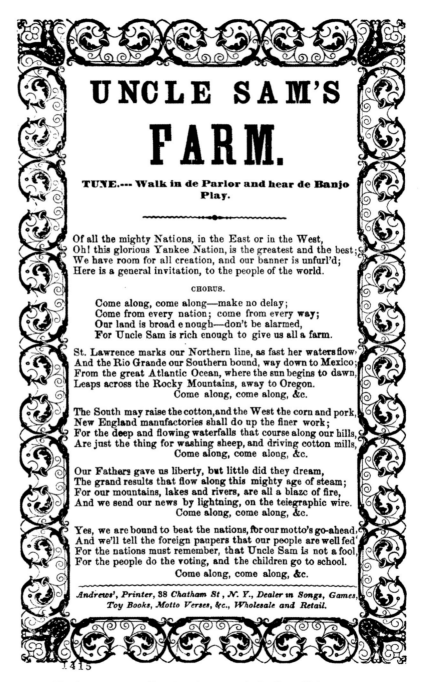

UNCLE SAM'S
FARM.

TUNE.--- Walk in de Parlor and hear de Banjo Play.

Of all the mighty Nations, in the East or in the West,
Oh! this glorious Yankee Nation, is the greatest and the best;
We have room for all creation, and our banner is unfurl'd;
Here is a general invitation, to the people of the world.

CHORUS.

Come along, come along—make no delay;
Come from every nation; come from every way;
Our land is broad enough—don't be alarmed,
For Uncle Sam is rich enough to give us all a farm.

St. Lawrence marks our Northern line, as fast her waters flow,
And the Rio Grande our Southern bound, way down to Mexico;
From the great Atlantic Ocean, where the sun begins to dawn,
Leaps across the Rocky Mountains, away to Oregon.
Come along, come along, &c.

The South may raise the cotton, and the West the corn and pork,
New England manufactories shall do up the finer work;
For the deep and flowing waterfalls that course along our hills,
Are just the thing for washing sheep, and driving cotton mills,
Come along, come along, &c.

Our Fathers gave us liberty, but little did they dream,
The grand results that flow along this mighty age of steam;
For our mountains, lakes and rivers, are all a blaze of fire,
And we send our news by lightning, on the telegraphic wire.
Come along, come along, &c.

Yes, we are bound to beat the nations, for our motto's go-ahead,
And we'll tell the foreign paupers that our people are well fed,
For the nations must remember, that Uncle Sam is not a fool,
For the people do the voting, and the children go to school.
Come along, come along, &c.

Andrews', Printer, 38 Chatham St, N. Y., Dealer in Songs, Games, Toy Books, Motto Verses, &c., Wholesale and Retail.

Songs like this encouraged immigration to settle the Great Plains.

and was called "Calumet," the name of the ceremonial Indian pipe. The town itself was called De Smet, enshrining the name of a French Jesuit priest, a Black Robe who had ministered to the Lakota Sioux. It became the seat of the newly organized Kingsbury County. The first structure built in town was a saloon. Caroline Ingalls surely disapproved.

On April 1, 1880—no joke despite April Fools' Day—an energetic newspaperman hauled a printing press to De Smet by horse cart from Volga, a town thirty miles east and two months older, over the newly laid and as-yet-unused train tracks. The first issue of the *Kingsbury County News*, later renamed the *De Smet Leader*, came off the press later that month. It reported, "Business men looking for locations are now coming in with a rush. De Smet is on the boom." The first scheduled train reached De Smet on Tuesday, May 11, 1880, at 3:00 p.m. By the end of the month, mail arrived daily and a lumberyard was up and running.

Charles Ingalls was part of the boom, a one-man whirlwind of activity that year. He broke sod and planted his first crops of sod corn and potatoes, which didn't need a smooth seedbed. After waiting a couple of months for the grasses to start to rot, he would have "backset" his grain fields by re-plowing them in furrows perpendicular to the first. This crisscross plow pattern made a finer seedbed for smaller grains like wheat, oats, and barley. In town he bought two corner lots diagonally across from one another on Calumet Avenue. He built two commercial buildings out of wood salvaged from the now-unused railroad construction sheds. Nothing went to waste on the prairie, especially not scarce lumber. He built a shanty to house his family on his quarter section. It is exhausting to think about Charles Ingalls's work output that year.

In short order, Pa, Ma, and the girls moved out to the claim. On the way, or so goes the story, thirteen-year-old Laura caught her first glimpse of Almanzo Wilder, then twenty-three, driving his eye-catching team of Morgan horses. Almanzo, along with his older brother, Royal, and their sister, Eliza Jane, had filed claims on land north and west of town in August of 1879. (James and Angeline Wilder had moved their family from New York to Spring Valley, Minnesota, in 1873.)

That spring, the local wildlife was doing land-office business too. "Prairie

Prairie chickens, once abundant in North America, are a type of grouse with a loud mating ritual in spring. Males inflate unfeathered air sacs on either side of their necks to produce "booming."

chickens are contriving in getting up a boom of their own," the De Smet newspaper joked. (The males of the species display with a wild booming call to attract mates.) One Sunday the editor spotted a flock of thirty pronghorns—what he called antelopes—south of town. Another day, Pa must have exercised a hunter's bragging rights, as De Smet's news of the day boasted, "C. P. Ingalls shot a large white swan on Silver Lake one day last week. It measured six feet eight inches from tip to tip."

The sloughs and lakes, silver sheets of fresh water flung across the prairie in abundance, drew a profusion of birds. Wilder documents one of the great migratory flyways of North America. Birds animated Silver Lake with a bedlam of takeoffs and landings and a babel of honks. Ducks appear in the book in force: dabbling ducks like mallards and teals that frequented the shallows,

Fowl, fish, and other fauna gather in lakes and prairie potholes.

and diving ducks like the redheads, bluebills, and canvasbacks. Some walked—
or at least swam—like a duck, but weren't, like the mud hen, which is a coot,
and the hell-diver, another name for a small grebe. There were wading herons
and cranes, and a few, like gulls and pelicans, that seemed as if they would be
happier with an ocean closer by. Some ate mostly plants, including the geese
and swans; the others were omnivores, partaking of fish, frogs, and the like,
as well as vegetation.

The ghosts of the great herds of American bison lingered on the Dakota
prairie in the names of flora and terrain. As in Kansas, there were clumps of
wiry buffalo grass that the stock gravitated toward. But in this new place, Laura
also spotted buffalo beans, a low-growing plant with plum-colored flowers,
and buffalo wallows.

Buffalo bean, as its name suggests, is a part of the great botanical bean

American bison once filled Dakota Territory as in this image, circa 1855, with a herd stretching to the horizon near Lake Jessie in present-day North Dakota.

Buffalo bean is a member of the bean family that blooms each spring on the prairie.

family, the Fabaceae. Members of this tribe share a flower shape that is easy to pick out of a floral line-up. Uneven in shape and size, the two large upper petals form the banner, with two smaller wings tucked in below, and the smallest center petal, the keel, at the base. Without too big a stretch, the flowers resemble Lilliputian male turkeys—or prairie chickens—fanning their tails. Peas and beans, vetch and wisteria share the same floral structure, a structure that coevolved with its insect pollinators.

Find some buffalo beans with their purple flowers in spring, and you will witness this age-old love fest between bloom and bee. If you can hang around for a month or two more, you may see something munching the green leaves, likely the larval offspring of the small duskywing butterfly that lay eggs on this host plant. Wait longer still, and you will observe the plant's seed pods form and ripen, round like marbles, purple as plums. Some call the plant "ground plum" because of the fruit. Even the second half of its botanical name, *Astragalus crassicarpus*, translates to "thick" (*crassi-*) "fruit" (*-carpus*). (*Astragalus* is a Greek word for members of the bean family). No one recommends eating the fruit because it is difficult to distinguish from similar poisonous species, although the Lakota and Dakota peoples did.

A buffalo wallow with a man for scale, taken in Kansas in 1897.

A buffalo wallow full of violets seemed like magic to Laura and to baby Grace too.

In addition to buffalo beans, Wilder also took note of buffalo wallows. In *Pioneer Girl*, she described the one south of their house:

> It was grassed over and early in the spring the whole hollow was covered with beautiful purple violets, so fragrant that one could smell them before reaching the hollow and a saucerful of the blossoms would perfume a room.

If, as I did, you thought of a wallow as a wet muddy place in which animals roll, then you share my mistake. A buffalo wallow is a dry spot, where bison coat themselves with insect-repelling dust. The bison pick spots at distributed points across their grazing land to use communally. In each wallow over time

they rub out the plant life and grind the earth down into a shallow depression set, as Wilder put it, like a dish into the prairie. It was a big dish—the one she remembered from her family's claim south of the house was about two acres, roughly the area of two football fields. When the buffalo were gone, the hollows remained, collecting scarce prairie moisture and providing a perfect germination bed for violets as well as for imagination. The fictional Laura thought surely it was a fairy ring. Baby Grace, now a toddler, was drawn there too, wandering off to the buffalo wallow in search of its sweet violets.

More than violets spangled the green Dakota grassland. In *Pioneer Girl*, Wilder wrote of "may flowers, thimble flowers, wild sweet Williams, squaw pinks, buffalo beans and wild sunflowers, each blooming in its season." In *By the Shores of Silver Lake* she added others, placing them in her descriptions of the year like china ornaments on whatnot shelves.

Wild crocus are welcome as the first flower of the growing season.

The lily (4) stands tall on the prairie.

In early spring, the wild crocus or pasqueflower blossomed. It rises from the ground around Easter time in a resurrection of its own. (South Dakota, which joined the Union in 1889, designated it the official state flower.) Wild onions and the tangy sheep sorrel were edible and pretty, and, in summer, lilies the color of flames beckoned. Wilder did not gild this lily. Red as the prairie sunset, and taller than the grasses when it blooms, the lily was the center of attention. By late summer and into autumn the prairie erupted with gold as the various sunflowers began to open, such a cheerful sight that it is no wonder that Charles Ingalls sang a cheerful song about them.

Even with this procession of flowers, the Ingallses missed trees. Who doesn't enjoy sitting in the shade of a tree in the heat of a summer day? In addition to being a natural air conditioner, a tree is a thing of beauty, larger than human scale in both time and size. In a display case at the Laura Ingalls Wilder Historic Home and Museum in Mansfield, Missouri, are two landscape

pictures that Laura painted in the 1880s. One is a scene of a woodland water-fall. Another is a cottage in the woods. The caption in the case explains, "The paintings were inspired by her sister Grace, who, ten years younger than Laura, looked up from her reading and asked, 'What is a tree?'" Perhaps Pa heard the question too. He fetched some cottonwood saplings from along Lake Henry and carefully planted them around their latest little house.

Charles had good company in his tree-planting efforts. Eight years earlier J. Sterling Morton, a journalist who later became Secretary of Agriculture under President Grover Cleveland, inaugurated Arbor Day in Nebraska. In March of 1877, the *Chicago Tribune* reported, "Tree planting has become a mania with Nebraskans." The reporter went on to describe a scenario that rang true for Charles Ingalls in Dakota too:

> One of the first acts of the settler, after he has turned over the sod
> and put in his first crop, and after providing a place for his family, is
> to plant trees about his farm. Many species, especially cottonwood,
> grow very rapidly, and in three years form a strong barrier to wind,
> and yield in summer a grateful shade.

During the winter of 1880–1881, everyone in De Smet would wish for stronger barriers to the weather.

Wilder opened *The Long Winter* in summer. We hear Pa's mowing machine, south of the house in the buffalo wallow where bluestem grass grew in force. The air was infused with the smell of the fresh mowing, and Laura pitched in to help with the haying. Big bluestem was the bread-and-butter of the new Dakota farmer. Its seeds and stems were nutritious for livestock in any season. It dominated the tallgrass prairie along with other species like Indiangrass, switchgrass, and little bluestem.

If you tried to design the perfect prairie plant, big bluestem might be the result. Its height lifts its flowers to wave head-and-shoulders above its neighbors, meaning plenty of fertilized seeds will be spread around to reproduce. For an ecosystem prone to going up in flames, big bluestem shrugs off a burn, rebounding from the base and photosynthesizing faster. Even its seeds

Pa planted cottonwoods to grow up and shade the claim shanty.

germinate at a higher rate after a prairie fire. Its roots run deep, up to seven or eight feet down into the ground, providing built-in erosion control. These tenacious roots make it a sought-after plant for modern prairie restorations.

For the plant enthusiast, identifying big bluestem is a snap. It's big and it's blue, growing three to seven feet tall with narrow, blue-green leaf blades alternating up its sturdy stalks. The bases of the stems are an even brighter shade of blue. When in bloom, the skinny flower head splits into linear segments, usually three, which is why some folks, including Almanzo Wilder, call it turkey foot.

The grasses along the slough were, in comparison, less graceful but even more robust. Laura remembered them growing five or six feet high—well above her head—and called them sloughgrass or wild hay. Botanically it is *Spartina pectinata*, a grass that would become vital to the survival of the Ingalls family in the winter of 1881. Like the Ingallses, it is tough, and its dense stands survive drought, inundation, and insect infestation. Its thickness, both above and below ground, made it the best pick for sod bricks or to roof Pa's new barn. Muskrats liked to eat it, then and now, as do Canada geese and the larvae of a few species of moths that refuse to eat anything else. Sloughgrass offers habitat to mammals, birds, and bugs. For the Ingalls family, it was fortunate that, along with big bluestem, Pa cut so much of it in their first summer on the claim.

The cadence of autumn seemed strange that year, and it certainly had a fast beat. The frost came early, leaving the grasses brown and shriveling the leaves on the little cottonwoods. Lit by the morning sun, the prairie glistened. Glittered. Still, as Wilder wrote in *Little Town on the Prairie*, there was ambivalence. "She knew that the bitter frost had killed the hay and the garden. . . . It would leave every living thing dead. But the frost was beautiful."

Laura remembered that Pa had heeded the warning of an Indian in the general store in town about the hard winter to come. A Native American in this area would have been a member of a Great Plains tribe, likely Lakota Sioux. Their understanding of prairie meteorology would have been based on long experience. Starting in the late 1600s, tribal scribes recorded "winter counts," pictograms of significant events, on buffalo skins. They depicted incidents including weather, war, peace, famine, disease, visits, drought, and "deep snow

Big bluestem starting to open into its "turkey foot" shape.

The Long Winter instills a new appreciation for a green pumpkin.

As Laura grew up, she sometimes envied the birds their freedom.

winters." Historians and meteorologists still study them. Charles's neighbors should have paid more attention.

Charles brought in the scant harvest of their first growing season early that autumn of 1880. Laura remembered potatoes and corn, beans and wheat, tomatoes and pumpkins, but the pickings were, as they say, slim. Caroline stretched the produce in every possible way, including making pie out of the green pumpkin. And they moved into town, taking up residence in one of Pa's store buildings on Calumet Avenue.

Their move was just in time. The first blizzard that year was in the middle of October. Once the cold set in, the frigid air burned its way down Laura's nose into her lungs. The world shrunk in color to near monochrome. Gray skies, blue shadows, white snow, and when the sun shone, casts of pink and lavender. Still, the local paper did its best to keep up spirits. "Our school goes

Photographed and Published by ELMER & TENNEY, – WINONA, MINN.

E. & T. Minnesota Snow View Series of 1881.

Southern Minnesota Division, C. M. & St. P R'y.   Snow Blockade, March 29, 1881.

A stereoscopic image of snow blockading a locomotive in southern Minnesota during the Hard Winter tells the story of why trains couldn't get through to De Smet.

Twisting hay spelled survival.

bravely on," the editor cheered, and "Double up!" for the safety in numbers. (Caroline and Charles took in a young couple, George and Maggie Masters, and their infant son, though they were left out of Wilder's later novel.) One day the newspaper even printed the good-hearted query: "Have you a cold in your doze?"

Soon it was no laughing matter. Snow drifted into the cuts, and while the railroad paid anyone willing and able a dollar and a half a day to shovel, they couldn't keep up. The assorted settlers, be they farmer or shopkeeper or journalist, were left to fend for themselves. When flour ran out, the Ingallses and many of their fellow De Smet-ians resorted to the endless grind of running wheat kernels through their hand-crank coffee mills. (A flour mill wouldn't get up and running in De Smet until 1883.) "How much coal have you?" queried the newspaper one day. Firewood was scarce, and folks resorted to burn-

ing any available lumber, including, Laura remembered, telegraph poles. Soon the newspaper editor observed, "Hay fire is all the rage in town." To keep their place heated, Pa and Laura spent much of their time twisting the dried slough-grass hay into coils to feed the stove.

They were in the maw of endless winter. In blizzard upon blizzard, wind screamed and blinding snow fell as if the weather were trying to thresh the territory of its new inhabitants. On February 2, a storm hit and went on for nine days. Cattle froze. Tempers flared. Time stretched like a long length of sloughgrass, twisting back on itself. It seemed like it might snap, but it never did. Laura felt "as though we had been grinding wheat and twisting hay for years . . . Pa did not sing in the morning about the happy sunflower."

Starvation waited, like an uninvited guest. In a famous episode in *The Long Winter*, Almanzo Wilder took a perilous winter ride, along with his boisterous friend Cap Garland, to bring barrels of wheat from a country homesteader back into town. That wheat, distributed to the Ingallses and their neighbors, sustained them for the rest of the hard season. It brings the phrase "our daily bread" into high relief.

I am standing at the edge of the Ingalls homestead on a cold February morning in 2016. To be more precise I am leaning on a diagonal, as my right foot has broken through the top crust of ice, and that leg is sunk knee-deep in snow at the side of the road. Back in the dim reaches of my brain, there is an echo of my father warning me, then a new driver, to be careful not to end up in a ditch by letting the right wheels drift off the edge of some country road. So while I haven't driven off this particular unpaved road—for which I am thankful—I have stepped off of it, and I am thus akilter in a depression covered over in yesterday's Dakota blizzard. Very fine dry snow is sifting into the top of my boot and down my leg. I'm sure there is a reason why I didn't lace them up tighter before I set out from the Prairie Manor B&B in De Smet, though what that would be, I don't know.

For a moment, I wonder if there is a haystack around, in case I have to tunnel into it to ride out the rest of the winter. But then I think, as a friend of mine likes to say, what would Laura do? I inhale and look, trying to assume a "this is now" attitude.

The dried grasses are standing tall at the edge of the white expanse of the Big Slough, lit lavender in the diffuse light of an overcast sun. Nearby cattails in a sturdy crowd are erect as soldiers, and I remind myself to check whether Wilder ever mentioned them in her writings. All around me are the gentle hills and swales of the land where Laura and her family farmed. Pa's cottonwoods are profiled, dark bones against a bleached landscape of snow. Except for an occasional car along the state highway that now runs between the homestead and town, it is entirely still. As my original objective was to get a good picture of sloughgrass I uncap my lens and take a few shots before hauling myself back up to the terra firma of the road and into the rental car to thaw out. If I had been a De Smet settler over the Hard Winter, I doubt I would have made it.

—MM

Many cattle died, frozen in the unending blizzards of 1880–1881.

The weather finally broke in late April of 1881. The warm chinook wind blew, a prodigal welcomed without reserve. The weather bureau in Yankton reported a high of 79 degrees. By May 10, the snow melted enough for the trains to make it through. Soon the Ingalls family "moved home again," Laura remembered, "for the farm was home to us." It was spring, with its lengthening days, the smell of damp earth, the green of new grass, and the sounds of frogs peeping in the slough. The birds came back with mating in mind. Even Ma's sourdough quickened. The whole world seemed to be fermenting, as if anything were possible. It was a time to plant, a time to heal.

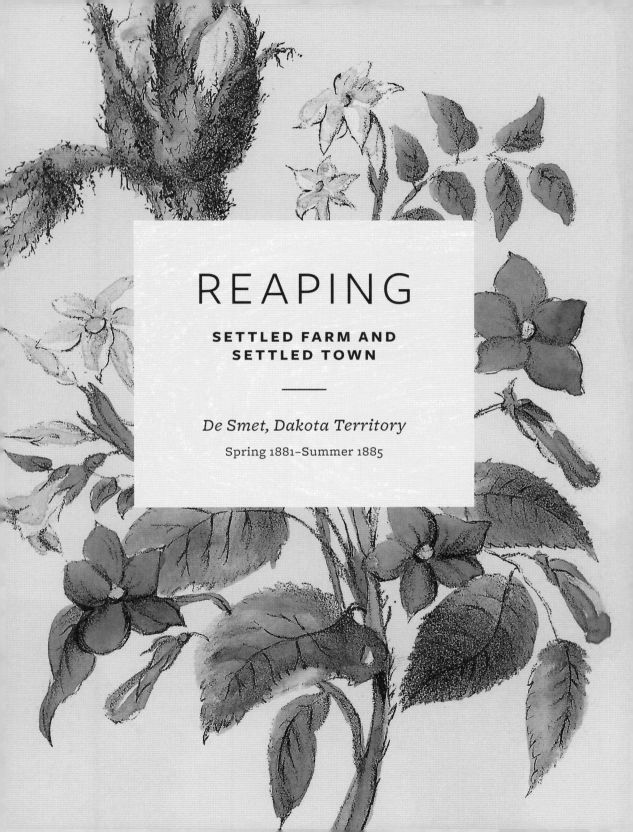

REAPING

SETTLED FARM AND SETTLED TOWN

———

De Smet, Dakota Territory

Spring 1881–Summer 1885

Charles Ingalls ended his odyssey on the Dakota prairie. When the tardy spring finally showed up in 1881, he was forty-five years old; Caroline was forty-one. Wilder remembered her father hankering to push on west, drawn by the magnet that was Oregon, but her mother's map of the world had requirements, limits. She put her foot down on his wandering foot. De Smet, this little town in Dakota Territory, would offer church, school, and a life among like-minded people. Charles and Caroline would be "stayers." They stayed on for the rest of their lives, finally putting down roots. And, of course, planting a garden.

For a gardener, the opening chapter of *Little Town on the Prairie* is cause for celebration. Of our now teenaged protagonist, we learn, "Ma took charge of the day's work for the rest of them, and best of all Laura liked the days when she said, 'I must work in the garden.'" Laura was an outdoor girl, a country girl, and the claim shanty—the one-room fourteen-by-twenty-foot wood and tarpaper house Pa built—was undeniably close quarters for her family of six. While the sightless but resourceful Mary took on the inside chores with Carrie and minded Grace, Laura enjoyed some one-on-one time with her mother out in the vegetable garden.

BIRD'S EYE VIEW OF
DE SMET, DAK.
COUNTY SEAT OF KINGSBURY COUNTY
1883.

By 1883 the town of De Smet was well-established with church and school as well as the depot, flour mill, lumber yard, and thriving commercial center along Calumet Avenue.

When the soil dried sufficiently that spring, Pa had prepared a substantial garden near the house with his latest acquisition, a new plow. Charles Ingalls, as portrayed by his daughter, did love a new and improved farm tool, by jingo. (If you haven't read the books, "by jingo" is just one of Pa's endlessly inventive exclamations.) Chances are he bought it on credit that spring at Fuller's Hardware—directly across the street from his store building where the family rode out the Hard Winter. An early photograph of Fuller's storefront shows the words "Farm Machinery" stenciled in an elegant script on the window.

Mr. Fuller didn't have a monopoly for long. Supplying agricultural equipment to farmers was big business in the nineteenth century, as it still is today. Edward Couse, another enterprising early arrival in De Smet, bought the other building Charles had built and opened a competing hardware store. Business was so lucrative that by 1885 he replaced Pa's wooden building with a two-story brick structure, complete with an opera house on the second floor. Couse advertised a machinery department "embracing nearly everything in the line of agricultural machinery from a bar to a thrashing machine. Some of the leading articles of stock are the Piano Binders, Moline wagons and buggies, Deere & Co.'s plows and cultivators, Victory thrashers, reapers, etc." Fuller countered with his own list of "Walter A. Wood Binders, Jackson wagons, Empire grain drills, Richard Champion seeders, J. I. Case thrashers." Everything a farmer could want. Maybe more.

The hardware stores served a growing market, as immigrants kept arriving at De Smet, much to Laura's chagrin. "I didn't care much for all these people," Wilder wrote. "I loved the prairie and the wild things that lived on it, much better." In this town of a little over a square mile, the population grew to over 500 people by the 1890 census, and the overall population of the southern half of the Dakota Territory tripled. But if the new people were taxing and the new construction seemed like a wound on the wild prairie, Laura's emerging social whirl soon gave her a new outlook. As well as school, church, and work—she had a job in town helping a seamstress—there were parties, Fourth of July celebrations, prayer meetings, sociables, and literaries.

The literary, an evening of culture complete with spelling bee that Wilder depicted in *Little Town on the Prairie*, took on a botanical theme. "Mimosaceous," referring to a plant related to mimosa, was late in the lineup of words for the final contestants. It is an unusual word, especially given the locale. The popular mimosa tree, with its dainty pink feather-fans of flowers, is not hardy in South Dakota. It does appear in *The Youth's Companion*—standby reading material for the Ingalls family—in descriptions such as this one: "The stars

Fuller and Couse both sold farm equipment for seeding, mowing, binding, and threshing. Laura eventually learned to drive a binder like this one. »

1883. SPECIAL CIRCULAR No. 2. 1883.

OUR WATCHWORD IS "PROGRESS."

WALTER A. WOOD STILL TAKES THE LEAD!

WALTER A. WOOD

IMPROVED HARVESTER

WITH

NEW IRON FRAME TWINE BINDER.

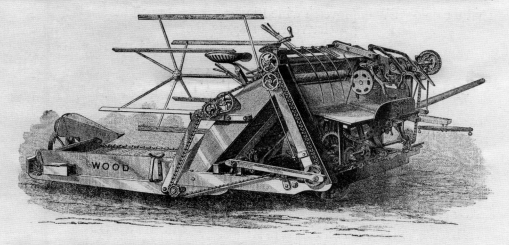

Facts Presented for the Consideration of Farmers,

WHO HAVE OCCASION TO PURCHASE A

SELF-BINDING HARVESTER

THE COMING SEASON

——BY THE——

WALTER A. WOOD MOWING AND REAPING MACHINE CO.

twinkled in the calm blue of the summer sky, and the soft night wind was heavy with the fragrance of mimosa." Native to southwestern Asia, the mimosa or "Persian silk tree" had been introduced in the United States over a century earlier, in 1745. By the time Laura was a teenager, the mimosa had nudged its way into the popular culture, though she had probably never seen one.

The last word in the evening's spelling competition, "xanthophyll," is a pigment in leaves. Xanthophyll is the yellow that emerges in autumn foliage when the green chlorophyll in leaf cells lays down on the job. Think xantho-phyll next time you see the yellow leaves of cottonwood in the fall. With this

A bouquet between two sisters.

Mimosa was a trendy exotic tree in the nineteenth century, known for its graceful leaf and flower. Now it is known to be invasive in some parts of the country.

1

2

Acacia mollis.

Gerachund delt.   M. Gauci lith.

Printed by Engelmann, Graf, Coindet & Co.

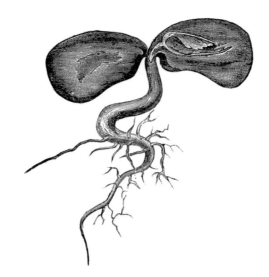

A germinating bean is a small miracle.

final round Pa won the contest, at least in the book. I have transcribed one of Charles Ingalls's letters with its somewhat inventive spelling, leaving me to wonder if Wilder stretched her facts a bit. "All I have told is true but it is not the whole truth," she later conceded.

What is true is that the Ingalls family was settling in on the new claim. Suppose yourself a bird, perhaps a meadowlark, soaring over their homestead in the early part of the 1881 growing season. Fields of grain, broken the year prior, stretch out in even rows of green, like warp threads on a loom. The garden near the house is a denser tapestry of color and texture. Wilder wrote of lettuce and radishes, onions and peas, potatoes, carrots, beets, and turnips, emerging in different shades of green. And, oh, the beans!

"Up from the bare earth, bean after bean was popping," she wrote, "its stem uncoiling like a steel spring, and up in the sunshine the halves of the split bean still clutched two pale twin-leaves." Wilder distilled the sheer joy of watching new life push up from the soil with a tiny lesson in seed germination. The halves of the split bean she described carry a temporary food reserve, a sort of backpack for a seedling. This clever backpack starts to manufacture

Ma started more than cabbages in wooden flats.

its own food when it hits the sun, turning green and photosynthesizing until the plant's first true leaves, those "pale twin-leaves," get big enough to sustain the plant.

Caroline Ingalls started her tomato seeds inside, then transplanted them outdoors as the summer temperatures warmed the soil and air. Laura kept an eye on the small tomato plants unfurling their leaves in the garden as she hoed around them. Alongside rows of tomatoes and hills of potatoes, the Ingalls garden boasted two more members of the nightshade family: small, sweet ground cherries and a purple variety of the larger husk tomatoes, now better known as tomatillo.

Ground cherries and tomatillos are closely related, two species of the genus *Physalis*. Native to the Americas south of the Rio Grande, their small fruits ripen inside papery husks. Laura thought they looked like hanging bells—maybe they reminded her of the church bell back in Walnut Grove that Pa had contributed toward, foregoing new boots. While the ground cherry is uncommon in today's vegetable gardens, an agricultural journal in 1858 singled it out, recommending, "In a new country where fruit is scarce, or a new home and garden, of which there are many in this great West of ours, it can be had the first season in abundance, and it is really delicious when used for pies and tarts, and more than passable eaten raw . . . It is also good for preserves."

A ground cherry grows inside its own wrapper.

When Carrie Ingalls was older and was living away, a letter from Ma instructed, "Plant your ground cherries in the house as you do tomatoes." She could have given the same instruction about the husk tomatoes. Dakota summers provide the heat needed to set flowers and ripen fruit, as long as the plants have had a head start indoors.

As the summer progressed in Caroline Ingalls's garden, cucumbers started to come in, and the surplus got salted. Salting draws the water from the cucumbers. The next step, pickling them in brine or vinegar, is a process of natural fermentation that stops them from spoiling.

Preserving food was a part of life for the Ingalls family in their Dakota home. In *Little Town on the Prairie* Pa moved the root vegetables from the claim into the cellar of the store building. (The family moved back into town for the winter of 1881–1882, which turned out to be mild.) Ma and the girls dried corn and made more pickles and preserves. At the Thanksgiving fundraiser for the

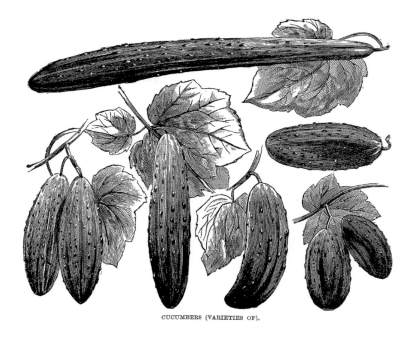

CUCUMBERS (VARIETIES OF).

Cucumbers were popular for pickles.

church, the spread at the mouth-watering "New England Supper" included three kinds of pickles—cucumber, beet, and green tomato—and footed glass bowls brimming with red tomato preserves and chokecherry jelly, a reasonable local substitute for jellied cranberries.

Chokecherry, *Prunus virginiana*, is close kin to the wild plum that the Ingalls girls picked on Plum Creek. Its spring blossoms look like bottlebrushes and its fruit is smaller—pea-sized—hanging in clusters that darken from red to purple as they ripen. Eaten as a fresh fruit, the chokecherry is bitter and strangely astringent, resulting in its common name. Trust me, you will want to spit them out. Laura remembered eating them and their furry, unpleasant aftertaste. Cooking or drying tames their tannins—the chemical cause of their odd effect. Indian tribes across the Great Plains used chokecherry flour as an ingredient in pemmican, a sort of mince-meat that was cached for winter food. Sugar helps too, which is why most recipes add ample amounts or mix

Ripening chokecherries are tempting.

the cooked and strained chokecherries with an equal amount of ripe plums.

As a matter of necessity as well as culinary creativity, preserving ripe produce had long been a household practice. Containers of salted, spiced vegetables and sugared fruits were corked or covered with brandied paper, cloth, or, according to a cookery book from the 1850s, pieces of bladder. (The chapter entitled "Butchering" in *Little House in the Big Woods* includes another unexpected use for a pig's bladder—a children's ball.) A damp piece of bladder was cut to shape, stretched, and tied over a crock. As it dried it would shrink and tighten, making an airtight seal. Voilà!

Preserving got easier after 1858 when John Landis Mason, a Philadelphia tinsmith, patented threaded glass containers with screw-on zinc lids. They still generically carry his name (Mason jars). It took some time to work the kinks out. The ensuing decades are papered with patents for various kinds of closures and seals—clamps, rings, springs, bails, and clips—until, in 1915, Alexander Kerr worked out the two-piece sealing lid with a threaded metal band that continues to dominate the market for home canners.

Mason jars were a giant step forward for home canning (left). Two-piece lids were a later improvement (right).

In my family, when it came to foraged food and the preservation thereof, the division of parental labor followed one that Laura would have recognized. Dad acquired the food; Mom preserved it. She dutifully "put up" jam from the buckets of wild berries deposited on the kitchen counter. The phrase "to put up" food was, I have learned, in contrast to putting it down in a cellar, but for years I thought it meant "to endure" because of my mother's summer jam-making marathons. It always seemed to be the hottest day of year, the box fan whirring in the kitchen door that opened to the screened porch. Quantities of fruit and sugar cooked on the ancient black stovetop, bubbling in the pot like a purple caldera on the verge of eruption.

My mother, like Caroline Ingalls, was the soul of thrift. Buying purpose-made jars being contrary to her character, an assortment of jars came out from Mom's under-sink stash to contain the resultant jam.

When her jam was ready she shooed us out of the kitchen, either out of safety concerns or, more likely, because we were a nuisance. Hot jam went into jars. A half inch of melted wax went on the top of each to seal out air, floating suspended on the jam. When cool, the jeweled preserves went down to the basement.

She never complained about the influx of berries. Each spring she prepared young pokeweed shoots by boiling them in three changes of water—to make them safe to eat—and amply seasoning them with bacon. She coped with his annual harvest of dandelion greens and enjoyed the supply of black walnuts that he wrested from their shells each fall. But when he showed up one summer morning with a bag of daylily buds gathered along the roadside—someone had given him a book by naturalist Euell Gibbons called Stalking the Wild Asparagus*—she balked. She preferred to see the orange flowers in bloom rather than sitting on her plate, thank you very much.*

—MM

By 1885, Charles Ingalls had improved the little house at the claim enough to make it a year-round residence. Until then, they would move out to the prairie for the growing season and back to the as-yet-unrented store building in winter. Every year Caroline looked over her garden seeds, because every year a garden is something new. She would plant up her garden, and help it grow. Her girls were growing up too.

Like all adolescents, then and now, Laura's teen years were a period of change. She dealt with the issue of body image, thinking herself "the homeliest girl ever." Still, she could best the boys at their games. She assessed the mirror and concluded that her waist was as round as a tree, albeit a young one. A corset was the means of correction in vogue at the time, though one that she undid given the chance. Helping Pa with the haying was a perfect excuse to loosen those stays. During these years, Mary left for her seven-year program at the Iowa College for the Blind. Laura studied hard, got her teaching certificate, and left home to take charge of the Bouchie School, a country schoolhouse twelve miles away. She eked out her two-month term of teaching, staying with a family in their claim shanty where—spoiler alert—she had to deal with a depressed, knife-wielding woman. She didn't stay there for long.

The main event in Laura's life was her emerging, sometimes reluctant, relationship with Almanzo Wilder. The importance of this particular farmer boy suddenly clicks into place. In both *Little Town on the Prairie* and *These Happy Golden Years* their courtship seems connected to flowers, especially violets and roses.

Helping with the hay meant loosening corset laces and sunbonnet ties.

Violets are a consistent floral element in Wilder's books, appearing in every novel except *Little House on the Prairie*, though violets *do* grow in Kansas. By the time we get to the Dakota Territory—the setting for many of her novels—they take on a more important role. The fictional Laura expresses a dislike of being conspicuous. Violets are anything but. In one of nature's quirks, many of the flowers that appear each spring go unpollinated and do not reproduce. Luckily violets have an effective backup plan, with self-fertile, seed-producing flowers that are hidden from view, generally underground. Seeds are deposited at or below the soil, and presto, baby violets.

Over a dozen species of violets are native to South Dakota, including the fragrant hookedspur violet, though it is now found only in the western part of the state. The most common near De Smet are the prairie bird's foot violets with deeply incised leaves that suggest the dainty feet of small birds, and the common blue violet, which is sometimes—confusingly—also called the prairie violet. The latter is a candidate for the mass of bloom that filled the Ingallses' buffalo wallow each spring, because it is abundant and favors disturbed soils. If you are in the United States anywhere east of the Rockies and grow a lawn, you might have thought of these little violets as weeds. At least until now.

Despite its solitary, self-pollinating habits, the blue violet's definition as listed in an 1855 floral dictionary consisted of one word: love. As the violets of spring gave way to the roses of summer, love was in the air for Laura Ingalls and Almanzo Wilder. "In June the wild roses bloomed," Wilder wrote in *Pioneer Girl*. "They were a low-growing bush and, when in bloom, the blossoms made masses of wonderful color, all shades of pink, all over the prairie. And the sweetest roses that ever bloomed."

The wild rose that provided the visual and olfactory backdrop for Laura and her new beau grew on low, dense bushes less than two feet tall. It was one of the handful of roses native to the Midwest that go by nicknames like "wild rose" and "prairie rose." The species that Laura enjoyed was, according to tax-

« And then there were boys, including Almanzo Wilder whom Laura and Grace spotted on top of his brother Royal's hay wagon.

Nothing sweeter than the prairie rose.

The prairie bird's foot violet (*Viola pedatifida*, 2) is native to the prairies near De Smet.

onomical officialdom, *Rosa arkansana*. Meriwether Lewis sent back specimens of this rose from Fort Mandan in 1805, collected the prior October in the area near the mouth of the Cannonball River, in what is now North Dakota. But by the time this rose was botanically baptized in the 1870s by Thomas C. Porter, a professor of botany at Lafayette College in Pennsylvania, he used a specimen he had gathered from the Arkansas River in Colorado and conferred its specific epithet accordingly.

Laura's rose, if we may call it that, blooms once a year, in early summer. The flowers have five pink petals that open wide to reveal the golden centers. Their pollen-packing pistils curled up like Laura's "lunatic fringe," as she called the bangs of her new hairstyle, the latest thing. By themselves each rose is only an inch or two across, but they crowd together in clusters forming the masses of color and scent that left an indelible impression on the young couple. To have it be summer, and to be in love. Endless days, so much time.

ROSE, BLUE VIOLET, JASMINE, MOSS ROSE, BUD.

Your beauty, modesty and amiability,
Have drawn from me a confession of love

One of Laura's favorite poems, Tennyson's "Maud," referenced in *Little Town on the Prairie*, includes the line, "And the musk of the roses blown." While noses and perceptions of fragrance differ from person to person, the scent of rose has been prized for eons, at least since the time of the ancient Persians. As perfumers know, rose essence permeates its petals. Unlike the flowers of lilac or lily-of-the-valley, considered "mute" by the perfume industry, the essential oil or attar of roses can be distilled from its petals using steam. (The others require a more elaborate process using solid fats and alcohol.) Even so, not every wild prairie rose will smell as sweet. Fragrance depends not only on the variety of rose, that is, genetics, but also on growing conditions like soil, weather, and especially the moisture content of the air on any given day or time of day. It is why the roses in Tennyson's poem were especially fragrant for Maud in the morning when "the black bat, night, has flown" and in the evening, when Almanzo and Laura would often take buggy rides out on the prairie.

Sometimes they rode out around dusk, and Laura always remembered the red sunsets with their blazing clouds. What she did not know at the time was that the atmospheric fireworks were the lingering results of a massive volcanic eruption on the other side of the globe. When Krakatoa erupted on an Indonesian island in August of 1883, it ejected so much dust and ash that blood red sunsets were reported across America and around the world. The phenomenon persisted for several years. At the time, scientists were puzzled about the cause. On November 8, 1884, the editor of the *De Smet Leader* mused, "Brilliant red sunsets, like those which set the scientific world to wondering last year, have appeared again, and their return upsets all the theories then advanced to account for them. They have nothing to do with politics." Did Laura and Almanzo assume that the sunsets were an emblem of love?

They would steer the young Morgan horse team north from town to Spirit Lake, about ten miles away, with its mysterious Indian burial mound. Or they would drive the seven or so miles to the Twin Lakes, the smaller Lake Henry separated from its larger twin Lake Thompson by a thin spit of land. It was a perfect place for courting. Wilder remembered the lush plant life growing

Violets and roses make a bouquet of romance.

Prairie sunsets are spectacular, and in the mid-1880s they were even redder than today.

Twin Lakes was full of bloom for Almanzo and Laura.

The embossed cover of Pa's big green book hints at what is inside: people, places, plants, and animals.

along the lake shores—grapevines and juvenile cottonwoods, and chokecherry trees. While returning from the Twin Lakes one evening, Almanzo proposed and Laura accepted.

Carrie and Grace were now old enough to enjoy Pa's "big green book" on their own, as Mary and Laura had done. *The Polar and Tropical Worlds*, a three-inch volume bound in emerald cloth and embossed with gold, combined two natural history books by a popular science writer, Dr. George Hartwig. The book's animals were the biggest draw for the Ingalls girls, with its descriptions from arctic fox to zebra. But the book was also a repository of information on plants, geography, and much, much more. The subtitle of the book, *A Description of Man and Nature*, describes the author's holistic view, one that was passed on, consciously or not, to a future author.

Like Wilder's novels, Hartwig's chatty tome includes birds, fish, insects, and weather phenomena. There are native cultures and locales: the Cree with their bison hunts, the Inuit of the north, and the indigenous peoples of Patagonia in the south. There are Norwegians for whom, along the fjords in winter, "every family, reduced to its own resources, forms as it were a small commonwealth, which has but little to do with the external world, and is obliged to rely for its happiness on internal harmony, and a moderate competency." Words to live by, especially for a Dakota pioneer.

The big green book is replete with plants. There are the immense extents of Arctic conifers with an illustration of a "forest conflagration," not unlike Laura's memories of a Wisconsin forest fire. Iceland has peat bogs; Peru has cacti. The second half of the book has an entire section on plant life, shaded with trees like the banyan and palm, and bustling with commercial plants—sugar, coffee, cocoa, and spices. In his chapter on "the chief nutritive plants of the tropical world," Hartwig sweeps in an account of the history and uses of maize, including popcorn.

In *Little Town on the Prairie*, Wilder included a corn-planting proverb handed down from Pa to Laura, "One for the blackbird, one for the crow, and that will leave just two to grow." This traditional rhyme has many variants. "One for the mouse, one for the crow, one to rot, one to grow" is from New England in 1850. Other versions blame seed loss on the wind or the cutworm, though they all seem to stick to the rhyme, pairing "crow" with "grow."

It's possible that Laura also knew the rhyme from school. A popular book of recitations from the period was *Exhibition Days* by Mary Slade. Published in Boston in 1880, this collection for "grammar and high schools, and parish and parlor entertainments," includes the poem "Dropping Corn." Its farmer added a fifth kernel for good measure to his sowing strategy, and to the poem's refrain:

Blackbirds were not welcome guests.

Little Katie went with the gray, old squire
("Who was he?" Child, he was your grandsire.)
To the furrowed field, in the dewy morn;
"Now sing," said he, "as you drop the corn,
'One for the blackbird, one for the crow,
One for the cut-worm, and two to grow.'"

However many seeds are in the tally, gardeners still know that planting a few extras is a good idea. Pests happen.

Charles Ingalls continued to battle pests in his fields out on the claim, blackbirds figuring prominently. While he dealt with the "four and twenty" (and more) corn-eating birds with his gun, other homesteaders were trying to poison them with strychnine- or arsenic-laced grains. Complaints from farmers in the Upper Midwest during the 1880s were so pervasive that the U.S. Department of Agriculture commissioned an ornithologist to study the problem. He reported back that farms with blackbird problems were located on land in and around "wet marshes or sloughs" because that is where the birds nested and raised their young. Ecology and agriculture do not always make an easy fit.

Whether marauding blackbirds or mere restlessness was the cause, in the autumn of 1884, Almanzo took a trip south with his brother Royal, considering the possibility of a move. On November 19, Charles Ingalls wrote them a letter that they received somewhere en route. He reported on the De Smet weather in vivid detail: "Last Sunday was a bad day here cold and it blowed so hard that my back hair is all loose and it looks tonight as it would blow clear off." Charles continued, giving the brothers some advice on land selection and adding a tall tale:

> Now boys don't be discouraged but take time and look but first get far enough South to be out of these bad storms then good land is the next and good running water the lay of the land does not mater so much if it storms tonight I will send a dispach by the wind in your direction so you will know what we poor mortals up here in Dakota are getting.

Before the Christmas holidays Almanzo returned, resolved to stay in De Smet. The following year, the town paper carried the announcement of the wedding of Almanzo and Laura "at the residence of the officiating clergyman, Rev. E. Brown, August 25, 1885." The editor included commentary and good wishes, "Thus two more of our respected young people have united in the journey of life. May their voyage be pleasant and their joys be many and their sorrows few."

"Bessie" and "Manly" as they called one another, moved to his land north of town. Newly married and newly settled, she remembered being "a little awed by my new estate." Laura felt that she had found her place in the world.

Laura and Almanzo in their wedding photograph.

This illustration punctuated the close of the first edition of *These Happy Golden Years*, which, at the time, Wilder envisioned as the end of the series.

THRESHING

FROM GREAT PLAINS
TO OZARK RIDGES

———

*De Smet, South Dakota
(statehood, 1889) to Mansfield, Missouri,
with intervals in Spring Valley,
Minnesota, and Westville, Florida*

1885–1894

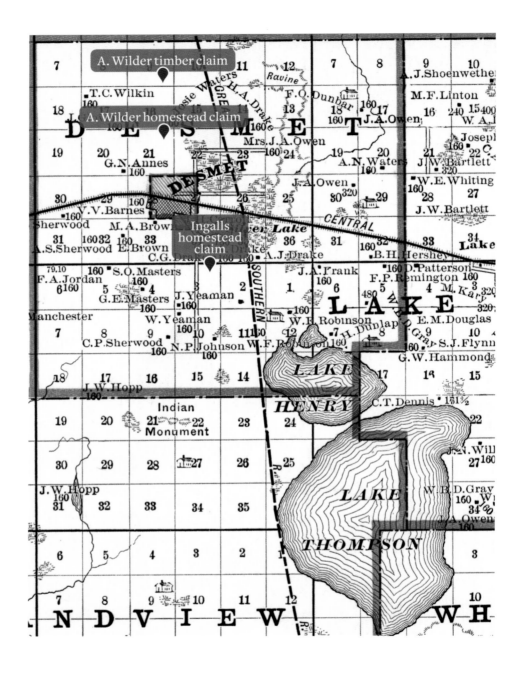

A detail of an 1884 map of Kingsbury County, marked with the locations of the Ingalls and Almanzo Wilder quarter sections. It shows the wetlands, streams, and lakes of the area, though the Big Slough was omitted.

> We'll always be farmers,
> for what is bred in the bone will
> come out in the flesh.
>
> —THE FIRST FOUR YEARS

Their marriage seemed like a happily-ever-after ending, but it was a story that was just beginning. When Laura and Almanzo married, they moved to a little house of their own. It was up on a small rise of land, affording it a view of the surrounding countryside. If they stood at the center of De Smet, say in front of Couse Hardware, her parents' place was about a mile and a half south, and slightly east. Their place was about two miles north. The Wilder newlyweds pictured a future life on a prosperous farm surrounded by children and shaded by a forest grove on Almanzo's tree claim.

Tree claims reflected economic ambitions for the region. Wood was a scarce resource, used for both fuel and building materials. Lumber was imported on boxcars, and De Smet soon had a lumberyard near the depot. Transportation costs made it expensive. Almanzo estimated that the lumber for a claim shanty cost $158.00, a substantial chunk of money for most homesteaders.

The Timber Culture Act of 1873 was a piece of follow-on legislation to the Homestead Act, and another example of the geographic crowdsourcing popular with Congress in the expansionist years after the Civil War. In short, the law allowed a settler like Almanzo another 160-acre tract in addition to his homestead claim, if he would plant forty acres of trees. On June 7, 1884, the editor of the *De Smet Leader* put forward this opinion, "Among the things that should be looked after in this new country is the planting of trees, both fruit and forest." Almanzo was doing his part, having already planted up his future forest.

On his tree claim Almanzo put in sturdy varieties native to prairie surrounds: the familiar cottonwood and willow, as well as boxelder, which is a maple in disguise. Boxelder, unlike most maples, has a leaf form that is compound, made up of three-plus leaflets joined with small petiolule stems. But its seeds are typical maple samaras with two wings that help the seeds disperse in the constant winds of the Great Plains. As seems appropriate for the Wilders' newly married state, boxelder is dioecious, with male and female flowers on separate trees. For fertile seeds, both sexes must apply.

Almanzo might have gotten some of his saplings from George Whiting, who settled in Yankton in 1879 and, along with farming his claim, started a nursery business to supply fruit trees and "forest trees, which were in demand for timber claims." But it seems likely that, like Charles Ingalls and his cottonwoods, Almanzo gathered seeds, cuttings, and saplings from the edges of the sloughs and lakes where he and Laura liked to drive their team of Morgan horses.

In order to "prove up," Almanzo had to keep the trees on his claim growing for eight years. It sounds like a good deal, a straightforward proposition, but the numbers are staggering. Forty acres planted with "timber, seeds, or cuttings" at twelve feet apart, as the law stipulated, amounts to twelve thousand trees. By the time Almanzo had to prove up on his claim, Congress had reduced the requirement from forty acres to ten, or three thousand trees total. Still a challenge in a region with weather that was inconsistent at best and where irrigation consisted of hauling water from a well.

Boxelder is a maple with an unusual leaf variant.

This detail of an 1883 perspective map of De Smet, with street trees and a timber claim on the outskirts of town. (Almanzo's claim was the other direction from the depot.)

In addition to timber claim holders like Almanzo Wilder, civic-minded De Smet townspeople soon started tree planting efforts of their own. It was a desire, unstated but understood, to recreate the aesthetic of the eastern half of the United States. In the same way that settlers built churches with steeples and schoolhouses with desks, they planted shade trees. In 1887, the *Leader* proudly announced, "Trees are being set out early on every lot on both sides of Third Street to the Baptist church. Let the good work go on."

My father involved himself in the good work of tree planting. He never bought a tree, though over the years he set out quite a few on our small suburban lot in northern New Jersey. Instead, he took the rusty Radio Flyer wagon that we had long outgrown from under the screened porch. Then with wagon, a cardboard box, and his well-used shovel, he walked down the street to the patch of scrubby woods wedged between the elevated railroad tracks and a creek that ran into the Passaic River north of town. It must have been a railroad right-of-way, or town easement. A little path ran through it, a cut through for people like my father who walked to and from the train station every day on their New York City commutes.

But this was the weekend, and instead of suit and tie, he was wearing worn jeans, a flannel shirt, and a red wool hunting cap with ear flaps that is still up in my closet somewhere. Back he would come, up the sidewalk, pulling a wagon filled with horticultural loot—a sapling and a box full of rich, black compost. I am sure the neighbors found this eccentric.

The trees he relocated were ordinary in a horticultural sense—pin oaks, native to the area, and Norway maples, already invading the local woods by the 1960s. His trees took. They appreciated the good holes he dug, the top-dressing with compost, and buckets of water applied during dry spells over the first few years in their new home. He mourned when utility companies pruned them badly. He sighed when some overzealous town workers removed one of his trees along the curb and replaced it with a nursery-grown specimen that promptly died.

The house is different now, sold years ago after my parents passed. The new owner moved the front door around the corner to the quieter side street, turned the screened porch into a room, and remodeled the inside from top to bottom, or so I am told. But one of Dad's pin oaks remains, standing straight, the tallest tree on the property and my own connection to home.

—MM

Almanzo top-dressed the trees on his claim, cultivating around them and adding manure. For water, they must have relied on rainwater and snowmelt, unless they were near the house and well. Laura could monitor the seasons by the cottonwood that grew on the north side, just outside her kitchen window.

Staring out the window at that cottonwood might have been what distracted Laura when making her first pie in her new kitchen. *The First Four Years* records a cooking disaster, when she forgot to sweeten the filling for the pie. It was filled with pie plant—rhubarb—harvested from the kitchen garden, which Almanzo had put in near the house. Rhubarb is delicious, but demands sweetening to be a palatable dessert because of its extreme acidity.

Almanzo's rhubarb was likely a division of his sister Eliza Jane's plant. She might have brought it from their parents' farm in Minnesota. The *De Smet Leader* of May 31, 1884, acknowledged, "Thanks are due to Miss Eliza Wilder for supplying the editor's family with some delicious pie-plant." Rhubarb is a sturdy plant that can be dug and split, and as Miss Eliza Wilder rode out to De Smet with her brothers, it is easy to imagine her carrying along a pot of rhubarb in soil or bare-root and rolled up in some damp cloth. It can be grown from seed, but why bother when the roots are so forgiving?

A plant scientist would tell you that rhubarb is a vegetable, though in the kitchen Laura treated it as a fruit. It originally grew on the Asian steppes in places like Mongolia and southeastern Russia, and made its way overland to Europe along trade routes. The ancient Greeks gave it the name, rhubarb, roughly translating to barb(arian) plant from beyond the Rha, or Volga, River.

The Greeks adopted it as a medicinal. Its roots, fresh or dried, are still valued in Chinese herbal remedies and were part of European and American pharmacopeia well into the eighteenth century. Rhubarb was prescribed to detoxify

Rhubarb is
a vigorous
grower.

the blood, treat stomach ailments, and dissolve kidney stones. In his almanac of 1756, "Poor Richard" (a.k.a. Benjamin Franklin) suggested that to recover from jaundice one could "chew Rhubarb a few Mornings." Franklin is credited with introducing the plant to America, sending seeds of what he called "Tartarian rhubarb" to his botanical and medical friends in the colonies from London in the 1760s. When Caribbean sugar production increased, making sugar more widely available and cheaper, rhubarb moved from the medicine chest to the kitchen pantry. Recipes for rhubarb desserts proliferated, leading to its linguistic makeover as "pie plant."

In *The First Four Years*, Laura's rhubarb pie is linked to threshing, as she served it to the threshing crew. A thresher was expensive, so often a more prosperous farmer would buy one and rent it out to neighbors. By the 1880s in Dakota Territory, new models were driven by steam rather than horses. Either way a threshing machine was efficient, but still required significant manpower to feed in the bound sheaves, stack the straw, and bag the grain. Local men shared work, an informal communal network in which farmers traded labor. It was hungry work, and threshing crews had the reputation of eating as though they had hollow legs. The farmer's wife provided the meal.

The timing of Laura's very tart pie seemed odd to me. Rhubarb is a spring seasonal ingredient—consider the classic pairing of strawberry with rhubarb—

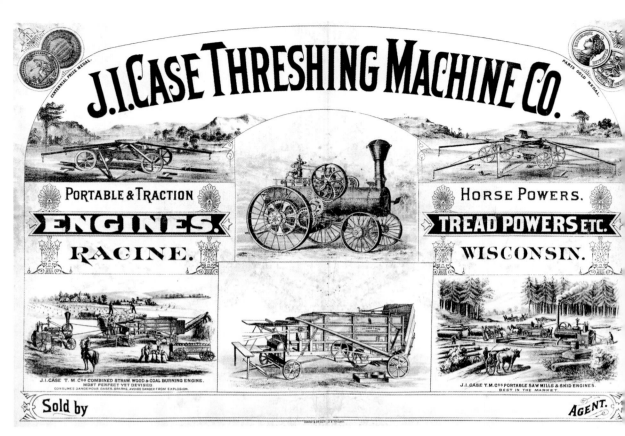

Threshing machines at the end of the nineteenth century could be powered by horses or engines, and it took an industrious crew to work the "thrasher."

while the wheat harvest would have been more of a summer-to-autumn event. But it turns out that rhubarb stalks can be lightly harvested until the first hard frost, as long as they are from a strong plant with enough oomph to get through the winter.

In their garden, Almanzo would have given the rhubarb plant elbow room. Its scrunched leaves pop through the soil in spring like small-fisted knuckles, then balloon out expansively. With its leaves, which are poisonous, and its stalks, which are not, it can spread to three-plus feet across. It appreciates high soil fertility, so while he was manuring the trees with black gold, shoveled out from the barn, Almanzo would have added some around their pie plants too.

Of the "gold" of the farm, Laura and Almanzo both remembered "Don't

Leave the Farm" from their singing school days, excerpted by Wilder in her
novel. The 1871 lyrics by Clara F. Berry allude to the extended Australian gold
rush, which spanned the second half of the nineteenth century, as well as com-
posted manure. The song extolled the virtues of the farm over the vices of the
city or business world, including this verse:

> You talk of the mines of Australia,
> They're wealthy in gold without doubt,
> But sh! There is gold on the farm, boys,
> If only you'd shovel it out.
> The mercantile trade is a hazard,
> The goods are first high and then low,
> Best risk the old farm a while longer,
> Don't be in a hurry to go.

While Almanzo was not in a hurry to go, Laura's attitude toward being
a farm wife and embracing the farm life is a mystery. In her last novel, published after her death, the fictional Laura set a four-year timetable for trying
to make a go of the farm. Whether this was a narrative device or a real discussion between wife and husband is unknown. But the unfolding of events in the
novel match those of their first years together.

A little over fifteen months after their marriage, their first child, Rose, was
born. Named for the sweet wild roses that scented the air in June, their blue-
eyed Rose arrived at the doorstep of winter, December 5, 1886, bringing joy
along with doctor bills that were beyond the family budget. By the following
spring infant Rose, with sunbonnet covering her blonde curls, lay in a clothes
basket near the garden while her parents sowed seeds.

Childbirth and childrearing did nothing to slow down the demands of the
farm. Almanzo was game to try new labor-saving farm equipment, which he
bought, often on credit. Charles Ingalls acquired a used twine binder that he
and his son-in-law repaired for the wheat crops. Laura was game too. "I learned
to do all kinds of farm work with machinery," she wrote, adding "I have rid-
den the binder, driving six horses." The binder delivered the hay in bundles

Laura and Almanzo named their daughter for the prairie rose (1) that they loved.

A daughter, Rose, was born to Laura and Almanzo in December 1886.

South Dakota harvesters in 1898, using the type of mower-binder Laura learned to drive.

neatly tied with twine. The time-consuming drudgery of gathering and binding sheaves by hand—methods Almanzo had learned from his father decades before—was gone.

By the time Rose arrived, her grandparents had won their bet with the government. Charles Ingalls proved up on his claim in May of 1886. He had farmed the land for six seasons and lived there, with the exception of two winters and two other short intervals when they moved to town to give the girls a shorter walk to school. His proof, the "testimony of claimant," that he filed at the land office in Watertown, outlined his improvements: a house—the original claim shanty with a good-sized addition—and barn, a good well and pump, and sixty acres of cultivated land. He also noted, "Apple trees bearing plum trees bearing small fruit in abundance, about 6000 fruit trees some of them 6 years old." By September of the next year, Grace Ingalls, by then ten years old, wrote in her diary, "We have had lots of fun eating plums but only have one tree of plums left." So Pa had been planting an orchard—with limited success—in addition to cottonwood trees.

The cottonwoods at her parents' place chronicled the years. To Laura, her parents never seemed to age, but the trees on their land were suddenly substantial. When Pa had planted them, they had been so small—just twigs with

The Ingalls family as adults, taken in the photographer's studio in De Smet. From left to right are Caroline, Carrie, Laura, Charles, Grace, and Mary. Laura is wearing the sensible black dress she made for her wedding.

a few leaves. They had been watered during droughts of course, and watched carefully each spring for signs of life, a green tinge, swelling leaf buds. Now they were robust, almost triple her height, and a healthy square of shade around the shanty. Looking at the trees, Laura could not deny the passage of time, and more changes were coming. In 1887, Pa built a frame house on Third Street. At Christmastime that year, he and Caroline, along with Grace, Carrie, and Mary who was home from school that year, moved one last time. They left the homestead for their new house in town. Out back, they planted more fruit trees and a big garden. Their days as farmers were done. Charles was almost fifty-two. Caroline had just celebrated her forty-eighth birthday.

Perhaps Laura envied them, or perhaps not. On Almanzo's land every-

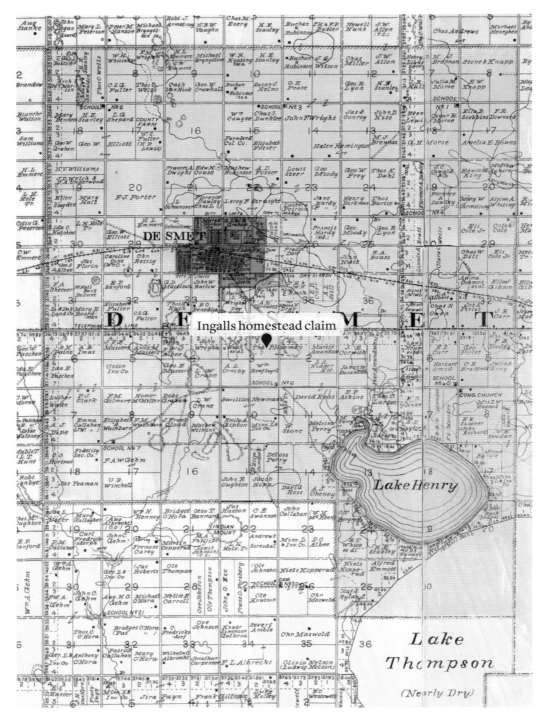

Ingalls homestead claim

By the time of this map in 1899, Charles and Caroline lived in town, and their original claim, the northeast quarter of Section 3, was owned by Thos. P. Norman. Years of drought had taken their toll. Silver Lake had vanished, the Big Slough was dry marsh, and Lake Thompson was marked "Nearly Dry."

This winter scene shows a variety of De Smet businesses: restaurants and a hotel, a grocery, livery, harness shop, and tobacco store—even a bowling alley and sweet shop. Note the wagon beds shifted onto runners for the snow. And the Wilders weren't the only ones who tried their hands at sheep.

thing seemed sunny at the start. He planted wheat and oats, raised horses and cattle, and, with the help of Laura's cousin Peter, tried his hand at raising sheep. She made butter, tended the garden, and collected eggs from her flock of hens. But calamity lurked, quiet in the shadows. "We could get rich on paper," Wilder later wrote, "IF, but the 'IF' was too big."

Drought, heat, and hail seemed to conspire against their crops. Harvests were meager. Taxes had to be paid on the homestead claim that had proved up. There was interest on loans for farm machinery and credit used for necessities like coal. Then, in early 1888, Laura and Almanzo came down with diphtheria. Almanzo, pushing himself to get back to work, had a stroke, like a terrible repeat of Mary's affliction. Even after recuperation, he was left with some lingering paralysis in his arms and legs. Everyday chores that had been rote were suddenly difficult.

The wealth of sorrow accumulated. Laura, pregnant again at the end of 1888, delivered a baby boy in August of the next year. He died on August 12, 1889, twelve days old. Later that month, their house on the timber claim burned to the ground, the result of an accidental kitchen fire. Almanzo was in

Almanzo and Laura pose in front of a saw palmetto (*Serenoa repens*) in Westville, Florida.

the fields. Laura saved Rose and the deed box. With some small exceptions, everything they owned was gone. Even her cottonwood near the kitchen window was dead.

A retreat seemed in order, so Almanzo and Laura packed their few belongings and set off with Rose for his parents' farm in Spring Valley, Minnesota, to recuperate body and spirit. During this brief interlude, they considered emigrating to New Zealand, a farther shore—they had some experience raising sheep after all—but soon another opportunity arose.

Peter Ingalls, Laura's cousin who had shared their sheep venture in De Smet, had made a homestead claim in Westville on Florida's narrow panhandle, a stone's throw from the Alabama state line. Peter could use some extra hands to work his claim. It seemed just the ticket as the cold—never Almanzo's preference—had become intolerable since his lameness had come on. So the family trio headed south.

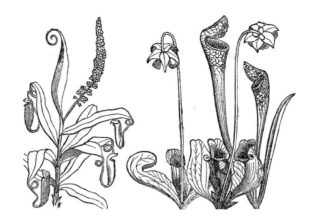

This image of carnivorous plants is from the botany textbook used at Franklin Academy in Malone when the Wilders attended.

The endless summer of Florida was as exotic as the pictures in Pa's big green book. The smells, the heaviness of air, the odd fauna and flora—alligators on the rivers, columnar pines, dense palmettos, and gargantuan live oaks bearded with Spanish moss. There were plants that ate insects for goodness sake, though that would have been undeniably useful during grasshopper days on the prairie.

Laura's notice of carnivorous plants was apt. The scrubland and marshes along the Gulf coastline of the panhandle are a hotbed of pitcher plants, specifically species of *Sarracenia*. These coastal wetlands are now protected, as some of the plants are endemic, occurring nowhere else in the world. Their mechanisms are elegant and deadly from a bug's-eye view. The insect falls for a combination of color, scent, and nectar, and, if it succumbs, falls inside the pitcher where it is digested by the plant over time.

Florida was not a good fit, especially for Laura. Like a replay of being the country girl in a class of town students, Laura found herself, as a Yankee woman, the subject of interest that bordered on suspicion. She did not fit in and could not tolerate a heat that struck her more like the pan than the panhandle. So in 1892, after about a year spent in Florida, the Wilders packed up once more and boarded a train back to De Smet.

They rented a house not far from her parents that seemed large to six-year-old Rose, who remembered its yard and a footpath through the short brown grasses. Working at her lessons in the "chalky schoolroom" with the beloved Miss Barrows, Rose absorbed words the way a plant absorbs sunlight. When school wasn't in session, Rose stayed at her grandparents' house while Laura worked for a dressmaker in town and Almanzo picked up odd jobs. They walked and rode on town streets shaded with maturing trees.

The gabled house where Rose's grandparents and three aunts lived on Third Street had tall windows and deep eaves. There was a pump outside the kitchen door and a big garden in the adjoining lot, with hens in a chicken coop. Grandpa Charles Ingalls tried his hand at a general store, took in fees for his duties as Justice of the Peace, and worked carpentry jobs. He didn't make much, but they made ends meet.

Rose remembered that her Grandma and the diligent Aunt Mary, now graduated from the Iowa College for the Blind, always kept busy. Caroline Ingalls canned produce from the garden and sold the excess. With different-sized shuttles, Mary netted a variety of objects in a variety of sizes. The largest were hammocks, one of which created an outdoor room of sorts in the simple yard on Third Street. It swung between two trees on the side of the house where Rose remembered lying in it on summer afternoons watching clouds and birds.

Notwithstanding this peaceful image, neither of Rose's parents seemed satisfied to settle in De Smet, a place that had to be a steady reminder of all they had lost. Prospects for getting ahead were dim. The prairie that had held so much promise looked already burned out, worn out. Crops failed year after year. Drought persisted. The land was increasingly prone to what Grace Ingalls called sandstorms. In a diary entry, she wrote, "To day the wind is blowing hard . . . it hasn't rained for a long while and the ground is dry as powder." It foreshadowed what would, four decades later, become the Dust Bowl.

In 1893 or thereabouts, the Wilders contracted what the local paper diagnosed among the broader populace as "Missouri fever." It seemed to invigorate them both. Friends of Almanzo's had taken a train to the Ozarks—some advance reconnaissance—and came back with good reports. One of them, Mr. Sherwin, brought Laura an apple, a huge, dark red apple. It was her talisman.

COME TO THE OZARKS!

The Land Of The Big Red Apple.

Where the summers are long and pleasant, and the winters short and mild. Where crop failures are never known and hot winds never blow.

Now is your chance to get a home cheap. We are situated on the South slope of the Ozark range twelve miles from Norwood Mo. We have some of the finest farms in Douglass County on our list. Our lands produce forty to sixty bushels of corn, twenty to forty bushels of wheat, one to two and a half tons of hay per acre and other crops in proportion.

The finest living water in the known world. Fine White Oak, Black Oak, Hickory, Walnut and Pine timber. Wood and fence posts no object.

Wild fruit such as Grapes, Blackberries etc. in abundance.

Free open range for all stock in most of countys.

Saw-mills, Grist-mills, Schools and Churches. The most hospitable people in America. The best Normal School in South-west Missouri is located at Ava the County Seat of Douglas county. Our teachers are among the best instructors in the State.

What is the use of you paying large rents when you can buy you a home for from five to twenty-five dollars per. acre?

If you want a home, now is the time to buy as land is going up by leaps and bounds. Write for list, or better, come and see what we have got.

Address
COATS and LEFLER,
Brushyknob.
Douglas Co.   Mo.

Promoters of Missouri farmland touted the "Land of the Big Red Apple."

She set it on the windowsill of their rental, to gaze upon and dream and plan. Rose recalled her mother's voice almost singing, "Just wait till you see trees!"

Always good at squeezing a nickel, Laura contrived to save $100, notable given she was earning a dollar a day for each twelve-hour shift she put in with the seamstress, and—on a good day—Almanzo cleared double that. For his part, Almanzo moved his old two-seater hack into the shade at the side of the house and fitted it out as a covered wagon for the trip.

On July 17, 1894, the Wilders embarked on their journey to Missouri. Almanzo was thirty-seven, Laura twenty-seven, and Rose seven years old. Laura carried with her a small five-cent memorandum book. Every day she penciled an entry, filling both sides of each page as she went. It was her first significant work of prose, though not, one presumes, intended for publication. (Rose transcribed it after her mother's death, bookending it with essays of her own. It was published as *On the Way Home* in 1962.)

The diary is silent, as Laura was regarding many sad events, about the leave taking on that July day in De Smet. Her parents were still reasonably fit, but graying. Her sisters were grown—even Grace had reached nominal adulthood. They all knew that the 650 miles that would separate them would not be trod lightly. The wagon was packed with some practical going away gifts: a hammock Mary had netted, a tin camp stove from Pa.

They didn't go alone. They convoyed with some friends, the Cooleys, who drove two wagons of their own. The Wilder rig included a squawking caboose of chickens, a makeshift coop attached to the back of the wagon bed, and Little Pet, the young colt. Perhaps they drove past Almanzo's homestead or the tree claim, or the old home place with its stand of cottonwoods. Perhaps a few last prairie roses bloomed near the little lakes that had figured so distinctly in their courtship.

Laura's diary begins with practicalities. In the second sentence of the diary, already on the road, she spotted a weed, newly infamous at the time, the Russian thistle. Better known in American popular culture as tumbleweeds, Russian thistles rolled through a generation of Hollywood westerns and launched into stardom with the cowboy song "Tumbling Tumbleweeds." But in 1894 when Laura commented on them, they were relative newcomers

Russian thistle, better known as tumbleweed, arrived in America after the Civil War.

on the prairie, though already a nuisance to farmers. Historians speculate that seeds of *Kali tragus* stowed away with flax seed, accidently carried to the Great Plains by immigrants in the 1870s. Almanzo once described a Russian thistle as "large as a bushel basket," rolling in the wind, catching on anything in its way, and scattering seeds every time it catches. (The "wheels of fire" described in *On the Banks of Plum Creek* were probably caused by a less invasive local plant with a similar habit, such as tumble mustard.)

The Wilders camped along the banks of the James River, in a place that was so agreeable it felt like home. The next day they crossed the river, turned around, and took in the view from the bluffs. "We all stopped and looked back at the scene and I wished for an artist's hand or a poet's brain or even to be able to tell in good plain prose how beautiful it was," Laura wrote. She was prophetic, about the prose in particular. She went on. "What is it about water that always affects a person? I never see a great river or lake but I think how I would like to see a world made and watch it through all its changes."

By the time they hit Kansas, the August dust covered the road like guilt or regret. It clung to them, sifted into their possessions. Kicked up by hoof and wheel and the incessant wind, it hovered around the wagon in a stifling, choking haze. "Dust is 3 to 5 inches deep on the road so all the time we are in a smother of dust." That night she wrote in her diary that they set up camp near a church, in dust. Still, she took time to note the plants. With the eye of an experienced forager, she reported the first hazelnuts they passed, and she pocketed a horse chestnut, a round ball of a nut that is inedible but so smooth and hard in the hand.

Laura tallied the hardwoods—hickories, walnuts, and oaks—and native fruit trees—wild crabapples, plums, and the downy hawthorn or "thorn apple" as she called it. Unusual trees caught her eye. "Along the roads are hedges of Osage orange trees, 20 or 30 feet high, set close together," she observed. "They are thorny." The fruit was puzzling, "like green oranges, but no good for eating nor anything else." She was right on both counts, though squirrels would beg to differ, as the numerous nuts inside each compound fruit have squirrel appeal. When mature, the heavy fruits fall from the trees with dull thuds, littering the ground like alien green brains. To be clear, fruits fall only from female trees as, like hollies or the boxelders on Almanzo's timber claim, Osage oranges are dioecious, with male and female flowers on separate plants.

The common name that Laura used resulted from the plant's native range matching original Osage Indian lands, in what is now Texas, Oklahoma, and Arkansas. Did the plants remind Laura of the Osage people who walked away all those years ago in Indian Territory? If so, she didn't say. Since the late 1840s settlers used close-planted Osage orange trees along the borders of their farms, creating, as the thorny wood filled in over some years of trimming, a

The giant fruit of Osage oranges coevolved with North American megafauna. Think woolly mammoths. »

living fence "horse-high, bull-strong and hog-tight." It was barbed wire in the days before barbed wire was invented.

Thus Osage oranges earned the alternate name "hedge apples." Still others called them by the more historic "bois d'arc"—wood for bow—as the Osage and other tribes used its hardwood for hunting bows, a practice soon adopted by French trappers. Laura may not have known that Lewis and Clark carried the fruits home from their expedition with the Corps of Discovery or that the trees—related to mulberry—were once cultivated with the thought of starting an American silk industry, but she would have been interested.

As the Wilders moved through the country they kept their eyes on the land. How were the yields? Was the water good? Was it tended by able farmers? Even if the land was idle or the gardens weedy, Laura was slow to judgment. She noted farm values in price per acre and crop prices by the bushel. If you know any statistical historians looking for a source of land and commodity values in the 1890s, they could mine data from Laura's diary. In Douglas County, Kansas, Laura wrote, "This is the best farming country we have seen yet, prairie with natural groves here and there and timber along the creek." And who knew? With all of the emigrants the Wilders were meeting, coming and going in steady cross currents, they didn't know if their Missouri plan would stick. Better to have an idea of some good alternatives if they ended up backtracking as her parents had done several times.

As one might have expected, Laura was taken with tree plantings in towns along the way. They called to her. Fort Scott, Kansas, had so many trees, she described it as a bower. After crossing into Missouri on the afternoon of August 22 at precisely 2:24 and 3/4, she and Almanzo were charmed by the fresh, clean city of Lamar with its shady, tree-lined streets. It must have been bliss to think of themselves living in a house shaded by trees on warm summer afternoons.

From eastern Kansas to western Missouri, the land started to fold, as if it were creasing for a fan or paper dolls. As the team pulled the wagon up the gradual grade into the Ozarks, the Wilders savored the scenery. They seem to have left the wind behind in Kansas. "The trees and rocks are lovely," Laura wrote. You can hear the smile come through her words. Almanzo said, "We could almost live on the looks of them." They forded the Turnback Creek and never turned back. Laura was convinced. "The farther we go, the more we like this country," she wrote. "Parts of Nebraska and Kansas are well enough, but Missouri is simply glorious." Almanzo interjected, "This is beautiful country."

If the prairie is an upside-down forest, the Ozarks are upside-down mountains. They are actually a plateau in a jigsaw puzzle of a landscape where, over eons, streams made deep cuts into the limestone. "The Ozarks are not really mountains, they are valleys," Laura reflected, sounding like the schoolteacher she once was. "So the skyline is always level and blue like the sea, and nearly always there is a lovely blue haze over the hillsides." The Wilders had left a sea of grass for a sea of sky.

They saw a forty-acre tract of land for sale outside Mansfield. Laura took "a violent fancy" to it. She said, "If she could not have it, she did not want any because it could be made into such a pretty place." A long hill climbed from the valley. A hill! After years of being flatlanders. The land was timbered and ridged with rocks and ravines. There were creeks and springs with good water. Four acres were cleared, and in late summer the crickets and katydids held their own singing school. There were birds and butterflies. After the heat and dust of the road, the breeze was a kiss. The one-room wooden house up on a hill wasn't much, but it would do. They had found Rocky Ridge Farm, their new center of gravity.

SAVING
SEED

ROCKY RIDGE FARM

———

Mansfield, Missouri

1894–1915

Juglandàceae. Walnut F.
Juglans. Walnut.
Juglans nigra L. Black Walnut.
     (*Leaf Half Size*)   *Taunton Oct. 3. 91.*

Of the black walnut Wilder once wrote, "No nut that grows equals it in richness and flavor …
Nature bountifully supplies this delicious nut, with no trouble or expense to us."

After years of farming on the prairie, getting started at Rocky Ridge Farm was literally an uphill battle. Ozark agriculture meant preparing and cultivating land at all sorts of angles where, as Laura put it, "we can farm three sides of the land thus getting the use of many more acres than our title deeds call for." Theirs wasn't bottomland. At its best the farm offered areas of so-called "bench" land where the ridges leveled out. With the exception of one field, the rest of the new Wilder property was timbered when Laura, Almanzo, and Rose arrived.

Laura got her trees. A predominance of oak, great for firewood and for building materials, supported a diverse local wildlife. The Ozarks are a veritable compendium of oak species—scarlet, northern red, shumard, black, and white oaks, so acorns were everywhere. When the Wilders took title in autumn of 1894, the black walnuts were also releasing their bounty of nuts. Tupelo, sassafras, and dogwood were blushing red. The ravine was crowned with golden leaves of river birch and redbud. In the crisp air was the richness of fallen leaves, that subtle and oddly pleasant scent of decay. It was a smell with the redolence of childhood for both Laura and Almanzo—Wisconsin for her, New York for him.

The Wilders had big plans for Rocky Ridge. They would open more acreage for pasture, enough to support a dairy herd. The cows would have a second job. Around the edges of their one cleared field, colonies of tiny eastern red cedars had popped up, their dormant seeds invigorated by the sun. Cows, in addition to producing milk, would keep unwanted tree seedlings in check. Chickens were a definite. Poultry was a steady source of protein and a common country currency, as eggs could be traded at the grocer. And they'd have fruit. While Mansfield touted itself as "Gem City of the Ozarks," Laura and Almanzo did not forget that they had made it to the "Land of the Big Red Apple."

Rocky Ridge Farm came with a bonus: a thousand small apple trees, mostly a variety called Ben Davis. The prior owner had purchased them through an agent, no doubt of Stark Bro's. This Missouri-based nursery giant, founded in 1816, was the dominant supplier in the Midwest at the time, employing over fourteen hundred "traveling solicitors" by the 1890s. It was, and still is, headquartered in the eastern part of the state in the little town of Louisiana. The thousand trees destined for Rocky Ridge would have arrived by train at the Mansfield depot in a sizable wooden crate, then been brought to the farm with a dray wagon and team.

Almanzo questioned the wisdom of his apple-buying predecessor. Who would acquire a thousand trees before preparing the land for them? Almanzo observed wryly, "he unloaded his blunder on me." The Wilders found this blunder planted out in two places on the farm. Two hundred were set in a worn-out cornfield. They covered the four acres in rows about ten yards apart. The rest had been heeled in, crowded into a temporary nursery bed. More land had to be cleared during the Wilders' first winter to make space for the rest of the orchard, though calling it an orchard at that point would have seemed a stretch.

New apple trees are, as they were then, sold as one- or two-year old whips, generally bare-rooted, with a single central stem about a half-inch in diameter. They look like sticks with roots, because that is what they are. A nurseryman grafts a piece of a young branch—the scion—of a given variety of apple onto hardy rootstock, cutting interlocking notches in each piece of wood, fitting them together and binding the join. Grafting is carpentry with living wood.

The Stark Bro's logo is reminiscent of the bear in *Little House in the Big Woods.*

The scion develops into the top part of the tree. The rootstock ensures vigor. Grafting is cloning horticultural-style, with speed and reliability guaranteed. In other words, the Ben Davis whips that Almanzo carefully tended would bear Ben Davis apples, because scions are all as identical as identical twins.

Long hailed as a "mortgage lifter," Ben Davis was an apple farmer's dream. Farmers all over the country—including Almanzo Wilder—loved the variety because the trees matured quickly and started to bear heavy crops of market-ready fruit in under ten years. One writer in the April 1895 *Kansas City Journal* stated that if he were to plant a thousand-tree orchard, first he would select "999 of the Ben Davis variety," and the last one "would be Ben Davis." This isn't literally true. To get the heaviest fruit set, Ben Davis trees appreciate pollination from another variety. In Almanzo's case, while the majority of his trees were Ben Davis, a portion were Missouri Pippins—another apple sold by Stark Bro's in the 1890s.

Shippers, processors, and grocers loved the Ben Davis because its fruit was tough as nails. It shipped and stored like a champ. The apple was so indestructible that one writer suggested it as a substitute baseball if yours went missing before a game. Round, red, and unbruised, it seemed to sell itself.

If you are wondering why Ben Davis apples aren't available in a produce

An illustration from a Stark Bro's booklet on pruning shows the size of young fruit trees.

The popular Ben Davis apple.

section near you, the explanation is simple. It was great for cider, more than adequate for cooking and drying, but not a palate pleaser as an eating apple. One writer said he "would almost as soon as try to eat a piece of sponge." He wasn't alone in his opinion. Another of the nicknames for the Ben Davis was the "cotton apple." Some suggest that it was northern-grown Ben Davis apples that earned the variety its tasteless reputation. It requires a long season to ripen, more Missouri than Maine. But regardless of the reason or the fairness thereof, the Ben Davis is seldom grown in orchards at present. It does survive, genetically speaking, in one of its offspring, the Cortland, still a favorite among pie makers in all fifty states.

I think of Almanzo and Laura Wilder as prototype sustainable farmers. Though he confessed to "a colossal ignorance" in the subject of growing apples, Almanzo had hard-earned practical experience in trying to get trees to grow on his timber claim. He was going to do his best to get this orchard off to a good start, from the ground up. When he drove to town from Rocky Ridge to sell loads of wood—their first cash crop—he filled his wagon with free soil amendments for the return trip.

KEEP THE SOIL FERTILE
HOW
1 - RAISE LIVE STOCK
2 - ROTATE THE CROPS
3 - GROW CLOVER. ALFALFA
         AND OTHER LEGUMES
4 - SAVE THE BARNYARD MANURE
5 - PASTURE ROLLING LANDS
         TO PREVENT WASHING
6 - ADD HUMUS —
         DON'T BURN THE STALKS
7 - SUPPLY NEEDED ELEMENTS

A page from *Farm Knowledge* (1918) lists the good soil practices that Almanzo was already employing.

Manure from the livery stable was a ready but acidic source of nitrogen fertilizer. Wood ashes from the mill balanced the acidity, adding lime as well as key nutrients like potassium and phosphorus. This chemical balancing act adjusted the soil pH, which in turn made nutrients available for the plant roots to take up. The wood ash had another unexpected dividend. While a neighbor's new trees were plagued with borers—various beetles that eat the roots and bark of apple trees—the Rocky Ridge orchard was unscathed. Almanzo later read that the lye in the ashes discourages the pests, though he also credited the wild quail, which were "thick in the orchard" and had a taste for the bugs. He never allowed quail to be hunted on his property.

Between the rows of juvenile apple trees, Almanzo seeded timothy and clover. This duo is a soil workhorse. Timothy, a cool-season grass with fibrous

A. J. Wilder making hay on Rocky Ridge Farm with Buck & Billy

Almanzo and his Morgan horses cutting the hay crop.

roots, holds topsoil in and holds weeds down. Red clover, a short-lived perennial, sucks up phosphorus and nitrogen and banks it in its root nodules. The following year's plowing disperses those nutrients to the benefit of the apple trees. The clover taproots also break up compressed soil structure. When the timothy and clover matured in summer, Almanzo cut it as a nutritious hay for the livestock, "making two crops out of the land."

Laura and Almanzo transplanted the rest of the saplings out of the nursery bed. They tended their apple trees, getting to know them as individuals. He wrote, "Wife and I were so well acquainted with the trees that if I wished to mention one to her, I would say 'that tree with the large branch to the south,' or 'the tree that leans to the north,' etc." The orchard became one of the accomplishments of Almanzo's life. The trees grew, just as their daughter was growing, and he did his best to shape them. Early each year, equipped with saw, and eventually with ladder, he sorted the tangle of the prior year's growth, selecting the best branches and cutting out the rest.

Each spring, Almanzo sowed field crops like corn. Laura put in a vegetable garden, planting the potatoes by the dark of the moon. Their little girl helped in the garden too, and played in the creek and the woods. She picked wild berries in summer and gathered nuts in the fall, and grew up rosy-cheeked and bright-eyed. Rose was clever, gifted even, and soon outdistanced the curriculum offered at the Mansfield public school. She borrowed books from the school library which she and her mother would read aloud in the evenings while her father made popcorn for everyone to share.

Within two years Almanzo built a small frame house on the farm and repurposed the old cabin as a barn. But the apples would take some time to start bearing. The family needed steady income. In 1898 their friend Frank Cooley died, and Almanzo took over his Mansfield delivery business. As much as Laura loved Rocky Ridge, the practical thing would be to move temporarily. So they relocated to a rental house near town, closer to the school for Rose and to the depot for Almanzo. It was a scant mile from the new house to Rocky Ridge, so they could keep up with the work at both places.

There are few photographs of the Wilders' town place. In one, a youthful Laura smiles out at the camera, standing at the edge of their front porch with its carpenter scrollwork and comfortable furniture. A willow bentwood rocker is on one side and a tall swing or glider on the other. A potted plant hangs from a hook in the porch ceiling. Below the railing, another flowerpot is set into the ground. It might hold seeds of morning glory or some other vine that would clamber up in summer. To the right of the porch stairs, a rose bush blooms. The grass is shaggy, as if it were cut with a sickle or scythe. Laura is wearing a pinafore with a big pocket, and looks the picture of health. Perhaps she had finished her chores for the day, or was taking a well-deserved break to pose for the photographer.

It was an easy walk to town, if Laura wanted to stop in to buy a few things or sell some eggs. Mansfield, like De Smet, was a railroad town, officially established in the 1880s when one of the "Frisco" lines put a watering stop along its newly laid tracks. The town didn't start from scratch—there was already a village. But it was the railroad that made the town, creating a hub for transporting freight. Unlike De Smet, Mansfield was named not for a missionary, but for a railroad investor, Francis "F. M." Mansfield, a Hartville attorney who had a

Laura looks so young in this picture on the front porch of their house in town that she could be mistaken for her daughter.

hand in platting the town and selling the resulting lots. Also unlike De Smet, Mansfield was laid out with an open square at its center, early on designated "Park Square," planted with trees and lined with sidewalks.

The idea of a central square is an early European import to America. Colonists from Spain, France, and England put them in the heart of new cities in places as far flung as Santa Fe, New Orleans, and Savannah. In Mansfield, businesses faced the square—general stores and drugstores, bank and blacksmith—and its residential streets extended out from there. Laura was pleased with their thriving small town, writing that the town had everything a person could want—except a Congregational church. The Wilders joined the Methodist congregation.

The apple trees at Rocky Ridge Farm started bearing around 1902. That same year Pa, Charles Ingalls, fell ill. Laura caught a train to De Smet and made it back in time to say her goodbyes. He died on June 8, leaving a legacy of stories and memories.

Changes to her family circle seemed to be the theme for Laura at the beginning of the new century. The following year, 1903, Rose first moved away from home. A restless teenager, she went to stay with her aunt E. J.—Eliza Jane—who had married and moved to Crowley, Louisiana. Rose finished high school there. It must have been bittersweet for Laura, who hadn't graduated from high school herself, to not be in attendance when her daughter received her diploma and delivered her commencement address in Latin. (As a benchmark of Rose's intellectual abilities, she learned four years of Latin in one year at Crowley.) While Rose returned to Mansfield briefly, long enough to learn telegraphy from the town's stationmaster, she was launched into an independent adulthood as a wage earner.

Rose moved, first to Kansas City and then to California, working her way up through a series of "bachelor girl" jobs: telegraph operator, office manager, journalist, real estate broker. Like many of her cohort, she abandoned corset and petticoat, shortened her skirts, and eventually bobbed her hair. In 1909, she married Gillette Lane in San Francisco. Whether she broke the news to Papa and Mama Bess, as she called her parents, before or after the wedding, no one knows. Nor is there any record of the emotions that surfaced the next

Downtown Mansfield was organized around a shady central square.

year when Rose Wilder Lane delivered a premature baby boy who did not survive. It was as though a cruel symmetry had been carved into generations of the Ingalls-Wilder-Lane family tree, always taking the firstborn son.

Financially and agriculturally, things improved for Laura and Almanzo. His parents gave them the money to buy the house they were renting. With what they saved, they had more to put into Rocky Ridge Farm. They were building up the place in more ways than one. Over the years they acquired several adjoining parcels, adding sixty-plus acres to their original forty. They bought and bred livestock—hogs, Durham cattle, and Morgan horses. By 1910 they moved back to the farm full time, and began building a new house on the hill. The *Mansfield Mirror* reported in September 1913 that, "A. J. Wilder is building a fine 12-room residence on his farm near Mansfield," adding, "Mr. Wilder is one of our most progressive farmers."

The farmhouse at Rocky Ridge Farm with the oak tree in front and the grape arbor in back. The chimney includes many fossils of seashells, making its own cabinet of curiosities.

Almanzo's orchard bore fruit.

Laura and Almanzo sited the house not far from the ravine in the lee of the ridge, among an oak grove they had thinned and carefully selected for the purpose. The oak trees with their ample girth and shady circumference form an entry to the house, as well as a living awning. Oaks from the farm's woodlot—cut, seasoned, and hand-planed—also furnished the lumber for the construction, beams and joists as well as the finish work. The paneling in the parlor, the beams in the ceiling, the floorboards, mantle, bookshelves, window seats, and staircase share the warm, honeyed surface of polished oak, as if they are talking to their brethren still growing outside.

Laura on the left and Rose on the right standing in the ravine at Rocky Ridge Farm.

Of her parents, Rose once wrote, "My mother loves courage and beauty and books; my father loves nature, birds and trees and curious stones, and both of them love the land, the stubborn, grudging beautiful earth that wears out human lives year by year." (Rose was clear in her intention not to be wed to the family farm, but would have an impact on its house and garden in years to come.) The farmhouse's fireplace is a testament to the accuracy of Rose's observations. Its chimney is full of fossils collected on the farm, stones that captured ancient, unspoken lives. The surround is made of great stone slabs that Laura found on the property and, after some persuading, Almanzo and the builders hefted into place.

The farmhouse was a part of the landscape. It seemed to emerge fully clothed from the hillside. Laura didn't curtain its windows so she could see the changing pictures of the world outside. Depending on the time of day, the

The stone fireplace was one feature that Laura insisted on for the new farmhouse.

season of the year, and the weather, the scenes framed in the glass panes shifted, but were a constant draw. She appreciated "the forest trees in the wood lot, the little brook that wanders through the pasture, the hills and valleys, and the level fields of the farm lands." Living close to nature was a fundamental thing. Along with love and duty, work and rest, nature was a key ingredient in her formula for a happy life.

Out back a honeysuckle grew over the well, and an arbor covered with vines formed a shady route to the kitchen door. In late summer it was laden with ripe round grapes, warmed by the Missouri sun. Laura wrote and asked Ma to send the directions for her concentrated grape juice. Caroline Ingalls replied with the recipe, layered with typical maternal commentary despite the fact that her daughter was now in her forties. "We are very glad and thankful

Grapes on an arbor made a shady, productive entrance to the kitchen at Rocky Ridge Farm.

that you are getting so well and strong again—but do not try to stretch the 24 hours you have and make yourself sick again. Take your time to sleep and sleep good." The recipe? Cook and strain the grapes as if you were making jelly, then add ½ cup sugar to each quart of juice and boil down until it thickens.

The grape arbor also masked the view of the farm buildings, including the barn and the chicken house. Rose once called her mother "a servant to hens." There must have been days when Laura also felt she was handmaid to her Leghorns, with their endless demands. "Believe me, I learned how to take care of hens and to make them lay," she once wrote. She was fond of them, really, their gossipy society. It must have put her in mind of the old home place, out on Pa's De Smet claim, where she hunted for eggs around the haystacks and in the thick prairie grass. All of the catchphrases that have drifted into English were true: pecking order, coming home to roost, chicken scratch, nest egg.

As nest eggs go, Laura's chickens were a part of the economic and ecological cycle that was Rocky Ridge Farm. Almanzo grew corn, millet, alfalfa, and oats, for poultry feed. After separating the cream from the daily milking, Laura put out some of the skimmed milk for the chickens. The rest went to the hogs.

A black walnut tree shades the barn.

Laura and Mary's old *Fifth Reader* included this picture of hens roosting and a cock crowing.

In her kitchen, vegetable parings, meat scraps, and the like were saved for the livestock too. The buckets were hidden in hinged wooden bins that Almanzo built close to the back door. She didn't waste a thing, and she liked to keep her kitchen just so.

She tolerated the wild birds sharing her berries, though their appetites sometimes struck her as gluttonous. Who would forgo their songs, their easy companionship, for the sake of some fruit? She had wished herself wings more than once. Of the chicken-thieving hawks, however, enough was enough. Laura was tempted to violate at least one commandment whenever she spotted a hawk making off with one of her fluffy yellow chicks.

Her chickens provided cash income—or credit at the grocers—but they also laid a golden egg, in that they launched Laura's writing career. She was invited to speak on her poultry at a local agricultural meeting, but was kept away by some sort of illness. She sent her speech to be read aloud, and it attracted the specific attention of one person in the audience, the editor of the *Missouri Ruralist*, a twice-monthly publication from Kansas City. The following year, 1911, her first article appeared there, entitled "Favors the Small Farm Home." In it, she developed one of her persistent themes, the feasibility of the self-sustaining farm, foreshadowing the work of American agricultural writers like Wendell Berry. Laura was forty-four years old.

She started slowly. In the first four years of her professional writing, twelve articles appeared in the *Ruralist*. Occasionally her work appeared in other local newspapers. On November 12, 1914, *The Democrat* of Monroe City, Missouri, published "How to Make Hens Lay During Winter," with the byline, "Mrs. A. J. Wilder."

In late summer 1915, Laura boarded the train in Mansfield and made the long journey to visit Rose and her husband, Gillette, in California. She missed her only child, and the feeling was mutual. Rose had written, "I simply can't stand being so homesick for you any more." Laura also hoped for some coaching from Rose and her literary friends on increasing the quality and quantity of her writing output. An extra enticement in 1915: the Panama-Pacific International Exposition, one of America's great world's fairs, was underway. Laura would be one of nearly nineteen million visitors that year, celebrating the opening of the Panama Canal and the redevelopment of San Francisco after the devastating 1906 earthquake.

Almanzo stayed at Rocky Ridge to work the farm. Laura worried about him and their dog, Inky—they always had a dog—as well as her garden. In her first letter, sent from Springfield, Missouri, on August 21 while she was waiting for her connection, Laura mused on the heavy rains and their effect on her plants. "How are you and Inky I wonder? The country here is awfully washed," she wrote. "Was the lettuce seed ruined? Perhaps you'd better look."

You may not have lettuce seed on your list of things to worry about when you travel. Lettuce is a member of the daisy family, and salads consist of

When Laura wrote articles for the *Missouri Ruralist*, she sometimes wrote about her friends' farms. Here she and Almanzo, on left, sit and visit on the front porch of a friend's farmhouse.

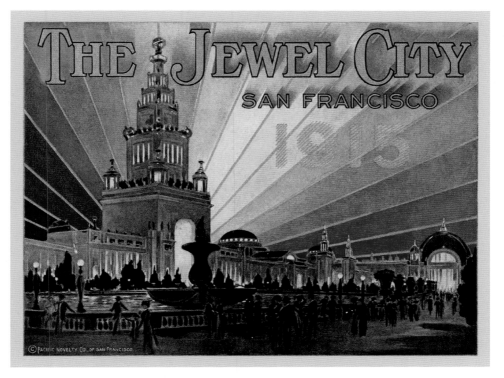

The centerpiece of the Panama-Pacific International Exposition that Laura visited was the Tower of Jewels, covered with crystals and lit at night with electric floodlights.

juvenile leaves of the plant. As it ages, the leaves toughen up and the milky sap gets bitter. If you grow it, you know that given hot weather the lettuce will "bolt," sending up flower stalks. Most gardeners yank it out at that point and consign it to the compost heap or—if they keep chickens—the chicken yard. Laura left hers. It bloomed with little starry flowers and set seed for the next year's garden. But if it rained too hard, the mature seeds would disperse, washing away or sowing themselves at random. Hopefully Almanzo was able to gather them in time.

When lettuce "bolts," it is producing seeds.

In her letters to Almanzo, Laura painted word pictures of the views from the train window—agrarian, picturesque, sublime—as she had so many years ago for Mary. There were farms with windmills, cattle, a cowboy with chaps. She mentioned when the flora or geology changed. Coming up to Denver she wrote, "Saw my first sage brush this morning. A dwarf variety. It is in little clumps all over the prairie." There were desert sands and alkali beds, mountains with "ramparts of rock . . . like those pictures of old castles in Austria we were looking at, and such wonderful fortified places they would make—such castles could be made on them!" On her moonlit ride across the Great Salt Lake, she was mesmerized. "It looked as though the train was running on the water. I undressed and lay in my berth and watched it, the moonlight making a path of silver across the water and the farther shore so dim and indistinct and melting away into the desert as though there was no end to the lake."

In San Francisco, Laura basked in the attention from Rose and her circle. They visited the fair over and over, and she sent home detailed accounts to Almanzo. Mother and daughter strolled the Japanese tea garden in Golden Gate Park, built for an earlier 1894 exposition, and went to Chinatown and Little Italy. They waded into the Pacific Ocean. Gillette took her to see the big trees in Muir Woods, dedicated by President Theodore Roosevelt in 1908, and named for naturalist John Muir.

Like Laura, John Muir, considered father of America's national park movement, remembered the Wisconsin wildflowers of his youth. He spent his boyhood about two hundred miles southeast of Pepin on a homestead in Marquette County toward the middle of the state. In 1865, as an adult, he tried—unsuccessfully—to buy forty acres of the Wisconsin family farm to "keep it untrampled for the sake of the ferns and flowers." He wrote that their beauty was "so pressed into my mind that I shall always enjoy looking back at them in imagination, even across seas and continents, and perhaps after I am dead." In 1912, with words that echo Wilder's, Muir had written, "Everybody needs beauty as well as bread, places to play in and pray in, where nature may heal and give strength to body and soul alike." Laura lived her life in harmony with his philosophy.

Meanwhile in San Francisco, Rose was sick with a hard-to-shake cold in the apartment at 1019 Vallejo Street. But she had the benefit of her mother's ministrations. In particular, Laura was "dosing her with snake root." While many native plants have been dubbed snakeroot, only one genus, *Echinacea*, is known as Missouri snakeroot. Several species of *Echinacea* are native to Wright County, where Laura might have harvested it or grown it in her garden, and all of them share a potent chemistry. Parts of the plant—leaves, flowers, and especially roots—are still popular ingredients in the herbal apothecary, used to boost the immune system and shorten the miseries of the common cold. If you walk into a pharmacy or health food store, you will find bottles of *Echinacea* with herbal supplements. If you walk into a nursery, you will find pots of

Echinacea, now usually called coneflower, with the garden perennials.

There are other indications that Laura used natural remedies, hardly surprising given the dearth of doctors in most of the places they had lived and the expense of medical treatment given their budget. Rose remembered as a child chewing elm bark, referring to slippery elm. *Ulmus rubra* is a small elm native to much of the United States. Its inner bark is slick with a mucilaginous goo that, mixed with water or saliva, coats the throat and the digestive tract. Like *Echinacea,* slippery elm is still used for sore throats and for various problems of the stomach and bowels that you hope to avoid. Later on, when she turned to fiction, Wilder wrote about her Aunt Polly steeping herbs for cousin Charley's fever in *Little House in the Big Woods.*

Rose, by then an established writer for the *San Francisco Bulletin*, worked hard at her craft. Laura was amazed by her daughter's dedication and the effort writing entailed. She confided to Almanzo, "The more I see of how Rose works the better satisfied I am to raise chickens." But Laura was writing more than letters. During the visit, Rose arranged for a few of Laura's poems to be printed in the *Bulletin*'s child-friendly "Tuck'em In Corner." Laura's poems are full of fairies and flowers. In one poem, she weaves in poppies from China—the showy perennial *Papaver orientale* originated in Asia. Japanese cherries are mentioned in another, and it is significant that, in 1915, the United States sent a gift of dogwood trees to Japan to reciprocate for the cherry trees sent three years earlier from Tokyo for Potomac Park in Washington, DC. Still another flower was Laura's subject for an entire poem, "Naughty Four O' Clocks."

Like the morning glory, the four o'clock is one of nature's timepieces, triggered by light and dark, temperature and humidity. Unlike the morning glory, which opens around sunrise, the four o'clock is, as you might expect, on the late shift. These circadian rhythms match their pollinators, four o'clocks being pollinated by night-flying moths. If you plant them in your garden, or write poems about them, you are bearing witness to coevolution and the plant-pollinator partnership.

Laura visited Muir Woods with her son-in-law, Gillette Lane.

1.

2.

3.

The Tuck'em In Corner

Naughty Four o' Clocks

By LAURA INGALLS WILDER.

There were some naughty flowers once,
Who were careless in their play;
They got their petals torn and soiled
As they swung in the dust all day.

Then went to bed at four o'clock,
With faces covered tight,
To keep the fairy, Drop O' Dew
From washing them at night.

Poor Drop O' Dew! What could she do?
She said to the Fairy Queen,
"I cannot get those Four o'Clocks
To keep their faces clean."

The mighty Storm King heard the tale;
"My winds and rain," roared he,
"Shall wash those naughty flowers well,
As flowers all should be."

So raindrops came and caught them all
Before they went to bed,
And washed those little Four o'Clocks
At three o'clock instead.

⌃ Laura's poem about four o'clocks, clipped from the *San Francisco Bulletin*.

⌃ Missouri snakeroot is another name for *Echinacea* or coneflower. The narrow-leaved coneflower, *E. angustifolia,* is the most common species in the state.

The four o'clock is easy to grow as an annual in Missouri or the Dakotas, but if you garden in a climate like central Florida it is a vigorous perennial. Its botanical name, *Mirabilis jalapa*—Jalapa is in Guatemala—and alternate common name, Marvel-of-Peru, give clues to its native locales. While no other evidence suggests that four o'clocks grew at Rocky Ridge, Laura was definitely familiar with them. It is an easy seed to share and save, and a popular "pass-along" plant, so I like to think they bloomed in her garden.

During her two-month stay in California she also completed several articles about the Exposition for the *Ruralist*. San Francisco in 1915 had its charms, but Laura was unconvinced. "The more I see of city life," she wrote to Almanzo, "the more I love the country." Rose hoped she might tempt her parents to relocate to the agriculture-rich Santa Clara Valley, inland just south of the Bay, but that was not to be. Her mother's thoughts were turning back to Missouri. Laura wrote, "I love the city of San Francisco . . . but I would not give one Ozark hill for the rest of the state that I have seen." East or, in this case, West, home really was best.

Of the exhibit for Missouri—the "Show Me State"—at the Panama-Pacific International Exposition, Wilder wrote, "We have 'shown' them." »

PUTTING
FOOD BY

THE ROCK HOUSE AND
THE FARMHOUSE

———

Mansfield, Missouri
1916–1957

In September 1917, Almanzo was a superintendent of the poultry department for the Mansfield fair.

The real things of life that are the common possession of us all are of the greatest value; worth far more than motor cars or radio outfits; more than lands or money; and our whole store of these wonderful riches may be revealed to us by such a common, beautiful thing as a wild sunflower.

—MISSOURI RURALIST

Laura returned satisfied to Rocky Ridge Farm in November 1915. She continued to manage her poultry flock and help Almanzo run the place. They showed the results of their labors, competing in the annual Mansfield Agricultural and Stock fairs. One year he won first place (fifty cents!) for best millet; another year she won a dollar for her Brown Leghorns. Sometimes they helped organize the events.

With her precious spare time, Laura was busy with church work, the Eastern Star lodge, her study clubs—the Justamere and Athenians prominent among them—and writing. Her written output increased, no doubt stimulated by the conversations with Rose, and she took on a regular feature in the *Ruralist* called "The Farm Home." Plus, every year she planted a vegetable garden.

Have you ever opened your mailbox on a winter day to find a promise of summer in the form of a seed catalog? It happened at Rocky Ridge too. One cold January, Laura described an annual ritual in her farm home. It would have resonated for her readers. Laura was "making garden" from the catalogs, performing blue-ribbon mental horticulture. "The vegetables one raises in the seed catalogs are so perfectly beautiful," she wrote. "We do grow beautiful gardens on cold winter days as we talk over the seed catalogs." It is an activity with innate appeal to any gardener, projecting green growing things onto a bleak midwinter backdrop. Wilder also saw the value in thinking through a planting plan during the slow season, concluding, "Our summer gardens are much more of a success because of these gardens in our minds."

It isn't known which seed suppliers Laura used for either her imagined or real gardens. Either she disposed of her old catalogs and seed orders, or donated them to some later paper salvage drive. At any rate, nothing survived with the exception of one advertising card from L. L. May, a seed house located in St. Paul, Minnesota. There were plenty of mail-order seed vendors for Laura to choose from in the 1910s and 1920s, including companies in the Midwest. There was Gurney Seed and Nursery, located at the time in Yankton, South Dakota. Iowa Seed Company, which advertised itself as "Seedsman to the American People," was in Des Moines. Tucker Seed Company was just one hundred miles due west of Mansfield in Carthage, Missouri. All of these companies relied on sumptuous catalogs delivered by the U.S. mail as the primary way to market their products.

When Wilder described browsing catalogs for seeds, she mused on intention, as important for a gardener as it is for a writer. By thinking through the "gardens in our minds," one could improve the actual results. She observed, "We grow many other things in the same way. It is truly surprising how anything grows and grows by talking about it."

Rocky Ridge Farm continued to grow and grow. Over time they bought more adjacent parcels, building the farm to two hundred acres. One can visualize Laura and Almanzo sitting at the dining room table, talking over planned

L. L. May & Co. of St. Paul, Minnesota, was a seed catalog familiar to Laura. »

L. L. MAY & CO.

ST. PAUL, 1896 MINNESOTA.

Two Hardy Climbing Roses.

* * * Crimson Rambler * * *

The most remarkable climbing rose that has ever been introduced. It is of Japanese origin, perfectly hardy, and the most rapid growing, free-flowering variety we have ever seen. Flowers are a beautiful rich crimson color and produced in great clusters throughout the entire season.

This is a rose that will please everyone and is highly recommended by the leading authorities in both America and Europe. Price 20c. each, 3 for 50c. postpaid

* * * White Rover * * *

A beautiful creamy white climbing rose that is a grand companion for the Crimson Rambler. The plant is a strong, vigorous grower, hardy in all sections of this country, and undoubtedly the most valuable white variety that can be secured. The flowers are of a good size, a delicate creamy white and borne profusely the entire summer. Price, 20c. each, 3 for 50c. postpaid.

THE ABOVE TWO ROSES FOR ONLY 35 cts., Postpaid.

Farm and Floral Guide

Seeds, Plants, Bulbs, Fruits and Seed Potatoes

Rocky Ridge Farm was home.

improvements. One came in liquid form when Almanzo piped in water, using gravity flow from an uphill spring. He ran one pipe into the reservoir of the cast iron cookstove in the farmhouse kitchen, delivering the luxury of hot water. Laura's cooking fires now did triple duty, heating food, the house, and water. But it got even better. "We revel in water!" Wilder exclaimed in the *Ruralist*. There were now spigots for the chicken coop, the barn, the "calf lot," and, at last, one in the garden. No more lugging water to give the plants a drink during dry spells.

Over the years, Almanzo experimented with crops to grow at Rocky Ridge. He added strawberries, becoming something of a local expert in cultivation techniques. He tried various kinds of legumes and grasses, always trying to perfect the hay he grew for his livestock. He planted Sudangrass—a drought-tolerant grass native to Africa, which the Department of Agriculture had just introduced. Sudangrass grows quickly in the middle of a Missouri summer, meaning it could be cut twice for hay. His eight-foot-tall plants motivated Almanzo to bring samples of both seed and grass into the town newspaper office, an event noted in the next day's edition. The agriculture teacher from the high school brought his class to Rocky Ridge Farm to learn about the various kinds of cover crops Almanzo grew.

In 1917, Laura took a part-time job as secretary-treasurer of the Mansfield Farm Loan Association, a job she held for about ten years. She was, in a real sense, participating in the next phase of American agricultural history. Just as Pa had claimed and qualified for the free land of the Homestead Act of 1862, his daughter was taking a direct role in the implementation of the Federal Farm

RUNNER.

Almanzo became a local expert in the cultivation of strawberries.

Loan Act of 1916. With the exception of Alaska, the country had effectively run out of arable land for homesteaders. The 1916 legislation was a way to provide low-cost, long-term credit for rural citizens who wanted to buy land for farming.

In April 1917, America entered the First World War, and food supply became a national issue. The U.S. Food Administration, run by a mining engineer and humanitarian named Herbert Hoover, started nationwide campaigns to encourage gardening, preserving food, and eliminating food waste. Laura, well-practiced in these habits of thrift, could easily march in step.

A glimpse of jars of food that Laura put up in one corner of the kitchen at Rocky Ridge Farm.

Growing, preserving, and saving food was important on the home front during the Great War.

The Mansfield Agricultural and Stock Show included a food conservation exhibit the following year. The new spirit of patriotic thrift echoed in Wilder's *Ruralist* columns. She wrote, "Out in the berry patch, the bluejays scolded me for trespassing. They talked of a food shortage and threatened terrible things to profiteers who took more than their share of the necessaries of life."

The Wilders bought war bonds and, with the bounty of Rocky Ridge Farm, supported Red Cross drives. The local paper reported Mrs. A. J. Wilder's donation of "15 thoroughbred Brown Leghorn eggs and a rooster to the Red Cross Auction held on the public square in Mansfield Center" on Saturday, May 4, 1918. Almanzo did his bit, providing another rooster, two hens, and a bushel of Irish potatoes.

In California, Rose and Gillette Lane divorced. She kept his name—not interrupting her authorial pen name of Rose Wilder Lane—but little else. Soon after the war ended, Rose began indulging her own version of the family wanderlust. She moved first to New York City, then to Europe where she traveled

˄ Laura raised Brown Leghorn chickens.

Wilder captioned the center photograph in this January 17, 1925, article for *The Country Gentleman,* "While you are kneading you can enjoy this view of hills and woods and pasture." »

widely, including the Mideast. To earn a living, she employed her pen, or more accurately her portable typewriter, sometimes freelance—fiction and opinion pieces—and other times as publicist for the Red Cross and similar relief organizations. She found romance abroad: with Arthur Griggs, an American living in Paris, and then with Guy Moyston, an old friend from San Francisco with whom she had a decade-long, sometimes long-distance relationship.

Rose continued to encourage her mother's writing efforts from afar, helping her place articles in higher-paying publications. In 1921 the *Mirror* announced "One of the leading articles in the June *McCall's* is by a Mansfield writer, Mrs. A. J. Wilder, whose articles have appeared in publications quite extensively. We have remarked before, and we remark again, that we believe no city its size in the United States has been or is the home of so many talented writers of national reputation as the Gem City of the Ozarks."

THE LITTLE DOOR LEADS TO THE DINING-ROOM SIDEBOARD

OUR REMADE KITCHEN IS MOSTLY CABINETS AND WINDOWS

My Ozark Kitchen

WE MADE a false start with the kitchen when we remodeled an old building into our Rocky Ridge Farmhouse. And I should have known better.

But my ideal kitchen had been made of ideas taken from women's magazines. It was almost the perfect room in which to cook, but when it was done it was not what I wanted. I had not realized that a farm kitchen must be more than merely a kitchen; it is the place where house and barn meet—often in pitched battle. My "city" kitchen was too small for the conflict and so placed that the sights and sounds and smells of the struggle penetrated the rest of the house.

I wanted a little, white, convenient, modern kitchen. I wanted it as badly as my neighbor, Mrs. Parsons, who made her husband get a job in the city machine shops because she wouldn't put up any longer with her farm-kitchen work. In a way I couldn't blame her, for the average farm kitchen is enough to break the strength and spirit of any woman.

But I meant, somehow, to bring my ideal kitchen to the farm. It had to be done by sheer brain power, for in the first place I could find no kitchen plans that provided for chickens' feed buckets, swill buckets, taking care of oil lamps, storage of foodstuffs and all my other problems. And in the second place we had very little money. But we country people are accustomed to using our brains; we must use them in our work. That is one of the great advantages of living on a farm.

Behind my unsatisfactory kitchen was a woodshed, separator room and junkshop combined. Here I had been meeting the barn, and trying to keep it from coming farther into the house. But in cold weather the skimmed milk and the swill buckets would freeze and have to be brought in to thaw at the kitchen stove. I studied this room for some time before I proposed that we finish it up for a kitchen. The Marf-of-the-Place is a very good jackknife carpenter, and I was an expert painter before that kitchen was done. We thought we could lessen expense by doing the work ourselves, and we did. The kitchen has cost just $49.84. But it took us a year to finish it, working at odd times.

Here's the Secret

WE BEGAN by putting wall board on the walls and ceiling; we cased the windows already there and put in others. Then we began to build cupboards. The secret of my kitchen is there—windows and cupboards.

"Why, this isn't a kitchen; it's a kitchen cabinet!" exclaimed the first friend who saw the completed triumph. The only wall space left of the original 12x14 room is the bit behind the range. All the rest is windows and cupboards.

The windows are large, with one clear pane of glass in each sash, and no curtains. They let in light and sunshine—and beauty.

The cupboards have several things in common. They are all built straight to the ceiling and to the floor, leaving no spaces beneath to be swept

THE WELL-LIGHTED MIXING CABINET HAS MATERIALS AND TOOLS CLOSE AT HAND

WHILE YOU ARE KNEADING YOU CAN ENJOY THIS VIEW OF HILLS AND WOODS AND PASTURE

By LAURA INGALLS WILDER

or above to be dusted. They are all closed with light doors, made of wall board framed in wood.

Every floor cupboard has a floor of its own, made of one broad three-quarter-inch board laid on the kitchen floor and sloped to set it at the cupboard threshold, and as the whole front of every cupboard is a door one whisk of the broom sweeps out the cupboard. There are no corners to clutch dust and no maddening obstacles over which it must be lifted with a whisk-broom.

Beginning with such windows and such cupboards, the only problem that remained was to arrange them to meet the needs of a farm kitchen.

The east wall looks toward the barn, with a glimpse of wooded hill beyond it, and the orchard and pastures to the north. All of this wall not occupied by the half-glass back door is filled by a large double window and the barn cupboards. These cupboards are under the sixteen-inch-wide window sill.

Places for Everything

THE swill buckets for the pigs, the skimmed milk for the hens, the lanterns and the kerosene can all have their places in these cupboards. There is a shelf for the shoe-blacking outfit. The cupboard doors shut them all out of sight.

On the top of these low cupboards is a hand basin and a jar of soft water. A towel rack is fastened to the window casing and a small mirror hangs against the double window.

Here I wash my hands and tidy my hair after excursions to the henhouse or hasty dashes to settle the affairs of colts or dogs. Here, too, the men wash up when they come in to meals on cold days. In the mornings I wash the lamps on this shelf and fill them from the oil can beneath it before I set them up in their own cupboard.

I chose the north side of the kitchen for my mixing and bread making because it has the best view. The two wide north windows give me hills and woods and the slopes of the sheep pasture to occupy my eyes and mind while I am kneading.

Between these two windows is my mixing cabinet. The lower part of it is a cupboard eighteen inches deep, holding baking pans and tins and cake board. The top of this is a wider shelf, 24x34 inches, and nineteen inches above this is the bottom of the shallow upper cupboard, which holds spices, baking powder, soda, and so forth.

Against the wall, under this upper cupboard, my egg beater, skimmer, wire strainer, spoons, paring knives and butcher knives, hang all in a row. Not all the spoons, and none of the knives, had anything to hang by, but the Man-of-the-Place put screw eyes in knife handles and with a small drill bored holes in the handles of the spoons.

Nor is this the whole of my mixing cabinet. Under the windows are built-in chests, 32x15 inches, their tops making the window sills. These tops are hinged and the fronts of the chests are doors, to allow easy cleaning. In the chests are white flour, graham flour, corn meal, brown and white sugar, all in tin containers. Weevils and all bugs that delight in flour bins are baffled, for when a container is empty I lift it out, scald and scrub and sun it. And before I put it back a whisk of broom and mop scrubs out the chest.

(Continued on Page 22)

Rose, posing in front of a garden she visited in Europe.

To Rose, her mother's apple pies were better than poetry.

In faraway France, Rose admired gardens, including those of Hyères, a town in the south of France where novelist Edith Wharton once made her home and garden. But of all the places she visited, she was smitten with the landscape and people of Albania. Still, she sometimes longed for home. Rose wrote to her mother, with the intense cravings of an ex-pat, "Could you fry a chicken and send it to us, please? These have been long, lank dry years, with no fried chicken. Some day we'll come home to fried chicken and on that day we get home for fried chicken it'll be a happy day."

One day, just before Christmas in 1923, Rose did come home to Rocky Ridge for an extended stay before heading back out to New York City. She ate more than fried chicken, feasting on apple pie—her mother's flaky crust filled with Almanzo's apples. What a combination. Rose sighed, "I would rather have made that pie than to have written a poem." Laura copied her daughter's words down for one of her *Ruralist* articles and added, "Thinking of pies and poems, I am more content with pie making, for surely it is better to make a good pie than a poor poem." Mother and daughter were just beginning their collaboration with words.

Laura and Almanzo had plenty of time to visit with Rose. By this point, they had started to reduce their agricultural endeavors at Rocky Ridge. "We are well as usual and have cut down our farming until we really don't do any," she wrote to a friend. "Just live on the Ozark climate and views." They did continue to have a large garden. Like her mother, Laura started the seeds for the warm-season vegetables like tomatoes in the house in late winter. In the height of summer she canned surplus berries and garden produce. But they had cut

On the back of this photograph Almanzo wrote, "Bessie picking peas note the high of them."

back on the orchard, field crops, poultry, and livestock, and increasingly relied on hired help for heavy chores. Almanzo was in his sixties, she in her fifties. The physical labor of the farm was increasingly difficult for them. Laura had been ill with what she described to her Aunt Martha as a "serious sickness, very close to nervous prostration." Perhaps it was brought on by overwork, as Rose thought. That year Laura had also lost her mother.

Caroline Quiner Ingalls had died on April 20, 1924, in the house on Third Street in De Smet. Mary lived with her, along with Grace and her husband, Nate Dow. Carrie had moved with her husband, David Swansey, to Keystone, a town in the Black Hills on the western edge of the state. Laura was in Mansfield, and did not return to South Dakota for her mother's passing or funeral. She was with Almanzo, and with her thoughts and memories of her parents.

The landscape of Rocky Ridge Farm was also changing, a change brought by progress that was both burden and boon to the Wilders. With the rise of the automobile, the Missouri highway department relocated the main road along Rocky Ridge, cutting into the hillside in front of the farmhouse. It changed the orientation of the property, so that the house now seemed to sit sideways to the road, as if it were looking away.

"The State Highway runs just north of the house now, just far enough away that the dust does not reach us," Laura wrote to a family friend. "People say that it has added $1000 in value to our farm, but we don't see it that way." Still, the pecan tree that Almanzo had brought back from his brother Perley's place in Louisiana was maturing nicely next to their driveway, along with the perpetual family favorite, a wild rose bush. He also moved some small cedars down along the right of way, to grow into a screen. And why complain about the road when Rose had bought them a car, a lightly used Buick (which Laura and Almanzo promptly named Isabelle)?

Rose had arrived home once again in January 1925, traveling with a friend, Helen "Troub" Boylston, whom she had met in Paris. (Boylston, a nurse and writer, later gained fame with the popular "Sue Barton" nursing series for young adult readers.) They stayed on through the summer, and in September, Laura, Rose, and Helen climbed into Isabelle and set off from Mansfield. They drove west to California, following the Old Santa Fe Trail along the banks of the Arkansas River through Kansas and Colorado. To Almanzo, who again stayed home to tend the farm, Laura wrote letters describing the landscape. In Kansas, she wrote of the prairie, full of buffalo grass. "It is strange to see the plains again with nothing to break the view in any direction as far as we can see," she wrote, recalling the last time they had traveled together from South Dakota by horse-drawn wagon. "Houses are miles and miles apart." The sunsets and prairie starlight brought her back, but Laura was happy they had left the incessant wind behind. "I am glad we are in Missouri for I could not stand to live in the wind." Further west, when the flora changed, she enclosed a sprig of sagebrush, sharing with Almanzo the scent of the desert in an envelope.

As they passed through Rocky Ford, Colorado, the three women feasted on the local specialty: cantaloupe. They could stop almost anywhere to buy one because the packing sheds were located roadside to facilitate transportation. The warm, ripe fruit was succulent. Laura thought the seeds so precious she

Isabelle, the Buick, performed well in the high mountains of Colorado, including the Tennessee Pass, elevation 10,424 feet. Rose is on the left, Laura on the right.

decided not to trust them to the mail. "We keep eating cantaloupe and saving the seeds for you," wrote Rose to her father. Then they decided to share the wealth more directly, shipping a case of Rocky Ford melons back to Almanzo at Rocky Ridge. Later in their journey, when they pulled into Green River, Utah— famous for its honeydews—Rose saved him seeds of those too.

Isabelle the auto cooperated on the rise into the Rockies. It was almost a miracle, given the condition of the roads at the time. This was decades and endless miles before the interstaes of the Eisenhower era. "Dear papa," Rose wrote on a penny postcard, "The car is going beautifully. Has climbed to 7980 feet on high without a murmur."

They had a hair-raising ride through the Rocky Mountain passes, drove through Yosemite, enjoyed visiting Rose's friends in California, and returned via the more placid southern route. Not long after their return to Missouri, Rose broke the news to her parents that she was returning to Albania.

When Rose and Helen arrived in Paris, they bought a 1926 maroon Ford Motor car, named it Zenobia, and drove the 1,200 miles to Tirana, the Albanian capital. Rose leased a small house, complete with a walled garden, and started sketching plans for a new villa to build in the nearby hills. It wasn't that she forgot about her parents. Far from it.

1915
SEEDS

Burrell's Select Rust-Resistant Rocky Ford Cantaloupe
If Its Only One—Make This THE One.

My prices are based on the market value of the produce from which these seeds were selected. For example, I cannot save the best cantaloupe seed and sell it for less than the melons would have brought and you do not expect me to do so. The most successful planters purchase the *best seeds*. The best are the cheapest in the long run.

D. V. BURRELL
SEED GROWER, ROCKY FORD, COLO.

Keep This Catalog to Order from Until You Get 1916 Catalog

By 1915 Rocky Ford, Colorado, was already known for its cantaloupe.

Rose fretted at a distance as Rocky Ridge suffered through years of drought. Her father had difficulty finding hired help for the remaining farm work. She commiserated, but what could she do? Her suggestion was to keep the grass cut and shrug off the rest of the work. "Anyway, as you say, you need not worry," she wrote, "Thank goodness Wall Street doesn't care whether it rains or not." Laura and Almanzo had followed her financial advice, putting their savings into "the Palmer account"— an investment fund—as she had done. They were basking in the sun of a stock market that seemed only to rise.

As the political situation in Albania frayed, Rose and Helen returned to Mansfield once more, in 1928. Having been thwarted at building a place of her own in the hills above Tirana, Rose focused her considerable, sometimes manic energy on Rocky Ridge. She envisioned transforming the farm into a writers' retreat, a place where she and her circle might gather and produce work amid the serene beauty of the Ozarks. Rose thought big. Her plans encompassed a new retirement home for her parents—close enough to walk but on the opposite side of the farm—plus a small house across the road for a farm manager, and a complete remodel of the farmhouse. "I love building," Rose once confessed. "Some women go mad in supermarkets, I go mad in a construction job."

For her parents, an English cottage. Rose could see it, nestled into a rise overlooking a wide meadow, so that dawn would catch the front each morning as it crested the ridge. Starting with a Tudor Revival plan from Sears Roebuck, she customized with the help of a Springfield architect, adding details that would make the place perfect for her Mama Bess and Papa. A local man, J. E. Garbee, did the construction. He added his signature masonry on the chimneys and exterior rock facing.

Like the farmhouse, Rock House blended in with its surroundings. The local stone on the exterior and the stone retaining walls moored it to the land. The property in front of the house fell off to a spring-fed stream and an open pasture, perfectly suited to her father's herd of goats. Almanzo built a spring house in the stream to store goat's milk and cheese at the perfect temperature.

Laura left the new house construction entirely in the hands of her daughter, husband, and the builder. She had more loss that season with the death of

Rock House is set into the hillside on the opposite side of Rocky Ridge, about a mile from the farmhouse.

her sister Mary. The first time Laura saw Rock House was just before Christmas in 1928, when Rose presented her parents with the keys. On January 4, 1929, the *Springfield Leader* reported, "Mr. and Mrs. A. J. Wilder, parents of the famous author, Rose Wilder Lane, have moved into their lovely new home on Rocky Ridge farm. The house with furnishings and the like is estimated to have cost around $11,000."

For my twentieth birthday, my mother and father got me a lawn mower. At least that is how I remember it. Unlike the Wilders, it wasn't the daughter who left home but rather the parents. Toward the end of his career, Dad's company closed his New York office. If he wanted a job, he would have to move himself back to the corporate office in San Francisco without benefit of a relocation package.

If management thought that my father, then in his mid-fifties, would retire, they didn't know him well. My parents packed up the car, handed me the house keys and the instructions for the new Sears mower, and headed west. Now, when I think of Laura's San Francisco connections, I am reminded that my parents relished their second California sojourn, a last great adventure that recalled their youth. They had, after all, met at a San Francisco skating rink during the Second World War. Mom said she fell in love with a uniform.

Then after he finally retired, my parents moved back to the house in New Jersey, drawn by the gravitational pull of five grandchildren. I happily yielded the lawn mowing into my father's capable hands once more. My mother's gardening efforts— never more than lukewarm—shrunk to harvesting from the clump of chives that grew along the post-and-rail fence and digging dandelions with an old kitchen knife.

Many years later when Mom was alone in the house, I resumed mowing her lawn. I was always in a hurry. By then in my late forties, busy with husband, home, and career, I had "too many irons in the fire," as she liked to say. When she came out to pick up sticks from the grass while I was mowing, I was annoyed. I was also oblivious. It wasn't until her younger sister came to visit that I learned a lesson. "Let her help," Aunt Donnie said. "She just wants to help." It was a gentle reprimand, but I felt it. I remember it still, with remorse, every time I pass the old house or pick up a stick in my own yard. Sorry, Mom. To Rose Wilder Lane, let me say, I understand.

—MM

Laura and Almanzo's view from the living room in Rock House.

One might fault Rose for relocating her parents from their custom-fit farmhouse, but Rock House had its advantages. It was undeniably easy to care for. The windows had steel sashes that didn't collect dust, and the tiled fireplace and sills could be dusted in a flash. The electric lights burnt clean. A furnace, water heater, and electric oven meant no need to split or haul firewood. Clever downspouts channeled rainwater from the roof into stone cisterns, gathering the soft water that Laura preferred for laundry. It was one-floor living.

Things might have been different had it not been for the Wall Street crash of October 1929. In its aftermath the Palmer account collapsed along with their savings. But the farm was paid off, and Rose was paying them rent for the farmhouse. Plus their ability to grow their own food was its own insurance. Almanzo kept busy in the vegetable garden—presumably a new one plowed near Rock House—and tending his milk goats. The orchard was past its prime, but he cared for the remaining trees. They kept a cow or two, and probably some chickens.

Almanzo, always interested in the latest farm equipment, captioned this photograph, "Bruce cuting hay with his tractor see the mowing machine behind."

Almanzo's goats with the shadow of his hat.

The stock market crash also sidelined many of Rose's building plans for the farmhouse, though she electrified it and added a new furnace and indoor plumbing. She consoled herself with adorning its grounds. She loved beautiful gardens, and she set out to make one. She planted a swath of irises overlooking the ravine. Bruce Prock, the hired man who occupied the small house that Rose had built across the street, leveled an area for a lawn.

Over the next few seasons, Rose seemed in endless pursuit of the perfect lawn. First she ordered bentgrass seed—by telegraph. That didn't fill in quickly enough, so the next spring she ordered a delivery of sod. To prepare the ground, she spread muck from the farm pond before she installed the rectangles of grass. She was trying again that fall, sowing bluegrass seed. For someone whose father and grandfather had broken prairie sod, she seemed to be expending a great deal of energy getting lawn grass to grow.

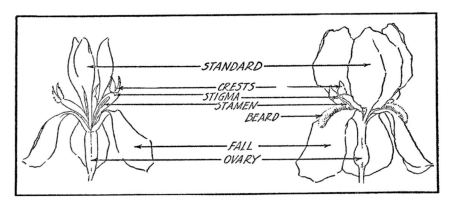

Laura's wild blue flags look like the irises on the left. Rose grew hybrid bearded irises as shown on the right.

Bruce dug more flowerbeds near the farmhouse. Over the years Rose put in larkspur, 'Miss Lingard' phlox, and myrtle, dahlias, and lilacs—lots of lilacs. Not everything succeeded. In a letter describing her garden to a friend, she wrote, perhaps archly, "Roses I can't cope with." The rhododendrons "went to Heaven with a lot of my love *and* money, tho' pampered with aluminum sulphate." Of her lilacs, she counted "of 75, only 19 survived." She added bulbs each fall to bloom the following year: snowdrops, glory-of-the-snow, and winter aconite for early bloom, muscari, hyacinths, and tulips for the height of spring, gladiolas for summer, though the "varmints ate the tulips . . . and gladioli died by scores." Rose would have nodded in agreement with a garden authority who once defined a gardener as someone who kills plants.

But her irises were a great success. "How cheering then," Rose wrote, "to see and smell great flocks & floods of iris, blooming with all their might, and whole blue lakes of myrtle & muscari." She planted a flowering tree across the road which Laura later described as a "tulip tree." Laura described the blooms looking like orchids. It was probably saucer magnolia, though one can't be certain. Several trees are called "tulip trees," including native tulip poplars.

Rose made a shrub border with the surviving lilacs, adding mock orange bushes, which she referred to as "syringas." When they bloomed, fragrant and

Rose worked on the lawn around the farmhouse, buying grass seed, sod, and a lawnmower.

white, Laura thought, "Lovely." Bruce, the hired man, made a rock wall along the edge of the new border and planted more myrtle along it.

In addition to buying plants, Rose bought gardening books. She also bought implements—pruning shears for $0.50, a rake for $1.25, a $7.25 lawn-mower. She always wanted the best tools for the job. Rose was in denial about the economic downturn—what came to be called the Great Depression—especially its consequences for her writing income. Helen, whose savings had evaporated with the last gasp of the Palmer fund in 1931, left Mansfield to go back east permanently, resuming work as a nurse and getting on with her own writing.

At Rocky Ridge, Rose kept gardening, growing vegetables too. Her diary from 1932 includes the first detailed list of what was grown for the larder at the Mansfield farm. Rose, always a stickler for details, even included many of the varieties:

Tomatoes	Earliana, Ponderosa, Bonny Best, Livingston's Stone
Corn	Golden Bantam
Beets	Detroit Red
Carrot	French Forcing, Oxheart, Chantenay, Danvers
Onions	Bermuda

Also on the list were lettuce and radish, and the perennial asparagus and rhubarb. She bought some of her seeds from the Farmer's Exchange store in town, but didn't say if, like her mother, she ordered others from the catalogs. (Most, though not all, of the varieties in Rose's list appeared in the 1932 *Seed Annual* from The Livingston Seed Company, Columbus, Ohio.)

It was a big vegetable garden. Rose put in thirty-six tomato plants. She sowed twelve hills of corn, planted every Sunday morning from the third week of May until the Fourth of July. She mixed radish and carrot seeds before she planted them. When she pulled the radishes it would leave more room for the carrots to grow. Obviously she had picked up techniques from her gardening books and her parents.

For beets, she spread the harvest. She sowed her first seeds in a hot bed—basically a cold frame set over a pit of composting manure to heat the soil—so that she would have transplants big enough when the ground thawed. Three later sowings of beet seeds, two in spring and one in fall, went directly into the ground.

With Rose in the garden and Almanzo out milking his goats, Laura looked for something new to occupy her time and her mind. Now sixty-one years old and living at Rock House, Laura sat down and wrote her autobiography, *Pioneer Girl*.

If writing were plants, Laura and Rose had a symbiotic relationship. They depended on one another like *mycorrhizae*, the microorganisms that colonize tree roots. These little fungi get a steady diet of food from the trees, while in turn giving the trees an assist by pulling in micronutrients and water. It is mutuality rather than an either-or proposition. For the Wilder women, Rose

Of raising and preserving food, Rose once wrote, "Give me seed and earth and weather permitting, I can harvest, thresh, stack, or dry and string and store them safely too."

lifted Laura's writing career with her network in the publishing world, along with her editorial skills. Laura infused Rose's best novels with the richness of her first-hand experience—her stories and her story-telling.

Rose encouraged her mother's ambitions, offering sometimes overzealous coaching. She massaged Laura's manuscripts into marketable products, sometimes pruning her mother's work with embroidery scissors, other times with an ax. She also grafted on words of her own. Rose saw her mother's writing as a means to bridge her parents into a comfortable retirement. When *Pioneer Girl* didn't sell as a memoir, Rose fashioned a sample juvenile novel out of selections from it. Rose and her agent placed the book, eventually titled *Little House in the Big Woods*, with Harper's. The rest, as they say, is publishing history.

Rose also helped with research for later books. In 1932, while Laura was writing down Almanzo's stories for *Farmer Boy*, Rose took a car trip that included Malone, New York. It was October. She knocked on doors, visiting

April

Rent	50	.
Labor, John	4	.
Groceries	42	90
Electricity	10	06
Heat		
Laundry	11	64
Gas		
Telephone		
Incidentals:		
lawnmower	7	25
seeds	1	40
water heating stove, &c	16	52
rake	1	25
pruning shears		50
sink plunger pump		50
muffin pans		30
~~cigarette Herndon~~	15	80
John, balance on milk	1	05
butter	2	10
Inc.		
	30	87

When Laura was working on *Farmer Boy*, Rose visited Malone, New York, and shipped some wintergreen plants back to Mansfield.

Rose's expenses for April 1934 included more plants, gardening books, and tools. John—one of several boys she took under her wing over the course of her lifetime—helped with garden chores.

people who had known the Wilders. She wrote home, describing the landscape around the Trout River, the fairgrounds, and her Wilder grandparents' farm, now occupied by a new family. The barn complex was there. The house was the same, and Rose saw that the lilacs still grew outside. Rose sent a twig from the balsam fir, *Abies balsamea*, growing in the yard. It smelled like Christmas.

She also sent a box of wintergreen plants home from Malone by express mail. "Please ask the expressman to telephone instead of mailing you a card when they come, so you can get them and set them out at once," she instructed. "I believe they will grow here. Have Bruce help you fix some good places to plant them. I wish he would put a couple of them in pots for me, and take good care of them till I come. Tell him to have them outdoors in the cold but see that they get enough water till they are well rooted and growing." Rose's horticultural instructions to her father echo her writing advice to her mother.

The following year Rose and Laura took a drive to Oklahoma, trying to find the site of the family's short-tenured farm, the setting for *Little House on the Prairie*. While they didn't find the exact spot (which was actually in Kansas), they were able to soak up the landscape as background for the story.

Rose, approaching middle age, felt increasingly trapped in Mansfield. but her career took a decided uptick. She published two books in the 1930s, *Let the Hurricane Roar* and *Free Land*, that were fictionalized versions of her mother's stories. Despite hard times, both hit the bestseller lists. When money started coming in again, Rose moved away from Rocky Ridge for the last time, first to Columbia, Missouri, then back to New York City. Her parents, in short order, moved back into their farmhouse. They shut off the furnace that Rose had installed, preferring the woodstove. Sometimes they shut off the electricity too.

Laura continued producing novel after novel, working with Rose by mail. She was reliving her childhood through writing, though sometimes her memory needed refreshing. She wrote her sister Grace, asking about wildflowers. The observant Grace responded, noting sad changes that settlement and farming had brought to the prairie. Of the flowers, she wrote, "Some are here yet, but lots of kinds we don't see any more." But she remembered many of them. Laura wrote to Rose that Grace's letter had come, then proceeded to transcribe her sister's list, beginning with, "The crocus came first in the spring . . . and the prairie used to be white with the blossoms of wild onions."

Grace itemized blooms by season, continuing with purple and yellow violets, sheep sorrel, yellow buttercups, "and white anemone, common name is wind flower." She added purple and blue wild peas, wild parsley, wild clover, and capped the recitation with "tiger lillies in low places." It is interesting that she wrote, "There were no sunflowers, goldenrod nor dandelions until much later." By that, Grace might have meant later in the year, as both sunflowers and goldenrod bloom in summer. Or she may have meant later in history, as the dandelions would have taken some years to show up. The dandelion is a European immigrant that spread across the country in the wake of the settlers. Almanzo had once told Rose that when he first broke the sod on his homestead, there were no weeds.

Grace's letter brought memories of wildflowers back to Laura, like wild crocus emerging from the prairie each spring.

The Dakota prairie of her youth bloomed again for Laura with Grace's prompts. How could she have forgotten? She found herself waking up in the middle of the night and going into the little study next to the bedroom to jot things down, memories that, in sleep, had drifted back into reach. Laura confessed to her daughter, "The sooner I write my stuff the better," then added, "You remember the roses of course and have heard us tell about them."

Rose did remember, and was planting more roses in new gardens of her own. In early 1938, she bought a small farm property with an old white house on a south-facing slope in Danbury, Connecticut. Her letters home now bore the return address Route 4, Box 42, King Street. During her first spring there, forsythia bloomed, and daffodils. The small apple orchard had five ancient gnarled trees. Not long after she moved in, she wrote in her diary, "For the first time a normal happy feeling of coming home. Rooted here already more than ever on Rocky Ridge."

Laura and Almanzo continued to travel, including back to De Smet for
Old Settlers Day in 1939.

To Rose, who suffered chronic and severe emotional swings, her Danbury garden was an anchor. She surrounded her home with flowers. There were shrubs: flowering quince, lilacs, mock orange, deutzia, bridalwreath spirea, and, of course, rose bushes. The redbuds and dogwoods were glorious in spring and fall. Honeysuckle twined up the side of the house, filling the window of her sewing room with fragrance. She loved her Japanese maple with its elegant red leaves. Her perennial garden was filled with bleeding hearts and peonies, followed by irises and phlox, followed by daylilies and hollyhocks.

Rose added a grape arbor, raspberry, blueberry, blackberry, and currant bushes, plum and cherry trees. She even tried a tangerine tree. When it didn't set fruit, she wrote to her mother, "One thing about gardening, it acts like the legendary carrot on the stick before the donkey, keeps you always going on to next year. Though I bet that never worked on any donkey; donkeys have more sense." (As a child, Rose rode a donkey named Spookendyke back and forth from Rocky Ridge Farm to school.) Rose's Danbury garden was so extensive that one year, during the Second World War, she put up eight hundred jars of produce, filling the shelves in her stone-walled, brick-lined cellar with what she called her "genuine social security." In Harlingen, Texas, her last home, she designed a lovely Spanish revival garden of patios, ironwork, and formal plantings, though by then both her parents were gone.

Almanzo died in 1949, weakened by a heart attack that summer, and taken by a second in October. Laura stayed on in the farmhouse alone. It was home, despite the gaping hole left by his absence. Every year she waited for the winter to end. Well into her eighties, she wrote to an admirer, "Spring has come to the Ozarks. The hills are green with new grass, buds are swelling on the trees, spring flowers are blooming. Our winter has been very mild, still I am glad it is over." She had always found the color green restful. The flowers reminded her of Almanzo and the bouquets of wildflowers he had picked for her. She had her harvest of memories. "I have been well," she wrote, "really astonishingly so. I am still living by myself, doing all my own work." Friends and neighbors pitched in, and Rose visited when she could.

Laura Ingalls Wilder lived to see her eight books reprinted many times, translated into many languages, and released in a new edition with illustrations by Garth Williams in 1953. Of her many honors, she seemed to enjoy most the letters from children around the country and, in some cases, around the world. She died at home on February 10, 1957, just after her ninetieth birthday, in the white farmhouse among the oak trees. That spring, the violets on the shady hill at Rocky Ridge would bloom again. They bloom there still, every year.

Bird's foot violets (*Viola pedata*) bloom in the lawn at Rocky Ridge Farm, just as they did for Laura. The largest oaks came down in a tornado in 1945, but their offspring grow larger each season.

There are deeps beyond deeps
in the life of this wonderful world
of ours. Let's help the children
to see them instead of letting
them grow up like the man
of whom the poet wrote,

A primrose by the river's brim

A yellow primrose was to him
and nothing more.

Let's train them, instead, to
find "books in the running
brooks, sermons in stones and
good in everything."

—MISSOURI RURALIST

WILDER
GARDENS

For much of Laura's early life, the prairie was her flower garden.

VISITING WILDER GARDENS

L aura once used the term "tin can tourists" to describe folks who, like Almanzo and herself, enjoyed getting behind the wheel or into the passenger seat to see America by car. Because she lived so many places in her ninety years, Laura Ingalls Wilder provides a ready-made itinerary for modern day tourists of the tin can variety. Her various homes, plus the Wilder farm in Malone, New York, occupy different ecosystems, each made up of those simple things she encouraged her readers to appreciate—the land, plants, wildlife—shaped by people who lived there, who live there still.

So whatever the season, and whether you are an armchair traveler or you share Pa's itchy foot for new surrounds, take time, as Laura did, to venture into nature. See your own prairie sunset. Hear the birds in their dawn chorus, or watch a wedge of geese pointing north or south among the clouds. Splash in a creek or a walk among the wildflowers. Sit in the shade of a tree, and wait. Laura's wild and beautiful world is still out there, if you take the time to find it.

In planning your own trip, start by getting a copy of William Anderson's *The Little House Guidebook*. As you lay out your expedition, here are a few added suggestions.

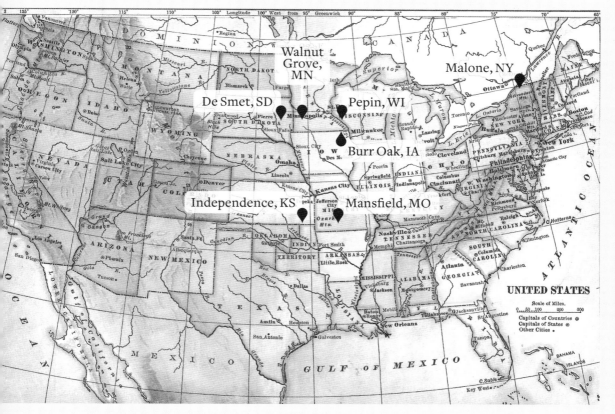

Walnut Grove, MN

Malone, NY

De Smet, SD

Pepin, WI

Independence, KS

Burr Oak, IA

Mansfield, MO

The Laura Ingalls Wilder trail.

NEW YORK

Farthest afield is Malone and the Wilder Farm, run by the Almanzo and Laura Ingalls Wilder Association. An ancient sugar maple that dates at least as far back as the Wilder family graces the front of the original house. Behind the house huge lilacs, likely the original, grow alongside an old garden rose, 'Harison's Yellow', that is said to have been Angeline Wilder's. There are demonstration gardens growing the vegetables that the Wilders grew and a small orchard of heirloom apples. If you want to see a hay cradle or a yoke for oxen, you will find a fine collection of period farm tools on exhibit in the reconstructed barns, as well as displays on dairy cattle, Morgan horses, and sheep. The barn complex was rebuilt recently based on a sketch Almanzo made as an adult, complete with dimensions. An archeological dig confirmed the accuracy of his recall.

Across the street from the house and barns, the museum maintains a path that leads down to the beautiful Trout River. There are raspberries that ripen along the meadow's edge in summer and woodland wildflowers in spring. Sitting along the riverbank, it isn't hard to conjure up a little boy named Almanzo clambering over the rocks or poised at some quiet spot with fishing pole in hand.

About a half-hour car ride south of Malone is the Adirondack Visitor Interpretive Center of Paul Smith's College. On its extensive and well-marked trail system you can get a sense of the varied wild landscapes that Almanzo knew in his childhood. See plants that played their part in *Farmer Boy*—wintergreen, moosewood, and blueberries, to name a few—on paths through the forest and boardwalks through the bog. You won't be disappointed.

Just outside the Wilder home in Malone, red geraniums bloom atop the old well by the kitchen door, and an ancient sugar maple shades the lawn.

Brook, bog, and mixed forest along the Boreal Life Trail at Paul Smith's Visitor Interpretive Center. »

WISCONSIN

Some thousand miles to the west is Pepin, Wisconsin, and Laura's first little house, giving some gauge of the breadth of the continent as well as the distances that the Ingallses and Wilders covered over the course of their lives. When you visit the Little House Wayside, take time to drive along the Great River Road around Lake Pepin. At scenic overlooks with easy access, interpretive signs describe the geology and natural history of the region. You may spot an American eagle overhead, which seems both appropriate and auspicious. The area is a part of the Upper Mississippi National Fish and Wildlife Refuge, and whether you fish, bike, hunt, kayak, or prefer to "take only pictures (and maybe a few pebbles), leave only footprints," your opportunities are abundant.

The Wayside includes a replica log cabin to commemorate Laura's Wisconsin birthplace. When a Laura Ingalls Wilder Memorial Society was formed in the 1970s, it organized the reconstruction and also planted trees, mimicking the lost setting of *Little House in the Big Woods*. There are oaks of course, one for Mary and the other for Laura, along with walnut, maple, and locust trees. Stand quietly and watch. Birds may appear, many of the same birds that Wilder described in her book. There isn't a garden, but the backdrop to the site is a large field, ready for plowing. Across the road, a sign on the barn reads "Good Turn Farm."

≫ Lake Pepin's colorful pebbles, smoothed by the rapid inflow of the Chippewa River into the Mississippi, fascinated Laura too.

≫ Trees surround the Little House Wayside in western Wisconsin.

Wild plums have lavish blooms in spring in the Eloise Butler Wildflower Garden.

MINNESOTA AND IOWA

Minneapolis is only ninety minutes away, so consider planning a stop at the Eloise Butler Wildflower Garden and Bird Sanctuary, part of the city's park system. Founded in 1907, it is the oldest public wildflower garden in the country. There, rounded up in a single fifteen-acre site, you will see many of the flowers, grasses, shrubs, and trees that Wilder mentioned in her series. Every week from spring until the first hard frost of winter you will see something different in bloom. The sanctuary is named for the local teacher who established the garden and acted as its curator for many years. I think Laura would have liked that. Just south of Minneapolis is the Nerstrand Big Woods State Park, a place that retains a remnant of old growth forest, the sylvan setting that surrounded Laura and Mary when they were growing up in the Wisconsin woods.

Along the way to Burr Oak, it is easy to detour to South Troy, Minnesota, where Laura and her family visited their Ingalls relations in 1876. While the exact location of her aunt and uncle's farmstead is not known, the area remains one of thriving agriculture, as if Charles Ingalls's dreams of wheat had all been granted. The local roads around the Zumbro River traverse farm fields so black and rich that you may be tempted to fill a suitcase with soil to bring home for your garden. Roll the car windows down and you might hear the sounds of cows and birdsong. The banks of the river are full of flowers in spring, green with grass that seems a perfect pasture. You can picture a nine-year-old Laura playing there on her way to bring in the cows for the evening.

The Masters Hotel, now part of the Laura Ingalls Wilder Park & Museum, still sits atop a rise along the main street of Burr Oak, Iowa. A long slope extends down to the now much-tamed Silver Creek, waiting for children to explore it. The museum staff has added small gardens near the hotel—a bur oak sapling on the side, a bed of old fashioned perennials out front, and a collection of herbs in back with an explanatory sign describing "The Pioneer Garden of Yesterday." A small planting of local native wildflowers gives a glimpse of the bouquets that Laura gathered in her Iowa days. Just down the street from the historic buildings is a cemetery on a hill. Laura liked to walk there, to read the old tombstones and enjoy the shade of the trees. Today several

The productive fields and big skies of America's heartland.

large specimens of bur oak grow there, your best chance to collect some of its unique acorns.

From Burr Oak, you are practically next door to Heritage Farm, the headquarters of Seed Savers Exchange in Decorah, Iowa. If you are interested in growing the types of fruits and vegetables that Ma, Pa, Laura, Almanzo, and Rose grew, this is a must-see. Seed Savers is a national leader in all things related to heirloom seeds. Its Heritage Orchard has more than nine hundred varieties of apples with a special section that features Midwestern cultivars including 'Ben Davis' and 'Missouri Pippin'. In addition to the demonstration gardens surrounding the visitor center and a barn with heritage poultry, eight miles of walking trails wend through its nearly nine-hundred-acre property. You can stroll along Pine Spring Creek and see many of the birds and flowers that Laura remembered so fondly from her time in Burr Oak.

Between Burr Oak and Walnut Grove, swing by Spring Valley, Minnesota, where Almanzo's parents settled after they left Malone and where Laura, Rose, and Almanzo recuperated before they went to Florida. Father and Mother Wilder's home is gone, but the church where they worshipped is now the Spring Valley Methodist Church Museum and includes exhibits about the family. On the day my husband and I visited, a bank of lilacs was in full, luxuriant, and heady bloom, reminiscent of the lilacs in Malone from *Farmer Boy*.

Mankato, never mentioned in Laura's books but familiar to any fan of the *Little House on the Prairie* television series, is also along this route. It is a lovely city, sited where the Blue Earth River flows into the Minnesota. Explore Rasmussen Woods and its many nature trails. Along the extensive river walk is a marvelous old depot, built in 1896—after the Ingallses' time in the state—but still in use by the Chicago & North Western Line, which is the railroad that Pa worked for in Dakota Territory. Watching the sunset is lovely from there.

We enjoyed a stop at the August Schell Brewing Company in New Ulm, just as the Ingallses did on their way to Walnut Grove in 1874. Schell built his brewery in 1860 in the forested hills along the Cottonwood River. The original brick building—the "large, square house" Wilder described in *Pioneer Girl*—is still there, today used as offices rather than family residence and workplace. Hops are trellised in front, a reminder to those on the Wilder circuit that in

Large specimens of bur oak grow in a cemetery that Laura liked to visit.

Columbines nod in shady places in spring across the Midwest, including the trails at Seed Savers Exchange.

the first years of their marriage Charles and Caroline grew hops as a commercial crop in Wisconsin, as did James and Angeline Wilder in Malone. Now the building is dwarfed by the larger operations of this robust regional brewery and by the elegant house and garden built by August Schell's son in 1885. There is a well-curated museum, and the company continues to be family-owned, operated by the sixth generation.

In Walnut Grove, the Laura Ingalls Wilder Museum and Tourist Center on 8th Street is organized around a courtyard of prairie plants and a new food garden featuring grains and vegetables grown by Laura and her family. A replica of the dugout offers a chance to step inside, though you will have to imagine the morning glories on the exterior.

Once you've enjoyed the museum displays, do not miss Plum Creek with the site of the original dugout, just down the road. It is a simple place, which is one of its charms. Although the Ingalls homesite is located on private property, the visitor is invited to drive in behind the neat and prosperous Gordon farm. A small lockbox at the entrance asks each driver to deposit a modest per-car entry fee. Down an unpaved road is a small parking area with a few picnic tables close to the creek. There are well-maintained walking trails. A prominent wooden sign marks the spot where the dugout nestled into the hillside. When you cross the new footbridge and stand on the banks of Plum Creek yourself, it will be clear how the Ingallses stayed above flood water, even after heavy rains. The banks are so high that the doorsill of the dugout must have been some fifteen feet above the creek bottom.

The configuration of rocks where the girls used to play has changed, but the spring is still evident. It rises right below the dugout, and joins the stream as the water flows downward. There are willows and thickets of wild plums. The land rises further beyond the creek, though the "table land" Wilder remembered is not evident. One supposes that some past owner might have leveled it in the interest of more efficient farming. The Gordons have restored a few acres along the creek with native prairie grasses and wildflowers. They keep paths mowed through the planting and have posted interpretive signs with color photographs to help visitors with flower identification.

The lilacs in Spring Valley seemed to be blooming for the Wilders.

A robin is right at home nesting on the old schoolhouse at the Laura Ingalls Wilder Museum in Walnut Grove.

Charles Ingalls would be amazed to see the thriving farm on his Plum Creek property.

SOUTH DAKOTA

Between Walnut Grove and De Smet, the drive along Highway 14 parallels the railway that Laura, Ma, Mary, Carrie, and Grace rode on their way to Tracy to meet Pa. Once you cross the state line, Brookings is well worth a visit. The South Dakota Agricultural Heritage Museum is on the campus of South Dakota State University, located in the school's old Stock Judging Pavilion built in 1918. There you can see the types of farm equipment that the Ingallses and the Wilders used over time. The permanent exhibits include an actual claim shanty built by homesteaders seventeen miles northeast of De Smet in 1882. Because none of the Ingalls or Wilder claim shanties survived, this provides a measure of the type of places they called home. (Should you share Laura's sweet tooth, the SDSU Dairy Bar has incredible ice cream.) Also on campus are the McCrory Gardens, with botanical collections and display areas including the Prairie Centennial Garden featuring native plants and the Prairie Medicinal Garden. The collection of willows is magnificent.

Two landscapes preserved by The Nature Conservancy are the thirty-acre Aurora Prairie and the two-hundred-acre Sioux Prairie, both less than a half-hour drive from downtown Brookings. In *These Happy Golden Years* Wilder wrote, "Laura thought how wild and beautiful it must have been when the twin lakes were one, when buffalo and antelope roamed the prairie around the great lake and came there to drink, when wolves and coyotes and foxes lived on the banks and wild geese, swans, herons, cranes, ducks and gulls nested and fished and flew there in countless numbers." In preserved landscapes like these, you can see the wildlife and walk among the tall grasses and unique wildflowers of the prairie that Wilder loved. Of course, these wildflowers are not for picking.

In De Smet, the Laura Ingalls Wilder connection is clearly evident, starting with the wooden "Welcome" sign at the town border. On top of the sign is a carved covered wagon bordered with the words "Little Town on the Prairie." On the bottom it reads "Est. 1880." The layout of the town is still the one that Laura remembered from her childhood, oriented to the railroad. Though many buildings have changed, she would still recognize the streetscape of the commercial blocks along Calumet Avenue from her visits with Almanzo during

Huge willows shade the McCrory Gardens in Brookings, South Dakota.

The best time to see the snow geese in South Dakota is in late winter.

their retirement years. The Laura Ingalls Wilder Memorial Society runs tours that include the house Pa built on Third Street, shaded by trees that the early town planners would have favored, and the Surveyors' House, moved decades earlier from its site near Silver Lake. Vestiges of Silver Lake are visible during winter thaws and wet spells, but it has mostly vanished, drained in the 1920s to "improve" the land. The Twin Lakes, Spirit Lake, and the Big Slough are still easy to find, as is the location of Almanzo's tree claim north of town, marked with a memorial plaque.

Aldo Leopold, an environmentalist best known for essays about his Wisconsin farm, wrote, "There are two spiritual dangers in not owning a farm. One is the danger of supposing that breakfast comes from the grocery, and the other that heat comes from the furnace." The Ingalls Homestead is a good way to avoid those dangers. Grab your sunbonnet and straw hat because Pa's original claim—the quarter section of rolling lands with its old cottonwood trees—has been repurposed into a hands-on pioneer activity center. Children of any age can twist hay, grind wheat, shell corn, drive a team, and wash clothes on a washboard with lye soap made on the premises. There are chickens, long-eared mules, Percheron horses, ponies, and every year a new calf named Bright. If you book ahead, you can spend a night in a covered wagon.

In 1999, the family who owns the Ingalls Homestead took one hundred acres of the property that had been in soy and corn production back to prairie, putting back the sod that Pa originally busted. They reseeded with a mix of six local native grasses. Adjacent fields of wheat and corn are sowed each year with a mule-drawn seeder called the John Deere 999, so christened because it missed only one seed out of a thousand. Joan, one of the owners, lovingly grows an heirloom vegetable garden near the visitor center. If you camp on the grounds you are invited to pick your own produce for your supper, with her compliments. Joan, by the way, orders her seeds from Seed Savers Exchange.

Pa's mature cottonwood trees lead the way to the monument that marks the original Ingalls claim in De Smet. This acre of the original homestead is maintained by the Laura Ingalls Wilder Memorial Society.

A taste of pioneer life on the original Ingalls claim awaits the visitor at the Ingalls Homestead. »

NEBRASKA AND KANSAS

If you plan to head south toward Kansas two targets are along the way: Homestead National Monument of America in Beatrice, Nebraska, with the oldest restored prairie in the National Park System, and the eleven-thousand-acre Tallgrass Prairie National Preserve in the Flint Hills of Kansas. With their vistas of sky and undulating prairie, these are landscapes that turn back time. The latter reintroduced a herd of bison, the first to roam the prairie in this part of America in over a hundred years. Visit in early spring, and you might witness a "controlled burn," a modern corollary of the wildfires that were so frightening to Laura, but so important to the health of the prairie. On a warm day in late summer, you can smell the sharp fragrance of prairie plants and stand listening as they shush and murmur in the wind. I heard my first dickcissel there, chirruping as it balanced atop a tall blade of grass.

Like the Tallgrass Prairie National Preserve, the Little House on the Prairie Museum near Independence, Kansas, is part of Prairie Passage, a corridor that extends from Texas to Minnesota. A partnership of government agencies—local, state, and federal—and non-profit organizations have pieced together, preserved, and restored sections of tallgrass prairie to support the plants and animals, birds, and bugs that Laura cherished. There isn't much of the original left. Of the uninterrupted grasslands that once covered an area roughly the size of Texas only about 4 percent remains. Across the road from the museum and a little closer to town is a small cemetery, a peaceful place, next to a small prairie meadow rich in flowers. There is a connection to Wilder's novel as Mr. Mason, the likely candidate for the character Mr. Edwards, is buried there. Still further down the road, the narrow gray leaves of willow blanket the little creek where the Ingallses fetched water until Pa dug the well.

A hint of the immensity of America's grasslands at the Tallgrass Prairie National Preserve.

The Little House on the Prairie Museum in Kansas is part of Prairie Passage, a patchwork of habitats for the plants and animals that appeared in Wilder's writing.

MISSOURI

Keep your eyes peeled on the drive from Independence, Kansas, to Mansfield, Missouri, and you should see Osage orange trees growing alongside the road. As you cross the state line, the land begins to pleat like the ruffles on a dress, rising in grade as it approaches the Ozark Plateau. On your way into town, take time for a stop at Bakersville, the seed farm and pioneer village that is the brainchild of Jere and Emilee Gettle of Baker Creek Heirloom Seeds. It is a gem of a place, set among Laura's beautiful Ozark hills. The trial gardens are luscious, and in addition to a seed store you'll find a mercantile, an heirloom garden museum, and heritage livestock.

Mansfield's town square is shaded with large trees and now boasts a gazebo as well as a bust of Laura Ingalls Wilder. She would be pleased to see the "public conveniences" behind the gazebo, an issue that she lobbied for when she was active in town improvement. Rocky Ridge Farm is about a mile out of town, now graced with a new museum building. In front of the new building, volunteers planted wildflowers native to Missouri.

The farmhouse is much as it was when Laura, Almanzo, and Rose lived there, thanks to Rose herself and the other members of the Wilder Home Association, established in 1957. Inside the house, you can see the custom cabinets where Laura kept her preserving kit and the countertop where she kneaded her dough. Flowers bloom all over the interior of the house: the wallpaper in the kitchen, the vinyl on the bedroom floor. Her Haviland china is strewn with roses. Willows weep on the blue willowware that were her favorite dishes. There are flowered doilies and pillow tops, Laura's work over countless hours sitting in the sun-filled windows. Morning glories clamber up one of the last quilts she pieced. At the end of his life, Almanzo added to the mix, hooking rugs in floral motifs to keep his hands occupied. Rose, who became an expert on the history of American needlework, designed some of the rug patterns for her father. It is easy to picture Almanzo and Laura working in comfortable companionship in the oak living room with the stone fireplace.

The grape arbor is gone, but the apple varieties that Almanzo grew are replanted in a small demonstration orchard. A new flock of hens has a fine

Volunteers planting Missouri natives in front of the new museum building at Rocky Ridge Farm.

Gardeners from Baker Creek Heirloom Seeds tend the garden at Rocky Ridge Farm, with vegetables and flowers like these dahlias.

coop, and some of the folks from Baker Creek Heirloom Seeds maintain a period garden.

In spring, lilacs bloom. Long-lived shrubs, they may be survivors from the many that Rose planted during her years of making gardens near the farm-house. A Japanese maple, red-leafed and elegant, came as a small transplant from Rose's house in Danbury, Connecticut, lovingly moved to Rocky Ridge Farm in 1963 by Roger MacBride, Rose's adopted grandson. In summer you can just make out the ravine, a cleft in the hill behind the house. It is more tree-covered than it was in the Wilders' day. The spring no longer flows freely there, due to prolonged droughts over the years and Rose's failed attempt in the summer of 1931 to create a larger pool in the ravine with the help of Bruce, the hired man, and some dynamite.

The place that Laura called home for most of her life.

On the other side of the property is Rock House with its fine view of the distant ridge. Almanzo's spring house nestles in the creek below the pasture. The house remains the quiet refuge that Rose intended. Depending on the season, you may be able to walk the mile between the two houses across the hill, part woods and part open pasture, as Laura and Rose once did. The views from the top are superb, and Laura treasured the early hours there, watching as the dawn built the day.

The lawn in front of the farmhouse is still shaded with oak trees. Birds nest in their branches. In spring they flower, with drooping catkins. Their leaves green up in summer and drop in winter, long after the acorns. They stand sentinel outside the uncurtained windows that lent Laura moving pictures of nature, always present and always changing.

GROWING A WILDER GARDEN

Plant for the pollinators and for the pleasure.

You can join Laura in the garden, whether you have acres of land or only a windowsill. Gardening is something one does with the heart, as well as hands and head. If you plant a few bean seeds and watch them every day, you will witness the small miracle of germination, each "stem uncoiling like a steel spring," just as she did. Grow popcorn like Almanzo, or plant a lilac like Rose. I plan to put in some red clover between the rows of my vegetable garden to build the soil, taking a page from Almanzo's sustainable farm practices.

With the interest in heirloom vegetables on the rise, it is easy to grow varieties that were available to the Ingalls and Wilder families. Then you can save some seed, imitating Laura and Almanzo with their lettuce. Saving seed also means you can share it, the way Mrs. Boast did with Ma on the Dakota prairie. Or if your gardening habits, like mine, are less tidy, you can let the lettuce bolt and sow itself. Every spring seedlings of 'Speckled Trout', an old Austrian romaine with distinctive markings, pop up at random in my community garden plot. Economy made manifest.

From the tiniest hoverfly to the brightest bird, the fauna will appreciate the flora.

There is so much to experience in the world outdoors.

If you plant a patch of prairie (or woodland, wetland, desert, jungle, or tundra, depending on your locale), you can do your part to support Wilder's beautiful world. It is an intricate web, though in its simplest form the bugs eat the plants, the birds eat the bugs, and so on. The most prominent of these partnerships in recent years is the monarch butterfly connection—no milkweed, no monarchs. If you are planning a "hometown habitat" for your farm, backyard, or public park, remember to research each plant's native range and match it to your own. The good news is that plants native to your locale are pre-programmed to survive your growing conditions.

We live at a time when wildflowers in wild places are scarce and should be left unpicked and in place. Seek out seeds or nursery-grown plants, now easily available by mail-order or via the web. Planting wildflowers—or grasses, shrubs, trees—means that you can share them, cutting a few bouquets as Almanzo did for Laura, and Laura did for the rest of us. Consider joining a native plant society near you. Laura knew the value of clubs for learning and getting to know like-minded people.

The love of gardening is planted early.

It is easy to grow sweet potato slips, just like Ma.

It can't always be summer, but you can capture its flavor.

Just as Pa did when he planted his cottonwoods, trees can commemorate. Many town environmental commissions, state forestry offices, and Audubon society chapters offer tiny saplings for conservation plantings. If you plant a tree near your window, you can watch the picture change, day by day, year by year.

Garden with a child, even if you need to borrow one. Children find every acorn of interest, and think pulling a radish out of the ground the most exciting thing ever. Plant extra flowers so that they can always pick a few stems. When they're old enough, you can teach them how to put up fruits and vegetables. Most gardeners remember a garden of their youth, a place and often a person that sparked a lifelong pursuit of plants and the world outdoors.

Wilder's books inspire many plant-related projects for children and former children. Last winter I started sweet potato slips in pint jars in my sunny kitchen window. As I write this, they are growing gangbusters in our vegetable patch. When the days shorten, I will go out to dig them with the help of my granddaughter, in hopes of a good harvest. Then maybe I'll gather some black walnuts, find some tools, and make a fresh attempt.

SOURCE ABBREVIATIONS

Abbreviations used in the plant table and the sources are modeled after "Editorial Procedures" by Nancy Tystad Koupal and Rodger Hartley in *Pioneer Girl*. The abbreviations include people and places, books by Laura Ingalls Wilder, other collections of Wilder's writings, as well as other sources. Full citation information is listed in "Sources and Citations."

AJW	Almanzo James Wilder
ALIWA	Almanzo and Laura Ingalls Wilder Association, Malone
BW	*Little House in the Big Woods*
FB	*Farmer Boy*
FFY	*The First Four Years*
FJ	*Laura Ingalls Wilder, Farm Journalist*
HGY	*These Happy Golden Years*
HHPL	Herbert Hoover Presidential Library
Letters	*The Selected Letters of Laura Ingalls Wilder*
LHOP	*Little House on the Prairie*
LIW	Laura Ingalls Wilder
LIWHM	Laura Ingalls Wilder Historic Home and Museum, Mansfield
LIWMS	Laura Ingalls Wilder Memorial Society, De Smet
LTOP	*Little Town on the Prairie*
LW	*The Long Winter*

Mirror	*Mansfield Mirror*
OWH	*On the Way Home*
PC	*On the Banks of Plum Creek*
PG	*Pioneer Girl*
RRF	Rocky Ridge Farm
Ruralist	*Missouri Ruralist*
RWL	Rose Wilder Lane
Sampler	*A Little House Sampler*
SL	*By the Shores of Silver Lake*
WA	William Anderson
WFH	*West from Home*

Violets appear in almost every book written by Laura Ingalls Wilder.

PLANTS FOR
A WILDER GARDEN

If you want to grow what Laura grew and knew, here is a list of plants mentioned in Wilder's writings plus those grown at Rocky Ridge Farm documented in Rose's diaries, family letters, and the like. For ease of use, the list is organized into categories, with garden flowers separated from wildflowers, vegetables from fruits, and so on. As plant experts distinguish prairie grasses from other wild perennials—the so-called forbs—they are separated here as well.

For the citations in the table, note that Rose Wilder Lane's diaries are in the collections of the Herbert Hoover Presidential Library (HHPL) in West Branch, IA, as is the majority of the correspondence written by Laura, Almanzo, and Rose. Unless otherwise noted, the published source for Laura Ingalls Wilder's letters is *The Selected Letters of Laura Ingalls Wilder* (*Letters*).

A word of warning about foraging for edible wild plants. Be sure to learn from an expert in the field and the kitchen. For example, all parts of the poke-weed plant are laced with oxalic acid and thus poisonous; the young green shoots are the only edible part of the plant, and only after boiling in multiple changes of water to remove all bitterness. Ground cherries are toxic until fully ripe. Buffalo beans bear a strong resemblance to several related toxic species, including locoweed. Your local botanical garden, native plant society, or cooperative extension service will have suggestions for classes. When in doubt, don't put it in your mouth.

The USDA maintains a database of wild plants reported by public and private partners at the state and county level. One can, for example, look up the wild onion mentioned in *By the Shores of Silver Lake*, and see that it is no longer reported in Kingsbury County, South Dakota, but still appears in neighboring Brookings County. The database may be found at plants.usda.gov. Here are some of the other online sources that are well worth a visit:

- wildflower.org/plants from the Lady Bird Johnson Wildflower Center

- kswildflower.org, part of the Kansas State University Libraries website

- minnesotawildflowers.info

- igrow.org, from the South Dakota State University Extension

- friendsofthewildflowergarden.org, maintained by the Eloise Butler Wildflower Garden

- mobot.org, the "Plant Finder" on website of the Missouri Botanical Garden

While Laura never lived in Illinois, many of the prairie plants she remembered also grow there, and the information on illinoiswildflowers.info is first-rate.

The bird's foot violet (*Viola pedata*) is native to Missouri and still grows at Rocky Ridge Farm.

PLANTS THAT LAURA GREW AND KNEW

Common name	Botanical name	Plant mentioned in	Grown at Rocky Ridge Farm?
Garden flowers (annuals, perennials, flowering shrubs)			
alyssum, sweet	*Lobularia maritima*	RWL diary 11/14/1929	x
azalea, Carolina	*Rhododendron carolinianum*	RWL diary 4/23/1930	x
baby's breath	*Gypsophila* species	RWL diary 4/23/1930	x
bluebell	*Hyacinthoides* species	RWL diary 4/6/1930	x
butterfly bush	*Buddleja davidii*	RWL diary 4/4/1934	x
chrysanthemum	*Chrysanthemum* species	RWL diary 5/2/1933	x
cinnamon vine	*Dioscorea oppositifolia*	RWL diary 4/29/1933	x
columbine, wild	*Aquilegia canadensis*	RWL diary 5/14/1933	x
cornflower	*Centaurea cyanus*	*LTOP*	
cosmos	*Cosmos bipinnatus*	RWL diary 5/13/1930	x
crocus	*Crocus* species	RWL diary 11/14/1929	x
daffodil	*Narcissus* species	RWL diary 5/14/1931	x
dahlia	*Dahlia* species	RWL diary 5/21/1934	x
delphinium	*Delphinium* species	RWL to unspecified 5/27/1935	x
forsythia	*Forsythia* species	RWL diary 4/29/1933	x
four o'clock	*Mirabilis jalapa*	*San Francisco Bulletin*, "Tuck 'em In Corner," 1915 (HHPL)	
foxglove	*Digitalis purpurea*	RWL diary 5/24/1930	x
geranium	*Pelargonium* species	*FB; FFY*	
gladiolus	*Gladiolus* species	RWL to unspecified 5/27/1935 (HHPL)	x
grape hyacinth	*Muscari armeniacum*	RWL diary 11/14/1929	x

Common name	Botanical name	Plant mentioned in	Grown at Rocky Ridge Farm?
hollyhock	*Alcea rosea*	*PG*; RWL diary 6/22/1930	x
honeysuckle	*Lonicera* species	LIW to Daphne Serton 5/26/1951; RWL to unspecified 5/27/1935 (HHPL)	x
iris, bearded	*Iris* species Rose mentioned growing hybrids from "two German brothers," probably referring to introductions from Hans and Jacob Sass.	LIW to Carrie Ingalls Swansey 5/21/1945; AJW to RWL 5/12/1939, RWL to unspecified 5/27/1935 (HHPL)	x
jonquil	*Narcissus jonquilla*	LIW to RWL 4/10/1939 (HHPL)	x
larkspur, garden	*Consolida ajacis*	RWL diary 6/11/1933	x
lilac	*Syringa vulgaris*	*FB*; LIW to RWL 6/1/1939; RWL diary 4/29/1932	x
lily, Easter	*Lilium candidum*	RWL diary 10/26/1929	
lily, regal	*Lilium regale*	RWL diary 6/3/1930	x
lupine	*Lupinus* species	RWL diary 4/18/1934	x
mignonette	*Reseda odorata*	*PG*; RWL to unspecified 5/27/1935 (HHPL)	x
moonflower	*Ipomoea alba*	RWL diary 4/10/1930	x
morning glory	*Ipomoea violacea*, including the cultivar 'Heavenly Blue'	*OWH*; *PC*; RWL diary 4/10/1930	x
moss rose	*Portulaca grandiflora*	*PG*	
mullein	*Verbascum* species	RWL diary 5/3/1924	x
myrtle	*Vinca minor*	RWL diary 11/16/1933	x
nasturtium	*Tropaeolum majus*	RWL diary 4/18/1934	x
painted tongue	*Salpiglossis sinuata*	RWL diary 5/2/1930	x
peony	*Paeonia lactiflora*	RWL diary 3/28/1930	x
phlox, garden	*Phlox maculata*, including the cultivar 'Miss Lingard'	RWL diary 6/11/1933; RWL to unspecified 5/27/1935 (HHPL)	x

Common name	Botanical name	Plant mentioned in	Grown at Rocky Ridge Farm?
phlox, moss	*Phlox subulata*	RWL diary 4/29/1933	x
pink	*Dianthus plumarius*	RWL diary 4/2/1930	x
poppy	*Papaver* species	PG, *San Francisco Bulletin*, "Tuck'em In Corner," 1915 (HHPL)	
tulip	*Tulipa* species	RWL to unspecified 5/27/1935 (HHPL)	x
pansy	*Viola* species	RWL diary 5/2/1930	x
petunia	*Petunia* species	RWL diary 6/5/1930	x
rosebay, Catawba	*Rhododendron catawbiense*	FB; RWL diary 5/12/1930	x
rose, cultivated	*Rosa* species, including hybrid perpetual, polyantha, and *R. rugosa*	RWL diary 5/13/1930 and 5/23/1934; AJW to RWL photograph undated (HHPL)	x
snapdragon	*Antirrhinum majus*	RWL diary 6/4/1931	x
snowball bush	*Viburnum opulus*	FB	
spirea	*Spiraea* species	RWL diary 4/4/1934	x
spiderlily	*Hymenocallis* species	RWL diary 6/11/1933	x
syringa	*Philadelphus* species	RWL to unspecified 5/27/1935 (HHPL); RWL diary 3/22/1930	x
tiger iris	*Tigridia pavonia*	RWL diary 5/12/1933	x
zinnia	*Zinnia elegans*	RWL diary 4/23/1930	x

Wildflowers

Common name	Botanical name	Plant mentioned in	Grown at Rocky Ridge Farm?
anemone, wood	*Anemone quinquefolia*	RWL diary 4/24/1924	x
aster	*Symphyotrichum* species	FJ; RWL diary 6/26/1930	x
black-eyed Susan	*Rudbeckia* species	PC; RWL diary 6/15/1924	x
blue flag	*Iris versicolor* (MN), *I. virginica* (IA and MO)	FJ; PC; PG; LIW to L. Dale Ahern 6/18/1947	x
buffalo bean, ground-plum milk vetch	*Astragalus crassicarpus*	FJ; PG; SL	

Common name	Botanical name	Plant mentioned in	Grown at Rocky Ridge Farm?
buttercup	*Ranunculus* species	*BW*; *FB*; *LTOP*; *PC*; *PG*; RWL diary 4/26/1924	x
butterfly weed	*Asclepias tuberosa*	RWL diary late June 1924	x
crocus, wild	*Pulsatilla patens*	*SL*	
goldenrod	*Solidago* species	*LHOP*; *LTOP*; *PC*; RWL diary 8/1/1924; LIW to RWL 2/5/1937	x
grassflower	*Sisyrinchium* species	*BW*; *LTOP*; *PG*	
horsemint	*Blephilia ciliata*	RWL diary 6/15/1924	x
Indian paintbrush	*Castilleja* species	*FFY*	
larkspur	*Delphinium carolinianum*	*LHOP*	
may flower	possibly *Anemone canadensis*	*PG*	
onion, wild	*Allium* species, likely *A. canadense* or *A. textile*	*SL*; LIW to RWL 2/5/1937	
ox-eye daisy	*Heliopsis helianthoides*	*FJ*; *LHOP*; RWL diary 7/4/1924	x
parsley, wild	*Polytaenia nuttallii*	LIW to RWL 2/5/1937	
pea, wild	Unknown	LIW to RWL 2/5/1937	
petunia, wild	*Ruellia humilis*	RWL diary 8/1/1924	x
pokeberry	*Phytolacca americana*	*BW*	
rose, wild	*Rosa* species in MO; *R. arkansana* in SD	*FFY*; *HGY*; *Letters*; *LTOP*; *PG*; RWL diary 6/15/1924	x
rush	*Juncus articulatus*	*PC*; LIW to L. Dale Ahern 6/18/1947	
sheep sorrel	*Rumex acetosella*	*LTOP*; *PC*; *SL*; LIW to RWL 2/5/1937	
snakeroot	*Echinacea* species	*WFH*	
sow thistle	*Sonchus* species	*FJ*	
squaw pink	*Castilleja minor*	*PG*	
sunflower, wild	*Helianthus* species	*FFY*; *FJ*; *LTOP*; *PG*; *SL*; LIW to RWL 2/5/1937	x

Common name	Botanical name	Plant mentioned in	Grown at Rocky Ridge Farm?
sweet William	*Phlox maculata*	*FJ; PG;* RWL diary 6/15/1924	x
thimble flower	*Anemone cylindrica*	*BW; PG*	
tiger lily	*Lilium philadelphicum*	*SL;* LIW to RWL 2/5/1937	
violet, bird's foot	*Viola pedata*	LIW to George Bye 5/15/1941	x
violet, blue	*Viola* species, likely *V. pratincola*	*BW; FB; FFY; HGY; LTOP; LW; PC; PG; SL;* LIW to RWL 2/5/1937	
violet, prairie bird's foot	*Viola pedatifida*	*LTOP*	
violet, yellow	*Viola nuttallii* or *V. pubescens*	LIW to RWL 2/5/1937	
wild carrot (Queen Anne's lace)	*Daucus carota*	RWL diary 7/4/1924	x
windflower	*Anemone canadensis*	*LTOP;* LIW to RWL 2/5/1937	
wintergreen	*Gaultheria procumbens*	*FB;* RWL to AJW 10/7/1932 (HHPL)	x
wood sorrel	*Oxalis montana*	*FB*	
wood sorrel, violet	*Oxalis violacea*	*PC*	
yellow star grass	*Hypoxis hirsuta*	*BW;* RWL diary 5/3/1924	x

Domestic fruits

Common name	Botanical name	Plant mentioned in	Grown at Rocky Ridge Farm?
apple	*Malus domestica*	*BW; FB; FJ; OWH; PG; SL*	x
avocado	*Persea americana*	RWL diary 6/10/1932	x
cantaloupe, Rocky Ford	*Cucumis melo* var. *cantalupensis*	*FJ;* RWL to AJW 9/25/1925	x
cherry, sweet	*Prunus avium*	*FJ*	
crabapple	*Malus sylvestris*	*FB*	
cranberry	*Vaccinium macrocarpon*	*FB; OWH*	

Common name	Botanical name	Plant mentioned in	Grown at Rocky Ridge Farm?
honeydew	*Cucumis melo* var. *inodorus*	*FJ*; RWL to AJW 9/27/1925 (HHPL)	x
peach	*Prunus persica*	*FJ*; *OWH*; RWL diary 4/26/1924	x
pear	*Pyrus communis*	LIW to Carrie Ingalls Swansey 9/24/1932	x
plum, domestic	*Prunus domestica*	*FB*; *FJ*; *OWH*; *PG*; RWL diary 7/4/1924	x
strawberry, domestic	*Fragaria ×ananassa*	*BW*; *FJ*; *HGY*; *Mirror*; *OWH*; LIW to RWL 3/12/1937	x
watermelon	*Citrullus lanatus*	*FB*; *FJ*; *LHOP*; *OWH*; *PG*	

Wild fruits

Common name	Botanical name	Plant mentioned in	Grown at Rocky Ridge Farm?
blackberry	*Rubus allegheniensis*	*FJ*; *LHOP*; *OWH*; RWL diary 5/3/1924; LIW to Daphne Serton 5/26/1951	x
blueberry, lowbush	*Vaccinium angustifolium*	*FB*	
chokecherry	*Prunus virginiana*	*FFY*; *FJ*; *HGY*; *LTOP*	
currant	*Ribes aureum*	*FJ*; *OWH*; RWL diary 4/26/1924	x
dewberry	*Rubus flagellaris*	*FJ*; RWL diary 5/3/1924	x
elderberry	*Sambucus nigra* var. *canadensis*	RWL diary late June 1924	
grape, wild	*Vitis riparia*	*FB*; *FJ*; *FFY*; *HGY*; *OWH*	
huckleberry	*Gaylussacia baccata*	*FB*; *FJ*; RWL diary 5/3/1924	x
pawpaw	*Asimina triloba*	*OWH*	
persimmon	*Diospyros virginiana*	*FJ*; *OWH*	
plum, wild	*Prunus americana*	*PC*; *PG*	
strawberry, wild	*Fragaria virginiana*	*FB*; *FJ*	x

Common name	Botanical name	Plant mentioned in	Grown at Rocky Ridge Farm?
Vegetables			
asparagus	*Asparagus officinalis*	RWL diary 1932	x
bean	*Phaseolus vulgaris*	*BW*; *FB*; *FFY*; *FJ*; *LHOP*; *LTOP*; *LW*; *PC*; *SL*; RWL diary 4/26/1933	x
beet	*Beta vulgaris*	*BW*; *FB*; *FJ*; *LTOP*; *PC*; *PG*; RWL diary 4/26/1933	x
cabbage	*Brassica oleracea*	*BW*; *FB*; *FJ*; *LHOP*; *PG*; RWL diary 4/26/1933	x
carrot	*Daucus carota* ssp. *carota*	RWL diary 1932	x
corn, including pop-corn	*Zea mays*	*BW*; *FB*; *FFY*; *FJ*; *HGY*; *LHOP*; *LTOP*; *LW*; *OWH*; *PC*; *PG*; *SL*; LIW to Carrie Ingalls Swansey 5/21/1945; RWL diary 4/26/1933	x
cucumber	*Cucumis sativus*	*FB*; *HGY*; *LTOP*; RWL diary late July 1932	x
ground cherry	*Physalis heterophylla*	*LTOP*	
husk tomato (toma-tillo)	*Physalis philadelphica*	*LTOP*	
lettuce	*Lactuca sativa*	*FJ*; *HGY*; *LTOP*; *WFH*; LIW to RWL 3/12/1937; RWL diary late July 1932	x
onion	*Allium cepa*	*BW*; *FB*; *HGY*; *LHOP*; *LTOP*; *PG*; *SL*; RWL diary 5/28/1924	x
parsnip	*Pastinaca sativa*	*FB*	
pea	*Pisum sativum*	*FB*; *FJ*; *LHOP*; *LTOP*; LIW to RWL 3/12/1937; RWL diary 4/26/3	x
pepper	*Capsicum annuum*	*BW*; *FB*; *PG*; RWL diary 4/26/1933	x

Common name	Botanical name	Plant mentioned in	Grown at Rocky Ridge Farm?
pie plant (rhubarb)	*Rheum rhabarbarum*	*FJ; FFY; HGY;* RWL diary 1932	x
potato	*Solanum tuberosum*	*BW; FB; FFY; FJ; HGY; LHOP; LTOP; LW; PC; PG; SL;* LIW to RWL 3/12/1937; RWL diary 4/26/1933	x
pumpkin	*Cucurbita pepo*	*BW; FB; FJ; LTOP; LW; PG*	
radish	*Raphanus sativus*	*HGY; LTOP;* LIW to RWL 3/12/1937; RWL diary late July 1932	x
rutabaga	*Brassica napus*	*FB*	
sage	*Salvia officinalis*	*BW; FB; FJ; PG; SL*	
squash, winter	*Cucurbita maxima*	*BW; PG;* RWL diary 5/8/1933	x
sweet potato	*Ipomoea batatas*	*FJ; LHOP; OWH*	
tobacco	*Nicotiana tabacum*	*FJ; LHOP*	
tomato	*Solanum lycopersicum*	*FB; FJ; LTOP; LW; OWH;* LIW to Mrs. Carson 3/18/1948; RWL diary 5/8/1933	x
turnip	*Brassica rapa* var. *rapa*	*BW; FB; FJ; LHOP; LTOP; LW; PC; PG;* LIW to RWL 3/12/1937; RWL diary 4/26/1933	x

Grains and other crops

Common name	Botanical name	Plant mentioned in	Grown at Rocky Ridge Farm?
alfalfa	*Medicago sativa*	*FJ;* LIW to AJW 9/22/1925	x
buckwheat	*Fagopyrum esculentum*	*FB; FFY*	
castor bean	*Ricinus communis*	*OWH*	
clover	*Trifolium* species	*FJ; OWH*	x
cowpea	*Vigna unguiculata*	*FJ*	x

Common name	Botanical name	Plant mentioned in	Grown at Rocky Ridge Farm?
flax	Linum usitatissimum	OWH	
hops	Humulus lupulus	1870 census (WA, ALIWA)	
kafir, also called milo or Jerusalem corn	Sorghum bicolor	FJ	
millet	Pennisetum species, including P. glaucum	FJ; Mirror	x
oat	Avena sativa	BW; FB; FFY; FJ; HGY; LTOP; PC; PG; SL	x
rye	Secale cereale	FB; FJ	
Sudangrass	Sorghum ×drummondii	Mirror	x
timothy	Phleum pratense	FB; FJ	x
wheat	Triticum species	BW; FB; FFY; FJ; HGY; LHOP; LTOP; LW; OWH; PC; PG; SL	x

Prairie grasses

Common name	Botanical name	Plant mentioned in	Grown at Rocky Ridge Farm?
bluestem, big	Andropogon gerardii	FFY; LW	
buffalo grass	Bouteloua dactyloides	FFY; HGY; LHOP; SL; LIW to AJW 9/21/1925	
Spanish needle grass	Bidens pilosa	LTOP; PG	
wild hay, also called sloughgrass or marsh grass	Spartina pectinata	FFY; PC; PG	

Other

Common name	Botanical name	Plant mentioned in	Grown at Rocky Ridge Farm?
bluegrass	Poa pratensis	FJ; RWL diary 11/15/1931	x
cactus, Christmas	Schlumbergera bridgesii	OWH; RWL diary 6/10/1932; AJW to RWL 3/12/1937 (HHPL)	x
dandelion	Taraxacum officinale	OWH; FJ; PG; RWL diary 4/19/1931	x

Common name	Botanical name	Plant mentioned in	Grown at Rocky Ridge Farm?
fern	unknown	OWH	
lichen	unknown	FB	
poison ivy	Toxicodendron radicans	FJ	
ragweed	Ambrosia artemisiifolia	PC	
sagebrush	Artemisia tridentata	WFH; LIW to AJW 9/28/1925 (HHPL)	
sand bur	Cenchrus longispinus	LTOP; OWH; PG	
tumbleweed, also called Russian thistle	Sisymbrium altissimum (MN), Salsola kali (SD)	OWH; PC; PG	

Trees and shrubs

Common name	Botanical name	Plant mentioned in	Grown at Rocky Ridge Farm?
ash	Fraxinus species	BW; FB; FJ	x
beech	Fagus grandifolia	FB	
boxelder	Acer negundo	HGY	
buckberry	Vaccinium stamineum	FJ	x
buckbrush	Ceanothus cuneatus	LHOP	
buckeye	Aesculus species	OWH	
butternut	Juglans cinerea	FB; FJ	x
cherry, wild	Prunus serotina	FJ; OWH	
cottonwood	Populus deltoides	FFY; HGY; LHOP; OWH; PC; PG; SL	
dogwood	Cornus florida	RWL diary 4/26/1924	x
elm	Ulmus americana	FB; FFY; FJ; LIW to Carrie Ingalls Swansey 5/21/1945	x
hawthorn	Crataegus species	BW; FJ; OWH; RWL diary 4/10/1930	x
hemlock	Tsuga species	LIW to AJW 10/6/1925	

Common name	Botanical name	Plant mentioned in	Grown at Rocky Ridge Farm?
hickory	*Carya* species	*BW*; *FB*; *FJ*; *LHOP*; *OWH*; RWL diary 10/16/1929	x
holly	*Ilex opaca*	Correspondence with WA	x
ironwood	*Carpinus caroliniana*	*FB*	
maple	*Acer* species	*BW*; *FB*; *FFY*; *FJ*; *HGY*; RWL diary 4/26/1924	x
maple, Japanese	*Acer palmatum* var. *atropurpureum*	Correspondence with WA	x
moosewood	*Acer pensylvanicum*	*FB*	
oak	*Quercus* species	*BW*; *FB*; *FJ*; *LHOP*; *OWH*; *PG*; LIW to Carrie Ingalls Swansey 5/21/1945	x
oak, black	*Quercus velutina*	*FJ*	x
oak, blackjack	*Quercus marilandica*	*FJ*; RWL diary 4/26/1924	x
oak, white	*Quercus alba*	*FJ*	x
Osage orange	*Maclura pomifera*	*OWH*	x
pecan	*Carya illinoinensis*	Correspondence with WA	x
pine	*Pinus strobus*	*FB*; *FJ*; LIW to AJW 10/6/1925	
pussywillow	*Salix discolor*	RWL diary 4/4/1934	x
redbud	*Cercis canadensis*	*FJ*; RWL to unspecified 5/27/1935 (HHPL)	x
red cedar, eastern	*Juniperus virginiana*	*BW*; *FB*; LIW to RWL 1/25/1938	x
redwood	*Sequoia sempervirens*	*Letters*	
sassafras	*Sassafras albidum*	RWL diary 4/26/1924	x
serviceberry	*Amelanchier arborea*	*OWH*	x
spicebush	*Lindera benzoin*	*OWH*	

Common name	Botanical name	Plant mentioned in	Grown at Rocky Ridge Farm?
spruce	*Picea species*	*FB*	
sumac	*Rhus typhina*	*BW; LHOP; OWH;* RWL diary 7/4/1924	x
sycamore	*Platanus occidentalis*	*LHOP; OWH*	x
tulip tree	*Magnolia* species	LIW to RWL 6/1/1939	x
tupelo, black gum	*Nyssa sylvatica*	*OWH*	x
walnut, black	*Juglans nigra*	*BW; FJ; LHOP; OWH;* LIW to Carrie Ingalls Swansey 5/21/1945; RWL diary 4/26/1924	x
willow	*Salix* species	*HGY; LHOP; PC; PG*	

RECOMMENDED READING

Laura Ingalls Wilder, circa 1917.　　　Laura Ingalls Wilder, circa 1930.

By Laura Ingalls Wilder

NOVELS

Little House in the Big Woods (New York: Harper & Brothers, 1932).
Farmer Boy (New York: Harper & Brothers, 1933).
Little House on the Prairie (New York: Harper & Brothers, 1935).
On the Banks of Plum Creek (New York: Harper & Brothers, 1937).
By the Shores of Silver Lake (New York: Harper & Brothers, 1939).
The Long Winter (New York: Harper & Brothers, 1940).
Little Town on the Prairie (New York: Harper & Brothers, 1941).
These Happy Golden Years (New York: Harper & Brothers, 1943).
The First Four Years (New York: Harper & Row, 1971).

LETTERS AND MEMOIRS

On the Way Home: The Diary of a Trip from South Dakota to Mansfield, Missouri in 1894 (New York: Harper & Row, 1962).

West from Home: Letters of Laura Ingalls Wilder to Almanzo Wilder, San Francisco, 1915, ed. Roger Lea MacBride (New York: Harper & Row, 1974).

Pioneer Girl: The Annotated Autobiography, ed. Pamela Smith Hill (Pierre: South Dakota State Historical Society Press, 2014).

The Selected Letters of Laura Ingalls Wilder, ed. William Anderson (New York: HarperCollins, 2016).

OTHER COLLECTIONS

A Little House Sampler: A Collection of Early Stories and Reminiscences, ed. William Anderson (Lincoln: University of Nebraska Press, 1988).

A Little House Traveler: Writings from Laura Ingalls Wilder's Journeys Across America, ed. William Anderson (New York: HarperCollins, 2006).

Laura Ingalls Wilder, Farm Journalist: Writings from the Ozarks, ed. Stephen W. Hines (Columbia: University of Missouri Press, 2007).

The Rediscovered Writings of Rose Wilder Lane: Literary Journalist, ed. Amy Mattson Lauters (Columbia: University of Missouri Press, 2007).

About Laura Ingalls Wilder and Rose Wilder Lane

Anderson, William. *Laura Ingalls Wilder: A Biography* (New York: HarperCollins, 1992).

Hill, Pamela Smith. *Laura Ingalls Wilder: A Writer's Life* (Pierre: South Dakota Historical Society Press, 2007).

Holtz, William. *The Ghost in the Little House: A Life of Rose Wilder Lane* (Columbia: University of Missouri Press, 1993).

Ketchum, Sallie. *Laura Ingalls Wilder: American Writer on the Prairie* (New York: Taylor & Francis, 2015).

Miller, John E. *Becoming Laura Ingalls Wilder: The Woman Behind the Legend* (Columbia: University of Missouri Press, 1998).

Almanzo was justifiably proud of his apple crop.

About American Agriculture, Gardening, and Landscape History

Adams, Denise Wiles. *Restoring American Gardens: An Encyclopedia of Heirloom Ornamental Plants, 1640–1940* (Portland, OR: Timber Press, 2004).

Kline, Roger A. et al. *The Heirloom Vegetable Garden*, Bulletin 177 (Ithaca, NY: Cornell Cooperative Extension, 1981).

Leighton, Ann. *Early American Gardens: "For Meate or Medicine"* (Amherst: University of Massachusetts Press, 1970).

———. *American Gardens in the Eighteenth Century: "For Use or For Delight"* (Amherst: University of Massachusetts Press, 1976).

———. *American Gardens of the Nineteenth Century: "For Comfort and Affluence"* (Amherst: University of Massachusetts Press, 1987).

Lopez, Barry, ed. *Home Ground: Language for an American Landscape* (San Antonio, TX: Trinity University Press, 2006).

Madison, Deborah. *Vegetable Literacy* (Berkeley, CA: Ten Speed Press, 2013).

McGee, Harold. *On Food and Cooking: The Science and Lore of the Kitchen* (New York: Scribner, 2004).

Russell, Howard S. *A Long, Deep Furrow: Three Centuries of Farming in New England*, ed. Mark Lapping (Hanover, NH: University Press of New England, 1982).

Schlebecker, John T. *Whereby We Thrive: A History of American Farming, 1607–1972* (Ames: University of Iowa Press, 1975).

Smith, Henry Nash. *Virgin Land: The American West as Symbol and Myth* (Cambridge, MA: Harvard University Press, 1970).

Stiloge, John R. *Common Landscape of America, 1580–1845* (New Haven, CT: Yale University Press, 1983).

Sumner, Judith. *American Household Botany: A History of Useful Plants 1620–1900* (Portland, OR: Timber Press, 2004).

Watts, May Theilgaard. *Reading the Landscape of America* (New York: Macmillan, 1975).

About Plants, Pollinators, and People

Armitage, Allan M. *Armitage's Native Plants for North American Gardens* (Portland, OR: Timber Press, 2006).

Bennett, Chris. *Southeast Foraging: 120 Wild and Flavorful Edibles from Angelica to Wild Plums* (Portland, OR: Timber Press, 2015).

Holm, Heather. *Pollinators of Native Plants: Attract, Observe and Identify Pollinators and Beneficial Insects with Native Plants* (Minnetonka, MN: Pollinator Press, 2014).

Rainer, Thomas, and Claudia West. *Planting in a Post-Wild World: Designing Plant Communities for Resilient Landscapes* (Portland, OR: Timber Press, 2015).

Rose, Lisa M. *Midwest Foraging: 115 Wild and Flavorful Edibles from Burdock to Wild Peach* (Portland, OR: Timber Press, 2015).

Tallamy, Doug. *Bringing Nature Home: How Native Plants Sustain Wildlife in our Gardens* (Portland, OR: Timber Press, 2009).

Wasowski, Sally. *Gardening with Prairie Plants: How to Create Beautiful Native Landscapes* (Minneapolis: University of Minnesota Press, 2001).

Weaner, Larry, and Tom Christopher. *Garden Revolution: How Our Landscapes Can Be a Source of Environmental Change* (Portland, OR: Timber Press, 2016).

SOURCES AND CITATIONS

Please note that citations for the Laura Ingalls Wilder quotations used in the book appear first within each chapter's notes. Page numbers from Wilder's novels refer to the 1971 HarperTrophy edition. Other abbreviations are listed on pp. 336–337.

BW	*Little House in the Big Woods*, © 1932, 1960 Little House Heritage Trust. Text used by permission of HarperCollins Publishers. Please note: "Little House" ® is a registered trademark of HarperCollins Publishers, Inc.
FB	*Farmer Boy*, © 1933, 1961 Little House Heritage Trust. Text used by permission of HarperCollins Publishers.
FFY	*The First Four Years*, © 1971, 1999 Little House Heritage Trust. Text used by permission of HarperCollins Publishers.
HGY	*Those Happy Golden Years*, © 1943, 1971 Little House Heritage Trust. Text used by permission of HarperCollins Publishers.
Letters	*The Selected Letters of Laura Ingalls Wilder*, © 2016 by William Anderson. Letters © 2016 Little House Heritage Trust. Introduction, annotation, footnotes, explanatory text, photograph captions © 2016 William Anderson. Text reprinted by permission of HarperCollins Publishers.
LHOP	*Little House on the Prairie*, © 1935, 1963 Little House Heritage Trust. Text used by permission of HarperCollins Publishers. Please note: "Little House" ® is a registered trademark of HarperCollins Publishers, Inc.
LTOP	*Little Town on the Prairie*, © 1941, 1969 Little House Heritage Trust. Text used by permission of HarperCollins Publishers.
LW	*The Long Winter*, © 1940, 1968 Little House Heritage Trust. Text used by permission of HarperCollins Publishers.
OWH	*On the Way Home*, © 1962, 1990 Little House Heritage Trust. Text used by permission of HarperCollins Publishers.

PC   *On the Banks of Plum Creek*, © 1937, 1965 Little House Heritage Trust. Text used by permission of HarperCollins Publishers.

PG   *Pioneer Girl*, *Pioneer Girl* text © 2014 Little House Heritage Trust and South Dakota Historical Society Press. All rights reserved. Text used by permission.

Sampler   *A Little House Sampler*, © 1988 by HarperCollins Publishers, Inc. Text reprinted by permission of HarperCollins Publishers.

SL   *By the Shores of Silver Lake*, © 1939, 1967 Little House Heritage Trust. Text used by permission of HarperCollins Publishers.

WFH   *West from Home*, © 1974 by Roger Lea MacBride. Text used by permission of HarperCollins Publishers.

FRONT MATTER

"It is a": *HGY*, p. 289.
"The voices of": from "As a Farm Woman Thinks (19)," *Ruralist,* April 15, 1923, *FJ*, p. 288.

A Life on the Land

"Ma took charge": *LTOP*, pp. 7–8.

CLEARING THE LAND: THE WISCONSIN WOODS

"The sap, you": *BW*, p. 123.
"legend-haunted Lake Pepin": from Case, John F. "Let's Visit Mrs. Wilder" *Ruralist,* February 20, 1918, reprinted in Ketchum, *Laura Ingalls Wilder: American Writer on the Prairie*, p. 178.
"if he had gone": *PG*, p. 27.
"came to make": *PG*, p. 39.
"a steel blade fastened": *PG*, p. 52.
"Birds sang in" and "Buttercups and violets": *BW*, p. 155.
"She knit all" and "Father harvested his": from "The Farm Home (16)," *Ruralist,* January 5, 1920, *FJ*, pp. 209–210.

The University of Wisconsin-Madison Libraries provides a collection called "Wisconsin Pioneer Experience" at uwdc.library.wisc.edu/collections/WI/wipionexp, which includes transcriptions of many letters, diaries, and other primary sources.

Many of the nineteenth-century primary source books and periodicals are available via archive.org, the Biodiversity Heritage Library (biodiversitylibrary.org), and Google Books.

Apps, Jerry. *Old Farm: A History* (Madison: Wisconsin Historical Society Press: 2008).

Boustead, Barbara Mayes. Personal communication from November 2, 2016, regarding the weather in Pepin, Wisconsin, on Laura Ingalls Wilder's date of birth, February 7, 1867.

Carmichael, Marcia C. *Putting Down Roots: Gardening Insights from Wisconsin's Early Settlers* (Madison: Wisconsin Historical Society Press, 2013).

Chadde, Steve W. *Wisconsin Flora: An Illustrated Guide to the Vascular Plants of Wisconsin* (self-published, 2013).

Ernst, Kathleen. *A Settler's Year: Pioneer Life Through the Seasons* (Madison: Wisconsin Historical Society Press, 2015).

Favell, Angela Haste. "A Girl Pioneer in the Wisconsin Wilderness," *Milwaukee Journal*, August 7, 1932, available at wisconsinhistory.org.

Franklin, Benjamin. *Memoirs of Benjamin Franklin, Volume 2* (Philadelphia: M'Carty & Davis, 1834). The quote "The first is by" is on p. 439.

Garland, Hamlin. *A Son of the Middle Border* (New York: Macmillan, 1917).

Hachten, Harva, and Terese Allen. *The Flavor of Wisconsin: An Informal History of Food and Eating in the Badger State* (Madison: Wisconsin Historical Society Press, 2009).

Ingalls, Caroline Quiner. Letter to Martha Quiner Carpenter, October 6, 1861, available at wisconsinhistory.org, is the source of the quote, "And now about."

Kouba, Theodore F. *Wisconsin's Amazing Woods: Then and Now* (Madison: Wisconsin House, 1973).

Leopold, Aldo. *A Sand County Almanac* (New York: Oxford University Press, 1949).

McClelland, Peter D. *Sowing Modernity: America's First Agricultural Revolution* (Ithaca, NY: Cornell University Press, 1997).

Pauly, Philip J. *Fruits and Plains: The Horticultural Transformation of America* (Cambridge, MA: Harvard University Press, 2007).

Zunz, Olivier, ed. *Alexis de Tocqueville and Gustave de Beaumont in America* (Charlottesville:

University of Virginia Press, 2011). The quotes "a widespread hatred," "so rapidly that," and "There is no" are on p. 74.

PREPARING THE SOIL: A NEW YORK FARM

"Don't forget it": *FB*, p. 188.

"a well-known": *The [Malone, NY] Palladium*, November 3, 1871, p. 3, available via nyshistoricnewspapers.com.

Anderson, William. *The Story of the Wilders: A Biography of Almanzo Wilder and the Family from "Farmer Boy"* (privately printed, 1983).

Annual Report of the Regents of the University to the Legislature of the State of New York (Albany: Comstock and Cassidy, 1863). Page 375 lists textbooks used at Franklin Academy.

"A Suckling Squash," *American Agriculturist* 34:12 (December 1875). The quotes "has been for" and "somehow be fed" are on p. 450.

Beach, S. A. *The Apples of New York, Volume I* (Albany, NY: J. B. Lyon Company, 1905).

De Long, Eric. "Understanding Frost," an article of the Cornell Cooperative Extension, 2001.

Downing, Andrew Jackson. *Andrew Jackson Downing: Essential Texts*, ed. Robert Twombly (New York: W. W. Norton & Company, 2012). The quote "better preachers of" is on p. 213.

———. *The Fruits and Fruit Trees of America*, 2nd ed., ed. Charles Downing (New York: Wiley & Halsted, 1857). This book, cross-referenced with Beach's *Apples of New York*, provided the list of apples grown northern New York circa 1866.

Edinger, G. J. et al., eds. 2014. *Ecological Communities of New York State*, 2nd ed. (Albany, NY: New York State Department of Environmental Conservation, 2014).

Harvard Health Letter, July 2004, available via health.harvard.edu is the source of a "Table of calories burned by activity."

Keith, Patrick. *A System of Physiological Botany* (London: Baldwin, Cradock, and Joy, 1816). The quote "some tribes of" is on p. 453.

Ott, Cindy. *Pumpkin: The Curious History of an American Icon* (Seattle: University of Washington Press, 2012). Ott's book also led me to the article in the *American Agriculturist*.

Raymo, Denise. "Malone celebrates 200 years," *Press Republican*, June 30, 2002.

Russell, Howard S. *A Long, Deep Furrow: Three Centuries of Farming in New England*, ed. Mark Lapping (Hanover, NH: University Press of New England, 2003).

Wood, Alphonso. *Class-Book of Botany* (New York: Barnes & Burr, 1860). The quotes "botany combines," "charming retreats," "patiently smiles," and "Thus if wheat" are taken from p. 12 and p. 153.

HARROWING: THE PRAIRIE OF KANSAS, INDIAN TERRITORY

"The land that": *LHOP*, p. 75.
"Pa was no": LIW to RWL, March 23, 1937, HHPL.
"It was lonesome": *PG*, p. 1.
"Pa built a": *PG*, p. 1.
"I saw the prairie fire": *PG*, p. 16.
"Now it was": *LHOP*, p. 199.

The census that included Laura's family in Indian Territory is available via ancestry.com through its access to the National Archives and Records Administration. Note that the census taker spelled the family name "Ingles."

Barnard, Iralee. *Field Guide to the Common Grasses of Oklahoma, Kansas, and Nebraska* (Lawrence: University Press of Kansas, 2004).

Clement, Margaret Gray. "Research on 'Little House on the Prairie,'" unpublished manuscript in the collection of the Laura Ingalls Wilder Memorial Society, 1972. In this document Clement outlined her research of the likely location of the Ingalls farm, the southwest quarter, Section 36, Township 33 (Rutland, Kansas).

Duncan, Patricia D. *Tallgrass Prairie: The Inland Sea* (Kansas City, MO: Lowell Press, 1978).

Cronon, William. *Changes in the Land: Indians, Colonists, and the Ecology of New England* (New York: Hill and Wang, 1983). The quote "In a vacant" is on pp. 56–57.

Cutler, William G. *History of the State of Kansas* (Chicago: A. T. Andreas, 1883), available via kansascoll.org. The quote "Elevated mounds" is on p. 1,583.

Elliott, F. R. *The American Fruit-Grower's Guide* (New York: C. M. Saxton, Agricultural Book Publisher, 1854). The quote "[H]er prairies, her" is on pp. 15–16, available via Google Books.

Herndon, Sarah Raymond. *Days on the Road: Crossing the Plains in 1865* (Guilford, CT: TwoDot Press, 2003).

Hoover, Leo M. "Kansas Agriculture After 100 Years," *Kansas Agricultural Experiment Station Bulletin 392*, August 1957.

Linsenmayer, Penny T. "Kansas Settlers on the Osage Diminished Reserve: A Study of Laura Ingalls Wilder's Little House on the Prairie," *Kansas History* 24:3 (Autumn 2001), pp. 168–185, available at kshs.org.

Madson, John. *Where the Sky Began: Land of the Tallgrass Prairie* (San Francisco: Sierra Club, 1982). The phrase "daisyland" is on p. 89; sloughgrass as sod bricks, p. 212.

———. *Tallgrass Prairie* (Helena, MT: Falcon Press, 1993).

Madson, John, and George Olson. *The Elemental Prairie: Sixty Tallgrass Plants* (Iowa City: University of Iowa Press, 2005).

Manning, Richard. *Grassland: The History, Biology, Politics, and Promise of the American Prairie* (New York: Penguin Books, 1995).

Meinig, Donald William. *The Shaping of America: A Geographical Perspective on 500 Years of History, 1800–1867* (New Haven, CT: Yale University Press, 1993). The quote "almost wholly unfit" from Major Stephen Long's report is on p. 76.

Moulton, Gary E., ed. *The Journals of the Lewis and Clark Expedition 1803–1806* are transcribed and available via the University of Nebraska Electronic Text Center, lewisandclarkjournals.unl.edu. The quote "[It] is so abundant" is from *Part 3: Botanical Collections* by Meriwether Lewis, winter 1804–1805, No. 4.

Perry, L. Day. *Seat Weaving* (Peoria, IL: The Manual Arts Press, 1917).

Price, John T., ed. *The Tallgrass Prairie Reader* (Iowa City: University of Iowa Press, 2014).

Sargent, Charles Sprague. *Report on the Forests of North America* (Washington, DC: U.S. Government Printing Office, 1884). The quotes "a strip of" and "arborescent vegetation" are on p. 5.

Savage, Candace. *Prairie: A Natural History* (Vancouver: Greystone Books, 2004).

Skamarakas, Constantine J. *Peter Kalm's America: A Critical Analysis of His Journal* (Washington, DC: The Catholic University of America, 2009). The discussion of the watermelon and malaria is on p. 191.

Smith, Annick. *Big Bluestem: Journey Into the Tall Grass* (Tulsa, OK: Council Oak Books, 1996).

Snell, Joseph W, ed. "Roughing it on her Kansas Claim: The Diary of Abbie Bright 1870–1871," *Kansas History* 37:4 (Winter 1971), available via kshs.org. The quotes "You know my" and "This is the Osage" are on pp. 395–396.

Stephens, H. A. *Trees, Shrubs, and Woody Vines in Kansas* (Lawrence: University of Kansas Press, 1969).

Stratton, Joanna L. *Pioneer Women: Voices from the Kansas Frontier* (New York: Simon &

Schuster, 1981).

Vinton, Mary Ann. "Grasses," *Encyclopedia of the Great Plains*, ed. David J. Wishart (Lincoln: University of Nebraska, 2011), available at plainshumanities.unl.edu, is one source of the "upside-down forest" analogy.

MAKING A BETTER GARDEN: CREEKSIDE IN MINNESOTA AND IOWA

"Rich, level land": *PC*, p. 6.

"Each blue flag": *PC*, p. 19.

"I thought it": *PG*, p. 62.

"not much more room": *PG*, p. 64.

"perfectly round table land" and "Mary and I": *PG*, p. 67.

"Pa never took": *PG*, p. 74.

"as large as": *PG*, p. 76.

"light-colored fleecy . . . a shiny white": *PG*, p. 79.

"like hail in" *PG*, p. 79.

"A big old crab" and "nasty things": *PG*, p. 92.

"He walked because": *PG*, p. 81.

"Pa said he'd": *PG*, p. 94.

"The wagon was": *PG*, p. 94.

"a big, beautiful": *PG* p. 96.

"that was filled": *PG*, p. 108. The yellow-green of the willows is also from this page reference.

"[A] dead town": *PG*, p. 112.

"lonesome, longing music": *PG*, p. 112.

"I loved the poppies": *PG*, p. 141.

"Mary and I" and "did hate to": *PG*, p. 140.

"All through the": from "A Bouquet of Wildflowers," *Ruralist*, June 20, 1917, *FJ*, p.118.

The researchers in the Pioneer Girl Project, sponsored by the South Dakota State Historical Society, tracked down Pa's preemption claim in Minnesota: the northwest quarter of Section 18, Township 109, Range 38, Redwood County.

The American Memory Collection at the Library of Congress includes "Pioneering the Upper Midwest," available at memory.loc.gov/ammem/umhtml/umhome.html.

Atkins, Annette. *Harvest of Grief: Grasshopper Plagues and Public Assistance in Minnesota, 1873–78* (St. Paul: Minnesota Historical Society Press, 1984).

Chapman, Brian R., and Eric G. Bolen. *Ecology of North America* (Chichester, U.K.: John Wiley & Sons, 2015).

Chapman, N., M.D. "On Constipation," *American Journal of Medical Sciences* (Philadelphia: Lee & Blackchard, 1839), includes a recipe for stewed prunes as one prescription, pp. 103–104.

Curtiss-Wedge, Franklin, ed. *The History of Redwood County, Minnesota, Volume 1* (Chicago: H. C. Cooper Jr. & Co., 1916). Redwood County, by the way, is named for the eastern red cedar, *Juniperus virginiana*, and not the California redwood. Pages 266–267 provide the dates of the grasshopper years; the types of control methods are on p. 569. The quotes "a dark rich loam" and "on account of" are on pp. 460–461; "We stood helpless" is on p. 464.

Dewey, Lyster Hoxie. *The Russian Thistle: Its History as a Weed in the United States* (Washington, DC: U.S. Department of Agriculture, 1894). Map 2, pp. 38–39, shows principal distribution of the Russian thistle in the Dakotas and Nebraska in 1894.

Downing, Andrew Jackson. *The Fruits and Fruit Trees of America*. The quote "a late plum" is on pp. 381–382.

Hedrick, U. P. et al. *The Plums of New York* (Albany: J. B. Lyon Company, 1911). This includes a description of the frost gage plum on p. 216.

Hoyt, J. W., ed. "Important Work for July," *The Wisconsin Farmer* 17:7 (July 1865), p. 1. See also "The Common Flat Turnip," *The American Agriculturist* 17:7 (July 1858), p. 196. In 1948, well after Wilder had written her books, Harry Truman enshrined the date politically, calling Congress back to Washington for a special July "Turnip Session," based on the old adage from his home state of Missouri.

Jarchow, Merrill E. "Farm Machinery in Frontier Minnesota," *Minnesota History* 23 (December 1942), pp. 316–327.

———. "Farm Machinery of the 1860's in Minnesota," *Minnesota History* 24 (December 1943), pp. 297–306.

Kampinen, Andrea R. *The Sod Houses of Custer County, Nebraska*, Master's thesis, University of Georgia, 2008, retrieved from getd.libs.uga.edu.

Marin, William A. "Sod Houses and Prairie Schooners," *Minnesota History* 12 (June 1931), pp. 135–156, is the source of the quote "a well-built sod shanty."

McClung, J. W. *Minnesota as it is in 1870; its general resources and attractions for immigrants, invalids, tourists, capitalists, and business men* (St. Paul: published by the author, 1870). The quotes "the wife or daughter" and "round the door" are on p. 171.

Peterson, Fred. *Homes in the Heartland: Balloon Frames Houses of the Upper Midwest* (Minneapolis: University of Minnesota Press, 2008).

Pollan, Michael. *Second Nature: A Gardener's Education* (New York: Grove Press, 1991).

Schlebecker, John T. "Grasshoppers in American Agricultural History," *Agricultural History* 27:3 (July 1953), pp. 85–93.

Thoreau, Henry David. *The Writings of Henry David Thoreau, Volume 4*, ed. Bradford Torrey (Boston: Houghton Mifflin and Company, 1906). The quotes "fringed, recurved parasols" and "a little too" are on p. 92.

Upham, Warren. *Minnesota Geographic Names: Their Origin and Historic Significance* (St. Paul: Minnesota Historical Society, 1920). See p. 453 for information about Walnut Grove.

Wells, Anna Maria. *The Floweret: A Gift of Love* (Boston: Lee and Shepard, undated, circa 1842). The excerpts from the poems are from p. 17, p. 69, and p. 72; available online from the Cornell Library at hathitrust.org.

Wilder, Laura Ingalls. Handwritten notes on the grasshopper plague of 1874 for her Detroit Book Week Speech, 1937. HHPL Box 13 Folder 197.

RIPENING: THE DAKOTA PRAIRIE

"We're west of": *SL*, p. 60.

"out in the yard": *PG*, p. 53 and referenced on p. 142.

"nothing happened on": *PG*, p. 151.

"as though we": *PG*, p. 221.

"It was grassed": *PG*, p. 233.

"moved home again": *PG*, p. 229.

"may flowers, thimble": *PG*, p. 234.

The Library of Congress provides "Chronicling America," a database of vintage newspapers from across the country at chroniclingamerica.loc.gov. It is the source of the quote from the *Canton [Dakota Territory] Advocate* September 18, 1879. "Good water, good wells" is from *Daily Press and Dakotaian*, May 20, 1880, which also reported daily mail delivery and the lumberyard in De Smet on May 26, 1880. "Chronicling America" also includes Missouri newspapers such as the *Mirror*, referenced in later chapters.

"Tree planting has" and "one of the first" are from *The Chicago Tribune*, March 28, 1877, p. 5, accessed via newspapers.com, another site that provides online access to period newspapers.

Allexan, Sarah S., et al. "Blindness in Walnut Grove: How Did Mary Ingalls Lose Her Sight?" *Pediatrics* 131:3 (March 2013), accessed via pediatrics.aappublications.org.

Boustead, Barbara E. "The Hard Winter of 1880–1881: Climatological Context and Communication via a Laura Ingalls Wilder Narrative," Ph.D. dissertation, University of Nebraska–Lincoln, 2014, available at digitalcommons.unl.edu.

Cather, Willa. *My Ántonia* (Boston: Houghton Mifflin Company, 1918). The quote "the train flashed" is on the opening page.

Emmons, David M. *Garden in the Grasslands* (Lincoln: University of Nebraska Press, 1973).

Gallo, Kevin, NOAA, and Eric Wood, USGS. "Historical Drought Episodes Recorded by Native Americans," *Great Plains Research* 25:2 (Fall 2015), pp. 151–158.

Hufstetler, Mark, and Michael Bedeau. "South Dakota's Railroads: An Historic Context" (Pierre: South Dakota State Historic Preservation Office, 2007), accessed via history.sd.gov.

"John No Ears' Winter Count," State Historical Society of North Dakota, Unit 3: Set One SHSND Mss 20167, is the source of "deep snow winter," available at history.nd.gov.

Lange, Cindy "South Dakota's Most Famous Trees," *South Dakota Magazine* (September/October 1996), pp. 30–37.

Laskin, David. *The Children's Blizzard* (New York: HarperCollins, 2004).

Over, William H. *Flora of South Dakota* (Vermillion: University of South Dakota, 1932).

Potter, Constance. "Genealogy Notes: De Smet, Dakota Territory, Little Town in the National Archives," *Prologue Magazine* 35:4 (Winter 2003), accessed via archives.gov. Includes the report from *Climatological Records of the Weather Bureau, 1819–1892*.

Schivelbusch, Wolfgang. *The Railway Journey: The Industrialization of Time and Space in the Nineteenth Century* (Oakland: University of California Press, 2014). This is the source of the quote from Victor Hugo, "The flowers by," p. 55.

Sherwood, Aubrey. *Beginnings of De Smet* (De Smet, SD: privately published, 1979). A collection by the longtime editor of the De Smet newspaper and early advocate for the Laura Ingalls Wilder Memorial Society. This is the source of the early quotations from the *Kingsbury County News*, later the *De Smet Leader*. The quote "Business men looking" is on p. 38, and "C. P. Ingalls" is on p. 39.

Wilder, Almanzo, and Rose Wilder Lane. Almanzo's description and sketch of turkey foot, as well as buffalo grass and sloughgrass, are on p. 9 of a seventeen-page questionnaire that Rose typed as background material for a novel. Her father supplied handwritten answers and hand-drawn diagrams. It is in the collection of the HHPL.

REAPING: SETTLED FARM AND SETTLED TOWN

"The place begins": *LTOP*, p. 61.

"Up from the bare earth": *LTOP*, p. 49.

"I didn't care" and "I loved the prairie": *PG*, p. 231.

"In June the": *PG*, p. 234.

"a little awed": *PG*, p. 324.

"the homeliest girl ever": LIW to RWL, December 29, 1937, *Letters*, p. 132. Wilder had earlier employed this phrase in *PG*, p. 245.

Anderson, William. *The Story of the Ingalls Family* (privately printed, 2006).

Berry, B. C. "Stealing Melons," *The Youth's Companion* 41:25 (June 19, 1879) is the source of the quote "the stars twinkled," p. 203.

Colman, N. J., and H. P. Byram. "The Ground Cherry," *The Valley Farmer* 10 (1858), p. 127.

De Smet News, March 19, 1897, clipping in Couse file, LIWMS, is the source of the quote "Walter A. Wood binders."

Earle, A. Scott, and James L. Reveal. *Lewis and Clark's Green World: The Expedition and its Plants* (Helena, MT: Farcountry Press, 2003). See *Rosa arkansana*, pp. 42–43.

Hartwig, George. *The Polar and Tropical Worlds: A Description of Man and Nature*, ed. Dr. A. H. Guernsey (Springfield, MA: Bill, Nichols & Company, 1872). The quote "every family, reduced" is on p. 123.

Leslie, Eliza. *Miss Leslie's New Cookery Book* (Philadelphia T. E. Peterson, 1857). The section on preserving fruit—or, as she called them, "sweetmeats"—starts on page 543.

Ingalls, Caroline Quiner. Letter to Carrie Ingalls, March 22, 1912, is the source of the quote "Plant your ground," LIMWS.

Ingalls, Charles. Letter to Almanzo and Royal Wilder, November 19, 1884, is the source of the quotes "Last Sunday was" and "Now boys don't." Used with permission from Laura Ingalls Wilder Historic Home and Museum.

Miller, M. F. "A Century of Missouri Agriculture," University of Missouri Agricultural Experiment Station, Bulletin 701 (May 1958).

Moser, JoAnn. *Mason Jar Nation* (Minneapolis, MN: Cool Springs Press, 2016). See the essay on the history of the canning jar, pp. 12–23.

Report of the Commissioner of Agriculture, 1887 (Washington, DC: Government Printing Office, 1888). The discussion of the blackbirds-in-the-corn study is on pp. 427–428.

Slade, Mary. *Exhibition Days* (Boston: Henry Young and Company, 1880). "Dropping Corn" is on p. 71. The verse quoted is the first stanza of a longer poem.

Speake, Jennifer, ed. *Oxford Dictionary of Proverbs*, 6th ed. (Oxford, U.K.: Oxford University Press, 2015). The corn planting rhyme is on p. 237 and, appropriately, includes a reference to Wilder's *LTOP*.

Wilder, Laura Ingalls. "A Letter from Laura Ingalls Wilder" reprint from the Laura Ingalls Wilder Issue, *The Horn Book Magazine* (December 1953), pp. 437–438, HHPL.

Williams, Susan. *Savory Suppers and Fashionable Feasts: Dining in Victorian America* (New York: Pantheon Books, 1985).

THRESHING: FROM GREAT PLAINS TO OZARK RIDGES

"We'll always be": *FFY*, p. 133.

"Trees are being": *The De Smet Leader*, April 30, 1887, clipping in Loftus file, LIWMS.

"We could get": LIW to RWL, March 23, 1937, *Letters*, p. 118.

"I learned to": *Sampler*, p. 9.

"We all stopped": *OWH*, pp. 23–24.

"What is it": *OWH*, p. 28.

"Dust is," "Along the roads," and "like green oranges": *OWH*, pp. 50–51.

"The trees and" and "We could almost": *OWH*, p. 65.

"The farther we" and "This is beautiful": *OWH*, pp. 68–69.

"The Ozarks are not really": *Sampler*, p. 89.

"a violent fancy" and "If she could not have it": from "The Story of Rocky Ridge Farm," *Ruralist*, July 22, 1911, *FJ* p. 18.

The claim papers for Charles Ingalls's homestead on the northeast quarter of Section 3 and Almanzo Wilder's on the northeast quarter of Section 21 in De Smet are available online from the National Archives at archives.gov. Almanzo's timber claim was the southeast corner of Section 9. See Miller, *Becoming Laura Ingalls Wilder*, p. 73.

On the Way Home is an illuminating book in terms of Wilder's views in 1894, when she was in her late twenties and embarking on the last major move of her life. Rose's introduction includes memories of her grandparents' house in De Smet including the footpath, hammock, and her schoolroom.

Berry, Clara F. "Don't Leave the Farm Boys" (St. Louis, MO: Balmer & Weber, 1871). The sheet music is available at the Library of Congress website, loc.gov, along with related teaching materials in its article titled "Rural Life in the Late 19th Century."

Foster, Luther. "Arbor Day: Why to Plant, What to Plant, How to Plant," *Dakota Agricultural College and Experiment Station Bulletin 3* (April 1888). Note that Bulletin 2, also published in April 1888, compares recommended wheat and oat varieties for the Dakota Territory.

Franklin, Benjamin. *Poor Richard Improved: Being an Almanack and Ephemeris for the Year of our Lord 1756* (Philadelphia: B. Franklin and D. Hall, 1756), available from Yale University's franklinpapers.org.

Hedin, Douglas A. "Foreword," *The Timber Culture Acts, 1873–1891* (Minnesota Legal History Project, undated). Available via minnesotalegalhistoryproject.org.

Ingalls, Grace. A transcription of Grace's diary is in the collection of the HHPL, transcribed by Rosa Ann Moore and Nancy DeHamer, and is the source of the quotes "We have had" and "To day the wind."

Kingsbury, George W. *History of Dakota Territory, Volume 5* (Chicago: The S. J. Clarke Publishing Company, 1915). The quote "forest trees" is on pp. 1,260–1,261, and also includes the biography of Yankton nurseryman George H. Whiting. Volume 3, p. 476, includes a list of tree species recommended in the 1880s for forestry and windbreak plantings.

Rikoon, J. Sanford. *Threshing in the Midwest, 1820–1940: A Study of Traditional Culture and Technological Change* (Bloomington: Indiana University Press, 1988).

Sherwood, Aubrey. *Beginnings of De Smet.* "Thanks are due" is from the *De Smet Leader* May 31, 1884, p. 26; "Among the things" and the discussion of the Calumet Avenue improvements, June 7, 1884, p. 26; "Brilliant red sunsets," November 8, 1884, p. 33.

United States Forest Service. *Possibilities of Shelterbelt Planting in the Plains Region* (Washington, DC: US Government Printing Office, 1935), p. 8.

Warnock, Alene M. *Laura Ingalls Wilder: The Westville Florida Years* (Leonardtown, MD: Heritage Printing & Graphics for the LIWHM, 2010).

Wilder, Almanzo and Rose Wilder Lane. Almanzo's description of Russian thistle as "large as a bushel" is on p. 10 of Lane's questionnaire, HHPL.

SAVING SEED: ROCKY RIDGE FARM

"We have a": from "Favors the Small Farm Home," *Ruralist*, February 18, 1911, *FJ*, p. 15.
"No nut that" and "We have 'shown'": from "And Missouri 'Showed' Them," *Ruralist*, December 5, 1915, *FJ*, p. 43.
"we can farm": from "Pioneering on an Ozark Farm," *Ruralist*, June 1, 1921, *FJ*, p. 250.
"How are you": *WFH*, p. 9.
"Saw my first": *WFH*, p. 11.
"ramparts of rock": *WFH*, p. 17.

"It looked as": *WFH*, p. 20.

"dosing her with": *WFH*, p. 48.

"The more I see . . . raise chickens": *WFH*, pp. 92–93.

"The more I . . . the country": *WFH*, p. 34.

"I love the city": *WFH*, pp. 116–117.

"the forest trees": from "As a Farm Woman Thinks," *Ruralist*, April 1, 1923, *FJ*, pp. 285–286.

"Believe me": quoting *Ruralist* editor John L. Case's interview with Wilder in 1918, *FJ*, p. 3.

For LIW's discussion of "my pictures" provided by her uncurtained windows see *FJ*, p. 87.

Agnello, Arthur M. "Apple-Boring Beetles" (Geneva, NY: State Agricultural Experiment Station Department of Entomology, 2006).

Anderson, William. *Laura Wilder of Mansfield* (privately printed, 2012).

Burford, Tom. *Apples of North America: 192 Exceptional Varieties for Gardeners, Growers, and Cooks* (Portland, OR: Timber Press, 2013).

Calhoun, Creighton Lee. *Old Southern Apples: A Comprehensive History and Description of Varieties for Collectors, Growers, and Fruit Enthusiasts* (White River Junction, VT: Chelsea Green Publishing, 2010).

Ingalls, Caroline Quiner. Letter to LIW, June 18, 1913, is the source of the quote "We are very." Used with permission from Laura Ingalls Wilder Historic Home and Museum.

Kindscher, Kelly. *Echinacea: Herbal Medicine with a Wild History* (New York: Springer, 2016).

———. ed. "The Conservation Status of *Echinacea* Species" (Lawrence: University of Kansas Biological Survey, 2006).

Lane, Rose Wilder. "A Place in the Country" *The Country Gentleman*, March 14, 1925, is the source of "a servant to hens," *Sampler* p. 129.

———. "Grandpa's Fiddle," a manuscript from HHPL, includes Rose's memories of chewing elm bark, *Sampler* p. 83.

———. "Rose Wilder Lane, By Herself," *Sunset*, November 1918, is the source of the quote "My mother loves," *Sampler*, p. 12.

Leshuk, David. "John Muir's Wisconsin Days," *Wisconsin Natural Resources* 12:3 (May–June 1988).

Mirror, September 25, 1913, p. 3, is the source of the quote "A. J. Wilder is building."

Muir, John. *The Yosemite* (New York: The Century Company, 1912). This is the source of "Everybody needs beauty."

———. *John Muir: His Life and Letters and Other Writings*, ed. Terry Gifford (Seattle, WA: The Mountaineers, 1996). The quote "keep it untrampled" is on p. 88.

Nathan, Manjula, et al. "Summary of Soil Fertility Status in Missouri by County, Soil Region and Cropping Systems," *Missouri Soil Fertility and Fertilizers Research Update 2007* (Columbia: University of Missouri Press, 2008) pp. 115–127. Reports Wright County soil pH as acidic (less than or equal to 5.3).

"Practical Apple Growing," *Kansas City Journal*, April 27, 1895. The quotes "999 of the" and "would almost" are from p. 10.

Proceedings of American Pomological Society, 33rd Session (Kansas City, MO: American Pomological Society, 1914) includes one of many examples of the Ben Davis apple being referred to as a "mortgage lifter" on p. 187.

Pursell, J. J. *The Herbal Apothecary* (Portland, OR: Timber Press, 2015).

U.S. Department of Agriculture. *Soil Survey of Wright County, Missouri* (Soil Conservation Service and Forest Service, 1981), available at nrcs.usda.gov.

Wilder, A. J. "My Apple Orchard," *Ruralist*, June 1, 1912, *FJ*, pp. 20–22. While it is widely believed that Laura wrote all articles with her husband's byline, she borrowed Almanzo's experiences as well as his narrative voice. This is the source for "he unloaded his," "making two crops," "Wife and I," and other related information about the orchard.

———. "Substantial Gates on Farm," *The Cape County Herald*, Cape Girardeau, MO, March 29, 1912, p. 7.

Wilder, Laura Ingalls (Mrs. A. J.) "Alfalfa Favored for the Poultry," *Mexico* [MO] *Message*, May 8, 1913, p. 3.

———. "Judgement Needed with Late Chicks," *Mexico* [MO] *Message*, July 24, 1913, p. 3.

———. "Tuck'em In Corner" poems from the *San Francisco Bulletin* are in HHPL, Box 14, Folder 203.

Zotta, LeAnn. *200 Years and Growing: The Story of Stark Bro's Nurseries & Orchards Co.* (Louisiana, MO: Stark Bro's, 2015).

PUTTING FOOD BY: THE ROCK HOUSE AND THE FARMHOUSE

"The real things": from "My Work," *Ruralist*, August 1, 1923, *FJ*, p. 291.

"making garden," "The vegetables one," "Our summer gardens," "gardens in our," and "We grow many": from "The Farm Home (17)," *Ruralist* January 20, 1920, *FJ*, p. 211–212.

"We revel in": from "So We Moved the Spring," *Ruralist*, April 20 1916, *FJ*, p. 58.

"Out in the berry": from "The Farm Home (26)," *Ruralist* July 5, 1920, *FJ*, p. 223.

"I would rather" and "Thinking of pies": from "As a Farm Woman Thinks," *Ruralist*,

March 1, 1924, *FJ*, pp. 306–307.

"We are well," "The State Highway," and "People say that": LIW to Meroe Stanton, December 17, 1924, *Letters*, p. 30.

"serious sickness": LIW to Martha Quiner Carpenter, June 22, 1925, *Letters*, pp. 33–34.

"It is strange," "Houses are miles," and "I am glad": LIW to AJW, September 18, 1925, *Letters*, p. 36.

"the sooner I" and "You remember the": LIW to RWL, February 5, 1937, *Letters*, p. 109. In this letter, Laura also quotes extensively from a letter, apparently no longer extant, from Grace Ingalls Dow describing wildflowers in South Dakota, the source for "Some are here," "The crocus came," "and white anemone," "tiger lillies in," and "There were no."

"Spring has come" and "I have been": LIW to Pomona Children's Librarians, February [March] 7, 1953, *Letters*, p. 348.

"One thing about": RWL to LIW, July 9, 1951, HHPL.

"genuine social security": Holtz, *The Ghost in the Little House*, p. 318.

William Anderson's work on LIW-related materials has been invaluable to a researcher. *Laura's Album* (New York: HarperCollins, 1998) includes a photograph of Laura's L. L. May & Co. trading card, p. 44. In *Letters*:

- Planting potatoes by the dark of the moon is noted in a letter to Rose, p. 28.
- Almanzo's cedar trees are mentioned in a 1938 letter to Rose, pp. 149–150.
- Laura refers to Rose's gardening books in 1939, p. 200.
- Rose's "tulip tree" and flowering shrubs are noted in a 1939 letter, p. 204.
- Violets blooming on the hillside at Rocky Ridge Farm are noted in a letter to agent George Bye in May 1941, p. 229.
- Laura starting tomato seeds indoors is noted in a March 1948 letter, p. 297.

A detailed explanation of the Farm Credit Act of 1916 is available at fca.gov.

Back-issues of the *Mirror* are the source of other information about what the Wilders raised at Rocky Ridge and their participation in the local agricultural shows and organizations. For example, April 20, 1922, p. 1, includes an advertisement for the stud services of the Morgan stallion "Governor of Orleans." Using chroniclingamerica.loc.gov, the most efficient search is: Missouri + 1900 to 1922 + "A. J. Wilder." The *Mirror* provided quotes and background information, including:

- July 29, 1915, p. 8, reported Almanzo's experimentation with Sudangrass.
- May 2, 1918, p. 8, is the source of the quote "15 thoroughbred Brown."
- June 5, 1919, p. 3, is source of the quote "One of the leading."

> March 10, 1921, p. 1, includes a short untitled article about the strawberry committee, listing Almanzo as one of its members, described as "people here that are thoroughly posted in growing and marketing the berries."

Lane, Rose Wilder. RWL to LIW, March 11, 1923, is the source of the quote "Could you fry," *Sampler* p. 127.

———. Rose's letters, manuscripts, and diaries in HHPL are rich sources of information about her travels and gardening efforts, including:

> RWL to AJW, September 25, 1925, is source of the quotes "We keep eating" and "Dear papa, the car is."
> RWL to LIW, October 7, 1926, is source of the quote "Thank goodness Wall."
> RWL to AJW, October 7, 1932, describes Rose's trip to Malone on a set of postcards and is the source of the quote "Please ask the."
> RWL draft letter to unknown recipient, May 25, 1935, is the source of the quotes "Roses I can't," "went to Heaven," "of 75, only," "varmints ate the," and "How cheering then."
> Danbury diary entry April 14, 1938, is source of the quote "For the first."
> "We Women Are NOT Good Citizens," *Woman's Day*, March 1939, quoted in Lauters, *The Rediscovered Writings of Rose Wilder Lane*, p. 109, is source of the quote "Give me seed."
> Untitled manuscript (probably written for *Woman's Day*, circa 1940) is source of the quote "I love building."
> RWL to LIW, July 9, 1951, describes her garden in Danbury, CT.
> Rose's garden diaries from Rocky Ridge Farm include many details on the lawn and garden. "Diaries & Notes, Item 22, circa 1924–25" includes Rose's diary entries on spring trees and flowers. "Item 36, 1929–1930" and "Folder 903, Item #41 1931–1932" include other garden-related entries. Note, some of the entries in the 1929–1930 diary appear to have been written by Helen Boylston. The 1933 diary includes the information about 'Miss Lingard' phlox on June 11 and the shrub border on November 16. Rose's budget book from 1934 (Box 22, Item 54) includes the tools and prices.
> Rose's diaries from the late 1930s through 1945 provide detailed information about what she grew in Danbury. Box 21 items 61, 64, 65, 66; Box 22 item 68; Box 23 item 69.

For more about Rose's adventures in Europe, read *Travels with Zenobia: Paris to Albania by Model T Ford*, written with Helen Boylston and edited by William Holtz (Columbia: University of Missouri Press, 1983). Rose's visit to the gardens of Hyères is described in a diary, HHPL, Box 20, Item 29.

For a flavor, albeit fictionalized, of Mansfield through the eyes of Rose Wilder Lane, try *Old Home Town* (Lincoln: University of Nebraska Press, 1985).

Springfield Leader, January 4, 1929, p. 9, is source of the quote "Mr. and Mrs. A. J. Wilder."

Wilder, Almanzo, and Rose Wilder Lane. Almanzo's comment on weeds, or lack thereof, is on p. 10 of Lane's questionnaire.

Wilder Gardens

"There are deeps" from "Look for Fairies Now," *Ruralist*, April 5, 1916, *FJ*, pp. 64–65. The passage, "A primrose by" is from "Peter Bell" by William Wordsworth, 1798; the passage "books in the" is, as noted in *FJ*, from Shakespeare's *As You Like It*.

VISITING WILDER GARDENS
"Laura thought how": *HGY*, p. 182.
"large, square house": *PG*, p. 62.
Anderson, William. *The Little House Guidebook* (New York: HarperCollins, 2007).
Winckler, Suzanne. *Prairie: A North American Guide* (Iowa City: University of Iowa Press, 2004).

GROWING A WILDER GARDEN
Hoose, Betty. *Laura's Flowers*, unpublished manuscript, 1995, in the collection of the LIWMS.

Louv, Richard. *Last Child in the Woods* (Chapel Hill, NC: Algonquin Books, 2008).

Lovejoy, Sharon. *Roots, Shoots, Buckets & Boots: Gardening Together with Children* (New York: Workman Publishing, 1999).

Root, Phyllis. *Plant a Pocket of Prairie* (Minneapolis: University of Minnesota Press, 2014).

Wenninger, Trina L. *Flora of their Writings: The Plants of Laura Ingalls Wilder and Rose Wilder Lane*, booklet printed 2003, in the collection of the LIWMS.

ACKNOWLEDGMENTS

To Kirke Bent, my Man-of-the-House as Laura sometimes called Almanzo, who had suggested my next topic be something in the south of France, but was equally pleased with the south of Dakota. You're still the one.

To Jenny Bent, agent and niece, who always knows and always understands.

To Tom Fischer, editor, I bow to the west in your general direction, and to Mollie Firestone for the triple play.

To Besse Lynch, publicist, and the world's best cheering section.

To Connie Neumann, friend in all things Potter, and mentor in all things Wilder.

To Thelma Achenbach, Jane Davenport, Sarah Hartman, Wendy Kohler, Linda O'Gorman, Gail Reuben, Sandra Swan, Jane Taylor, and Pamela Zave, readers whose eagle eyes and superlative input shaped the results.

To Yolanda Fundora, artist and designer, for your unerring hand in the illustration process.

To William Anderson, biographer, and Nancy Tystad Koupal, Director of the South Dakota Historical Society Press, for reviewing the manuscript and sharing encyclopedic knowledge of Laura Ingalls Wilder.

To the Laura Ingalls Wilder societies, associations, homesites, and fans, especially:

- The officers and of members the Laura Ingalls Wilder Research Association.

- Amy Ankrum and Joel McKinney of the Laura Ingalls Wilder Museum in Walnut Grove, MN. Thank you, Joel, for the able assistance on period maps and claim sites.

- Karen Carre and Sally Miller of the Almanzo and Laura Ingalls Wilder Association in Malone, NY. Thank you, Marilyn, for answering my research queries.

- Mrs. Jean Coday and the staff—especially Vicki, Rhonda, and Virginia—of the Laura Ingalls Wilder Historic Home and Museum in Mansfield, MO.

- Tessa Flak and the staff of the Laura Ingalls Wilder Memorial Society in De Smet, SD, especially for assistance in the archives and superb "Discover Laura" blog posts.

- Ann Lesch and Joan Sullivan at the Ingalls Homestead in De Smet, SD.

- Bonnie Tieskoetter at the Laura Ingalls Wilder Park & Museum in Burr Oak, IA, for the input and the phrase "the Wild Midwest."

- Audrey Helbling, Minnesota Prairie Roots blog.

- Jamie Martin, steadymom.com.

To the librarians and archivists, hats off to you and your profession, especially:

- Janet Evans at the Pennsylvania Horticultural Society.

- Spencer Howard and Craig Wright at the Herbert Hoover Presidential Library.

- Leora Siegel at the Chicago Botanic Garden.

- Stephen Sinon at the New York Botanical Garden.

- Kim Smith, Ken Stewart, Sara Casper, and Matthew Reitzel at the South Dakota State Historical Society Archives.

- The research librarians at the Library of the Chathams.

To so many others, for their expert assistance:

- Amanda Bachmann, entomologist for the South Dakota State Extension Service.

- Barbara Mayes Boustead, PhD, meteorologist.

- Dan Bussey, apple historian and orchardist at Seed Savers Exchange.

- Michael Davenport, Curator of Horticulture at the Lincoln Park Zoo, and plant wiz for everything from prairies to palmettos.

- Kelly Kindscher, PhD, Senior Scientist at the Kansas Biological Survey, University of Kansas, and *Echinacea* go-to guy.

- Becky Klukas-Brewer at Prairie Moon Nursery.

- Scott Kunst, geophytic historian and founder of Old House Gardens Heirloom Bulbs.

- Eric Lieberman, Esther Jackson, and the New York Botanical Garden Plant Info team.

- Kathy McFarland and Laura Stilson at Baker Creek Heirloom Seed Company.

- Cathy Messmer, historian.

- Debie Morris, fiber artist.

- Dave Ode, botanist for South Dakota Game, Fish & Park.

- Leah Scott, Conservation Forester, Kansas Forest Service.

- LeAnn Zotta at Stark Bro's Nurseries & Orchards.

And to my family who taught me about gardening, the prairie, and life.

My family poses in our great aunt's Illinois backyard, the flower garden that I imprinted on, in 1962. From left to right, Poppy, Jerry, Dad, Aunt Mary, Patty, Grandma, Kay, and Uncle Wayne. My mother was operating the Kodak Brownie camera, so I must have been standing with her.

PHOTO AND
ILLUSTRATION CREDITS

Pages 2, 218, 229, 237, 239, 241, 242, 243, 244, 245, 247, 250, 254, 257, 259, 269, 272, 274, 276, 281, 282, 283, 288, 292, 353 left, 353 right, 355: Herbert Hoover Presidential Library

Pages 5, 35, 71, 82, 89, 94, 95, 119, 161, 185, 192, 212: pictures © 1953 by Garth Williams, renewed 1981 by Garth Williams. Used by permission of HarperCollins Publishers. Please note: "Little House" ® is a registered trademark of HarperCollins Publishers, Inc.

Pages 12, 16, 19, 32, 51, 67, 93, 113, 121, 157, 164, 167, 176, 186, 196, 199, 332: pictures © by Helen Sewell. Used by permission of HarperCollins Publishers. Please note: "Little House" ® is a registered trademark of HarperCollins Publishers, Inc.

Page 22: from the Atlas of the Geological Survey of Wisconsin, courtesy of the Wisconsin Geological and Natural History Survey

Pages 28, 246, 279, 325, 327: Jimmie Lee Marler

Pages 29, 45, 47, 72, 74, 81, 87, 88, 102, 104, 105, 123, 126, 130, 135, 138, 144, 147, 149, 150, 154, 201, 210, 214, 221, 223, 262, 266, 268: courtesy of the Library of Congress

Pages 37 top, 58, 65, 69, 107, 133, 252, 287, 289, 301, 305, 306, 312 top, 312 bottom, 314 top, 314 bottom, 315, 317, 323 top, 323 bottom, 335, 338: Marta McDowell

Pages 37 bottom, 85, 115, 143, 145, 153, 158, 165, 189, 193, 310, 319, 329, 330: Christian Begeman

Pages 38, 59, 131, 225: The LuEsther T. Mertz Library of The New York Botanical Garden

Pages 54, 180: Kathy McFarland, Baker Creek Heirloom Seed Company

Page 60: U.S. Department of Agriculture Pomological Water Color Collection. Rare and Special Collections, National Agricultural Library, Beltsville, MD

Pages 62, 63, 114, 205, 230, 340: from the Rare Book Collection of the Lenhardt Library of the Chicago Botanic Garden

Page 76: Missouri History Museum, St. Louis

Page 78: Major Stephen H. Long Map of Arkansas Territory. Department of Special Collections and University Archives, McFarlin Library, The University of Tulsa. Tulsa, OK

Page 79: courtesy of the National Archives and Records Administration

Pages 92, 106: Nebraska State Historical Society (page 92: RG2608PH01094/10349, page 106: RG2608PH01249/10658)

INDEX